The Construction of Management

For my children, Elinor and Henry, who have shown me the art of the possible, and who have given me more than they can know.

The Construction of Management

Competence and Gender Issues at Work

Bronwen Ann Rees

Senior Research Fellow, Ashcroft International Business School, Anglia Polytechnic University, UK

Edward Elgar

Cheltenham, UK • Northampton, MA, USA

Published by
Edward Elgar Publishing Limited
Glensanda House
Montpellier Parade
Cheltenham
Glos GL50 1UA
UK

Edward Elgar Publishing, Inc.
136 West Street
Suite 202
Northampton
Massachusetts 01060
USA

A catalogue record for this book
is available from the British Library

Library of Congress Cataloging in Publication Data
Rees, Bronwen.
   The construction of management : competence and gender issues at work /
   Bronwen Ann Rees.
      p. cm.
   Includes bibliographical references and index.
   1. Management by objectives—Great Britain. 2. Performance. 3. Women
   executives—Great Britain. 4. Executive ability—Great Britain. 5. Management—
   Great Britain. I. Title.

HD30.65.R44 2004
658.4'012—dc21

2003049216

ISBN 1 84376 228 5

Printed and bound in Great Britain by MPG Books Ltd, Bodmin, Cornwall

Contents

Acknowledgements

Grateful thanks to all the organisations and the people in the organisations who helped me on this project. Without exception, they have all taught me a great deal about life in the modern organisation.

The financial support of the ESRC (Grant no. Roo0234869) for carrying out the empirical work in this paper is gratefully acknowledged.

Foreword

This book represents the culmination of ten years reflection and practice. It also represents a journey that began with the intellect, was nourished by the spiritual, and finally emerges as the first tentative steps into an embodied form. It represents my unfolding as an embodied woman. An unfolding that is learning to integrate theory and practice, the mind and the body, the group with the individual. An unfolding that at least hints at these possibilities.

The book itself is set out as a linear process, shaped and formed by the academic frameworks that have helped construct and delineate the society in which we live. It is also formed by the collective fiction necessary to bind the frameworks together: a collective fiction that necessarily depicts this book and its thinking as linear. It is useful at least to bring to consciousness the fact that it is a fiction – a myth that sustains and informs, and at the same time constrains the way in which we lead our lives. It is at once a freedom and an imprisonment.

Practically, the book offers up some alternative ways of enquiring into the world, of integrating rather than separating the mutual need for both autonomy and for interdependence. This need is a psychological and emotional manifestation of being human – and a fundamental question of how we develop as human beings. It is this need that underpins the way in which we relate to our bodies, and to each other as boys and girls, men and women. These are questions of separation and connection. They are moral and indeed emotional questions, and questions that can only begin with individual enquiry. Failing to examine these questions in the light of compassion can lead to disharmony, or the predominance of one way of being over the other. This can cause suffering to both men and women, as valuable and valid parts of their experience become 'written out' of the texts of our collective action.

This is an attempt to examine how this experience becomes 'written out' of our experience in the workplace. It shows how the tension between autonomy and interdependence is hidden in the technical language and practices of modern managerial strategies. Being hidden, it can cause severe discomfort and malfunction. My offering here is to attempt to uncover some of the many layers at which this tension is hidden, and to suggest possibilities for integrating, balancing, or even transcending this tension.

I have been helped by many people throughout that journey. First, by my parents, neither of them now alive to see this task come to fruition, but who have provided the set of conditions more than 'good enough', to enable me to want to, and to have the opportunity to examine 'how things are'.

On the academic side I owe a great debt to Elizabeth Garnsey who encouraged me in the possibilities for 'thinking outside the box' – but also taught me ways in which this could be incorporated into academic frameworks. Also for her friendship and continuing encouragement. To Chris Brewster for his unfailing support all the way through the journey, even in territories in which he was unfamiliar. To Hugh Willmott whose writings have informed much of the work here, and for the 5-hour grilling at an uncomfortable but extremely fruitful viva, which led me to change tack with some of the theoretical ideas. Also to Graeme Salaman and Paul du Gay, who provided me with some new ways of looking at the world.

I want to acknowledge too the help, support and encouragement of my women friends – Jen Tebensky, Helen Humphries and Kathy Willis in the village in which I live. To Jill Morgan who provided me with a remote farmhouse to begin the writing of this work, to Jennifer Frances for her feminist insights, for Kate Noakes for her very particular strengths. To Elaine Fear for knowing how to live in the world of organisations. To Katalin Illes for helping me find the inspiration to continue in academic life. Grateful thanks too to Liz Parker for carefully reading through a first draft of the original version.

The Western Buddhist Order has nourished me along the way, and also helped me make intellectual and spiritual connections that would otherwise not have been possible. First, to Dharmacharis Danavira and Atula – to Danavira for helping me continuously to realise how the heart and the imagination guide thinking processes, and to Atula for very subtly showing me that this book was possible, and perhaps, indeed, necessary. Second, to Dharmacharinis Akasasuri, Satyanandi and Varadakini who have provided me with the necessary spiritual friendship, and focused my intent, and my preceptor Ratnadharini, who has challenged me in ways that have brought out the courage to address this work in this particular way.

Finally, to my children, Elinor and Henry without whom none of this would have been possible. The book is completed because of them, and not (though it seemed so at times) despite them. I have been able to take these first steps into embodiment as a result of the insight that the most fruitful thing I could ever do was to bring two beings into a set of conditions in which they can learn to be both separate and connected.

Bronwen Rees (Dh. Sinhagupta)
Cambridge, January 2003

Introduction

Management and its discourses are playing ever more important roles in our lives. The political events in the UK of the 1980s and 1990s, growth of enterprise culture, reduction of manufacturing and an increase in the service sector has led to an increase in the numbers of people 'managing' (as opposed to producing). The discourse of 'new managerialism' carries in its wake an enormous swell of growth in business schools and academic and practitioner writings in the field. 'Managing' pervades our lives, and yet our understanding of the concept is problematic. It can be viewed as a set of ideas, an activity and a subject, depending on our perspective. Despite this conceptual ambiguity, however, the past decades in the UK have been characterised by increasing calls for furthering the 'development' of managers and building up a stock of trained and 'competent' managers in order to render the UK more competitive. Further, it seems that 'competent managers' are becoming the spearhead of globalising processes, and throughout the world 'international competencies' are being called for and developed in multinationals and their subsidiaries. The reach of 'competences' has developed at an extraordinary rate. The processes and language used to develop these 'competent' managers are the focus of concern in this book. In particular, I am concerned with the hidden action of power, and its potential impact on women managers.

At one level, views of what is good 'management' can be said to be changing. While there is growing reference in the literature to the importance in management of such qualities as co-operation, empathy, listening, nurturing, coaching etc., often explicitly associated with women (for example, Sharpe 2000; Ruderman *et al.* 2002) this recognition is not reflected in compensation practice or promotion policy towards women. The figures on the proportion of women in top management show little improvement over the past ten years (Oakley 2000). Recent statistics from the Equal Opportunities Commission (2002) show that, while the number of managers overall had increased by 20 per cent in the 1990s, women comprised only 30 per cent of managers in 2001, compared with a 45 per cent share of employment overall. They made up a higher share of managers and proprietors in agriculture and services (36 per cent) than that of the higher paid corporate managerial occupations. In spring 2001, women managers in middle and junior management earned 65 per cent of the average hourly workings of male managers (this was a wider gap than any other occupational group), and women directors and those in senior management earned 86 per cent of the average salaries of men.

This book explores how competence approaches represent and construct 'good management' and the impact this is likely to have on women managers. Do competence approaches encourage diversity? Or do competence approaches 'exclude' particular voices from reaching the boardroom? Competence approaches are largely vaunted because of their objectivity, in particular their gender neutrality. But is this the case and if not, what are the implications for women managers? In asking these questions, the more hidden underlying processes of power that may be setting up and reinforcing existing organisational structures and cultures are examined.

MAKING MANAGERS: THE MOVE TO COMPETENCE

Over the last two decades of the twentieth century, the intense globalisation and diversification of markets combined with the rapid growth of service industries has created a need to rethink organisation design and management within it. This redesign increasingly turned towards 'meeting the needs' of the customer. Organisational processes must have the flexibility to change to meet the vagaries of consumer desire – or even to construct consumer desire. This has spawned a whole new approach to 'managing' with an emphasis on creating a culture change that will enable real customer satisfaction. Managers have a pivotal role in securing change through fostering 'entrepreneurial values', first within themselves and then within their subordinates (Du Gay, Salaman and Rees, 1996). It is within this context that the notion of the 'competent manager' has arisen, and sophisticated ways of measuring this 'competence' have been developed.

As a means of developing and measuring managerial behaviour, 'competence' emerged in the UK in the 1980s. One of the major attractions of the competence approach is that it constructs and rewards particular types of behaviours that are deemed crucial to organisational success. Organisations draw up lists of behaviours (competence frameworks) which then become the basis for recruitment and promotion, underpinned by appraisal techniques. If, as a result of the appraisal process, it transpires that individuals do not meet the behavioural requirements, then they are encouraged to put themselves, or are sent, on various self-development courses, in order to be able to demonstrate the type of behaviour requisite for organisational success. Individuals are thus, in the language of competence 'empowered' to reconstruct themselves in line with organisational needs. By identifying and subsequently working on their own 'development needs' as clarified through the competence framework, individuals internalise the attributes required for organisational success.[1]

Not only are competences used in the training and development of managers, they can also be used in the performance management frameworks of organisations – measuring the behaviours of the chief executive downwards to manual workers. Further, competences are increasingly being used as the yardstick to measure the behaviour of different managers working in different cultures, in order to develop a 'transnational' organisational culture. Since the bases for the techniques are avowedly scientific, they moreover provide organisations with an 'objective' form of reward.

The question that this research sets out to ask is whether the competence frameworks really do provide the 'level playing field' that most practitioners claim for the approach. Do the particular assumptions in competence approaches foster diversity, or could they more subtly build on 'taken-for-granted' ways of structuring organisational hierarchies?

Management as Problematic

Theoretically, this book emerges from a growing critical corpus of writings that shows that management is a cultural, social and ideological phenomenon that should be critically analysed from a number of different perspectives other than that simply of making profit (for example, Knights and Willmott 1985; Miller and Rose 1990). It questions the notion that the neutrality and implied virtue of management is self-evident and builds on the work of these recent theorists who have exposed the workings of power in economic life to construct and shape identities (for example, Alvesson and Willmott 1996; Du Gay 1996). It is based in an understanding that profit and the effective use of resources to get profit are not the only issues in organisational study, but that there are other areas of equal concern: for example, creating meaning in the workplace, gender equality, or environment protection.

By questioning the perceived neutrality of competence, this book attempts to show that such assumptions can silence other voices – in this case those of women. This does not mean that there is no place for analysing, debating, and developing the technical aspects of managing, or that managers are engaged in some conspiracy to subordinate other groups. What is questioned here is whether impersonal, technical logic should be the prime basis upon which managers make decisions. Since competence frameworks are intimately connected with recruitment, reward and promotion, and vaunted for their scientific measurement of managerial behaviour, then it seems that competence frameworks will have a significant impact on who reaches positions of authority in organisations. This book examines the way in which competences are drawn up, and who will benefit from them.

Competence frameworks are rarely represented as disciplinary practices (with the exception of Townley 1993a, b, 1994, 1999; Du Gay, Salaman and Rees 1996; Rees and Garnsey 2003). Nevertheless the approach has features in common with classic approaches to discipline in organisations. Competence focuses on behaviours rather than tasks and processes, and as such may draw the individual into the realm of disciplinary power. Disciplinary power, according to Foucault, works through 'dividing practices' and also 'examination' and 'confession'. Do competence frameworks 'divide' and do they have elements of 'examination' and the 'confessional'? And if so, what is the likely impact on women managers? Furthermore, is there a way in which competence frameworks can work to become more all-embracing?

A Theoretical Plurality

This book draws on a plurality of theoretical and methodological perspectives. Critical management theory with its emancipatory intent and its tools for understanding broad historical processes provides a broad umbrella framework. However, in order to overcome the 'universalist' tendencies of critical theory, the approach here draws on feminist understandings to create a more sophisticated understanding of the 'embodied' subject. The 'subjects' of the study are psychologically and bodily conditioned by the fact of being born either male or female, yet also conditioned by ideological forces. These ideological forces run through gendered processes which: '… mean that advantage and disadvantage, exploitation and control, action and emotion, meaning and identity, are patterned through and in terms of a distinction between male and female, masculine and feminine' (Acker 1992, p.251). To uncover these ideological forces, and again to offset the more 'universalist' subject of critical theory, Foucauldian approaches to discipline are used as a framework to capture the hidden aspects of power. The book is underpinned by the understanding that:

> …politics of identity and identity construction is the deepest and most suppressed struggle in the workplace and hence the 'site' where domination and responsive agency are most difficult to unravel. … Prior to any analysis focusing on managers, workers or women and their various interests and reasoning processes is a concern with how these classifications come to exist at all. (Deetz 1992, p.28)

Unpicking the politics of identity construction necessitated a framework that could firstly examine how the classifications of 'best managerial practice' came into being, and then to analyse the impact of this on women managers.

Competences at Work

Case study material is drawn from six organisations: a university that was the instigator of 'open learning' techniques in the early 1970s; a major multinational in the oil industry; a multinational construction company; a semi-privatised national utility; a health and social services Trust and a beauty and cosmetics retailer and manufacturer. In order to access these processes, the book develops a variety of methods and tools of analysis. They represent a combination of textual and social analysis providing cumulative evidence to suggest that the identification and implementation of competence strategies is not as objective and straightforward as its adherents claim.

The interpretive repertoire is inspired and guided by insights from critical theory, feminism and post-modernism. However, in order not to fall into theoretical obscurity, and to provide some pragmatic advice for managers, it is also guided by a 'bilingual' position – keeping the critical dimensions in mind, but finding ways of working within and beyond the competence frameworks to expand their usefulness (Alvesson and Deetz 2000).

THE VOICE OF THE NARRATOR

This book represents an attempt at bringing together, both theoretically and empirically, two major areas of study to examine whether and how a gendered 'substructure' is built in organisations. This has necessitated developing a methodology and analysis that reflects this tension. The study represents a pioneering attempt to introduce new and more interpretative techniques into organisational research: it makes no truth claims. Because it is new there are undoubted pitfalls, which I return to in the final chapter. The freedom which I have exercised as researcher no doubt has its drawbacks: I do of course work within my own discursive constraints, and I do have my own political agenda. It is an attempt at what Foucault termed as the genealogical task of 'recovering the autonomous discourses, knowledge and voices suppressed through totalizing narratives' (Best and Kellner 1991, p.57) – here the narrative of organisational reform. It is an attempt at 'unearthing' ways in which the power of patriarchy filters through the introduction of competence strategies through the constitution of gender identity.

The book does not contest the processes of competence approaches themselves, but it does question the presumed neutrality of such approaches, and calls for a more critical approach to the way in which management models in general are introduced into the workplace. By prising open some of the assumptions in these models, it may encourage readers and management theorists to begin to examine some of the myths of modern management – or at least to articulate some of the unspoken questions.

Furthermore, since critical theory has an emphasis on reflexivity and self-transformation, I have attempted as a researcher and writer to surface my own fears and anxieties, in the hope that this may help others as we try to make sense of our world. The book has taken some 10 years in thinking and practice. It charts my own journey, or at least selective aspects of it. It has its own story, to which I return at the end. I hope that it opens up a way in which academic researchers can bring together theory and practice in more creative ways – and perhaps work across disciplines more freely. Organisational theorising can become tautological or conflictual, and relate little to practice at the workplace. Our views of the world can be shaped not by what is actually happening in the workplace, but in the heated debates of the ivory tower. In opening up the thinking and emotional processes that have guided this work (and breaking through my own fears), perhaps it paves the way for new and invigorating voices to be heard both in organisation theory and its practice.

ENDNOTE

1. This book does not focus here on generic concepts of competence such as those sponsored by UK-government-led initiatives for vocational training. Nor is it concerned with wider issues of strategy associated with developing 'core competences of the corporation' (see, for example, Prahalad and Hamel 1990). Rather, it is interested in the widespread introduction of competence methods as features of Human Resource Management (HRM) within organisations.

1. Ways of thinking about women at work: building a theoretical perspective

> Theories are developed and are accepted in human communities based on their ability to provide interesting and useful ways of conceptualizing, thinking and talking about life events. (Alvesson and Deetz 2000, p.39)

The theoretical understandings for this research are unorthodox, and represent the unfolding of a process, rather than the adoption of a theoretical framework as a 'rational' choice from the outset. Theories are drawn from a variety of disciplines, in order to elucidate processes of change, rather than to establish the universality at any point of the given theory. In that sense, it is a theory of praxis – a story of the iteration between research and theory building, including a process of self-transformation. Life is in constant flux, and our actions as human beings have an effect on the patterns within that flux. Theory is only useful where it can describe or illuminate phenomenon in an attempt to shape those changing phenomena in a positive direction. Along with Alvesson and Deetz (2000) we can consider theory to be a way of 'directing attention', 'organizing experience' and 'enabling useful responses'. This chapter represents an attempt at directing attention to certain theoretical views of the world, a way in which these can be organised to reflect upon the experience of competences, and finally to open up possibilities of providing some useful responses to that experience.

1.1   A THEORETICAL JOURNEY: UNTYING THE KNOT OF 'DIFFERENCE'

This research began with the observation that women appeared to be 'choosing' to work in positions that rendered them hierarchically subordinate to men. Why was it that women were clustered in occupations that were traditionally lower paid, or working part-time and thus rendering themselves 'unavailable' for the higher positions, or more money? Why was it that, despite the influx of women managers at middle management level, so many were failing to reach top-level positions? It seemed to me that this situation of imbalance was, and is, creating lack of understanding and hence disharmony between men and women in the workplace. However, the reasons for such imbalance seemed to lie as much in the 'choices' that women seemed to be making (that is to work in lower paid jobs) as in the structural conditions of the workplace. In other words, why was it that women seemed to choose to work in particular jobs that rendered them structurally subordinate to men?

Finding a theoretical home for addressing these questions was a long process. The first research area was the 'women in management' literature. Here there has been an on-going debate over differences both in the way in which women behave and the way in which their behaviour is perceived, or judged. For example, some research examines whether women use different power bases from men (for example, Johnson 1976). In the ongoing debate, some writers (for example, Donnell and Hall 1980) have ascertained that there are no significant differences between male and female managers. With few exceptions (Marshall 1984; Wajcman 1994; Statham 1988) these are set within the 'taken-for-granted' view that there is one best way of managing. Since these debates are set within a paradigm which assumes one form of 'masculine' reality, the argument is gendered from the start, and such work, despite the intention of promoting the position of women in management, may inadvertently do precisely the opposite. According to this perspective, women are socialised into feminine patterns of behaviour which are ill-suited to the managerial role. They lack the confidence, drive and competitiveness which are seen as key to effective performance as a manager. Women are said to be less instrumentally motivated, less interested in career advancement and less committed to work generally (Wajcman 1994). These characteristics are seen as the result of processes that occur outside of the workplace. Where there has been an explicit focus on 'men as men' and 'women as women', the focus on 'women' marks 'women' out as the problem – it is their inability or ability to 'fit' into the norms of organisational life that becomes the focus of the problem, not a question of the basis on which these norms are constructed (for example, Schein 1973, 1975; Donnell and Hall 1980; Ragins 1989).

Therein lies the theoretical problem. If we treat gender entirely as a social construction, then it may appear logical to remove any labelling of gender difference and move towards notions of a level playing field as much liberal 'women in management' theory has done. This apparently avoids treating women as 'other' and marginalising them. However, this also overlooks the possibility that women may be different as a result either of their particular social or biological conditioning, and may well negate certain qualities and experiences that are of value. Equally, if we suggest that women's experience arises out of an essential difference then emphasising such a difference may be taken as a reason for denying them equal treatment when they already have limited access to political resources. It is often, paradoxically, in the denial or advocacy of gender difference that power relations may be operating. Cockburn (1991) makes the point that: 'Men will say when difference is relevant'.

'Difference' too becomes an issue of politics and power at the level of practice. Examples of this can be found in the women working on industrial lines in the First and Second World War where women were deemed to be competent to carry out formerly 'male' jobs, but on the return of the men, they were quickly relegated to domesticity. In the same way, the current organisational acknowledgement of the strengths of women's 'interpersonal' skills may well be earning them places in the 'pink' personnel departments, while personnel practices are excluded from the boardroom. Even while in the twenty-first century, there has been a growing recognition of the qualities of co-operation, empathy, listening, nurturing, coaching etc., often explicitly associated with women which seems to be enhancing the performance of managers both in the business media and the research literature (for example, Sharpe 2000; Ruderman *et al.* 2002), the figures on the proportion of women in top management have shown little improvement over the past 10 years (EOC report 2002; Oakley 2000).

Webb (1997) shows how adopting this radical feminist agenda as a rationale for the promotion of women in management is a risky strategy, since it is based on a form of particularistic discrimination where women may still be expected, in such roles, to perform a public version of the patriarchally-defined role. Here the 'war' is an economic one and the 'strategic commanders' are the white male 'elite' who 'lead' the corporate firms in the competition for global resources, while the women serve faithfully in a national housekeeping role.

The dilemma is put clearly by Bacchi's (1990) historical account of the sameness/difference debate:

> The 'sameness' alternative is insufficiently critical of the status quo. The 'difference' option is critical ... but seems to conjecture that women can exist in some sort of separate world. Seeing women as the same as men prevents us challenging the model against which women are being compared; seeing women as different prevents us changing it ... by ignoring the connections between the marketplace and living arrangements, and the ways in which the two have been constructed as separate, it offers an inadequate political analysis. (p.262)

Thus feminist research in the workplace can become either polarised or marginalised. Rarely is attention paid both to the biological, social and thereby often domestic fact of being female, and how this intersects with the conditions in the workplace. A theoretical perspective was needed that could challenge the 'sameness' of organisational life (for example, how the notion of the 'manager' is constructed), yet also allow for 'difference' in the people working in organisations. This meant finding a way of bringing together theoretical perspectives that could make the connections between the workplace and living arrangements. It is in the shifting between domestic and the workplace, that a fault line in theory occurs, and the politics of gender sets in. A theoretical position which could address the issues of power and politics that were confusing and undermining the women in management literature was required.

1.2   POWER AND POLITICS IN ORGANISATIONAL LIFE: SOME THEORETICAL CONSIDERATIONS

The next port of call was to consider issues of power. Research that incorporates sophisticated analyses of power has emerged from epistemologies which have developed from outside the field of management; those of critical theory, and post-modernism. These philosophical positions have developed from different traditions such as social science, history, literary theory, radical and post-structuralist feminism and cultural studies. Massive bodies of literature have built up, many of which are highly theoretical, difficult to read, and even more difficult to apply at a practitioner level (Alvesson and Deetz 1996).

Critical theory and post-modernism were adopted much later in management and organisational research, with critical theory emerging in the late 1970s and early 1980s and post-modern approaches in the late 1980s. Both schools provide a critique of the specific socially and historically constructed conditions in which we find ourselves. 'Modernism' is considered to be problematic, in that its aims lie in the progressive evolution of science and technology, which may have positive effects, but which also contain dangerous forms of domination – dangerous because they are largely unseen and rarely made explicit. The emphasis on science and technology has pay-offs but also great costs. Technical solutions will not necessarily solve what has gone awry with modernism. While critical theorists see the flaws in modernist approaches, they also feel that these flaws can be addressed – through the judicious and careful use of reason. Post-modernists conclude that modernism has lost its way, and fail to see a future in pursuing it.

This is a crucial distinction. In post-modern thinking the idea that a unified world view will be produced by any department of knowledge or practice has disappeared. Rhetoric, quotation, irony, deconstruction, relativisation, all these are responses to the failure of science and its implied progress. While such responses expose the contradictions and power relations lying behind the dominance of reason, they are not underpinned by any search for 'value'. In the post-modern world, any sense of agency is lost in the circuitous conduits of power, and the individual is dissolved by the fragmenting of experience. Post-modernism calls for the end of epistemology, the individual and ethics (Giddens 1991, p.150). Post-modern studies focus on the fragmentation and disunity in any discourse, and cannot account for more embedded patterns of dominance.

Critical theory, on the other hand, affirms that human beings are not simply the puppets of the social machine (as Marxist theory would have it), while at the same time it recognises that for most of our history this social machine has dominated us and forced us along paths we may not necessarily have chosen. It emphasises that human action is a collective, not just an individual matter, and that the social relationships produced by a collective can take on a dynamic of their own. Beyond this, it can provide us with: 'working hypotheses, ways of looking at the world which we might find useful in explaining some, but not all of the things we want to study. It does provide an ethical and critical standpoint and an alternative notion of rationality' (Craib 1992). Thus it seemed that critical management theory held out some promise in being able to provide an alternative framework for investigating gender relations in organisations, yet one which could still integrate some feminist readings.

Origins

Critical theory emerged from the Frankfurt School, an institute founded in the 1920s in Germany as an independent research centre to employ researchers from a number of disciplines – philosophy, sociology, economics, psychology, with an aim to combine social science and philosophy into a politically and practically committed social philosophy. This school was one of the first to question whether social science could produce objective, value-free knowledge of society. Underpinning this was a concern to bring about reflection upon, and emancipation from the contradictions and restrictions inherent in modern societies.

One of the major targets of the Frankfurt school is instrumental reason. Instrumental here means a way of looking at the world and a way of looking at knowledge. To see the world as an instrument is to see its elements as tools, instruments by which we can achieve our ends. Craib (1992) uses our perception of philosophy as an example. He suggests that most people see philosophy as a way of looking at our lives, of finding meaning. If we, however, were to go to university to study philosophy, we would see that it is taught as an instrument – philosophy can help sort out the problem that science has run into: conceptual problems of theory. The Truth as a way of living has disappeared. Instrumental reason separates fact from value: it is concerned with discovering how to do things, not with what should be done.

Whilst the School embraced the emancipatory intent of Marxism, it did not believe that the proletariat would emerge as the revolutionary agent of social change – rather it believed that change would be brought about through the enlightened use of reason. Central to the thinking was an insistence on a psychological component to the Marxian theory of false consciousness. The first systematic integration of Freudian psychoanalysis into Marxist theory was undertaken by Erich Fromm, and with his work, analytical attention turned to the family. The family was the site of the development of subjectivity, where the home met work. As Fromm put it: 'the family is the medium through which the society or the social class stamps its specific structure on the child, and hence on the adult. The family is the psychological agency of society' (Fromm 1932/1978, p.98). Adorno and Horkheimer later posited that the former patriarchal authority was reproduced in family life through the internalisation of bourgeois authority. Unfortunately, this authority is not available to women, and as paternal authority waned under an increasingly administered society, it also became less available to males, thereby leading to the decline of the possibility of any emancipation (Marshall 1994).

While Horkheimer and Adorno showed how the spread of instrumental rationality increasingly subordinates all levels of existence – production, culture and personality – to its own logic and trajectory, Habermas introduced a more complex model of social development, drawing on developmental models of Piaget and Kohlberg (Marshall 1994). He incorporated a cognitive dimension into a model of societal evolution, and thereby re-introduced the possibilities for emancipation. His theory of communicative action is set out as a condition for empowerment and democracy (Habermas 1979).

The Basis of Knowledge

Habermas's ideas on knowledge-constitutive interests and the role of science and technology are especially helpful in understanding management from a different perspective (Habermas 1968/1971). Habermas distinguished between three types of knowledge. Knowledge is rooted in our relationship to nature. At the fundamental level, there is cognitive interest. This is based in man's need and desire to predict and control basic, unruly nature. Guided by this, different kinds of techniques are developed in order to control the world. In management terms, an example may be our attempt to understand, for example, motivation, through the Human Relations school. Many of the frameworks used by occupational psychologists are equally rooted in the assumption that we can control the psychological and motivational world of the worker. 'Branding' employees in line with the customer experience represents a further attempt at 'controlling' employee behaviour so that it 'fits' with the aims of the organisation.

A second level of knowledge is that of knowledge through understanding and communication. This would be encapsulated in the historical and hermeneutical sciences, and is characterised by a concern to understand mutual communication, so that we can understand each other's worlds. In management terms, an example may be a concern as to how people think or feel about how they are treated. Much interpretive work in organisations, such as that of storytelling, also fits into this category. This however, fails to take into account the historical and political forces that condition these worlds, and what might be affecting the processes of communication in a deeper way.

Thus, according to Habermas, there is a third type of knowledge, and that is a critically reflective knowledge, motivated by an emancipatory interest that pays attention to the relation between the exercise of power and the representations of reality. In this form of critical science, knowledge is generated that discloses the connections between power and the representations of reality, and shows where 'relations of dependence' become fixed. Thus, in organisational life, it may be that certain constructions of 'how we do things around here' may privilege certain workers over others – for example, it may be assumed, or even made explicit, that managers may need to display certain linear processes of thinking (such as strategic thinking), certain dominant ways of taking decisions (focus on task) which many men may find easier than many women.

As the world becomes more complex, and administrative systems become more complex, political and indeed organisational issues revolve around the functioning of more and more complex systems. Here citizens and indeed employees play only a small part in the decision-making processes, and hence it becomes more difficult to understand the relationships between action and consequences. But it is in these relations that power exerts its presence. To explain this, Habermas draws a line between social integration which is accomplished through immediate communicative action between those whose lives it co-ordinates (in the lifeworld), and systems integration where people have to co-operate through participation with a normative order that is imposed upon them at a distance by diverse experts and impersonal media (in the systems world). Systems integration is achieved through the use of the reward and punishments implicitly contained in frameworks rather than through the active, face-to-face consent of participants. In these situations where technical interests dominate, questions about politics or ethics fail to show themselves. The refinement of means becomes an end in itself. This has the effect of weakening the moral order of society. Such systems can be seen in the distant controlling of school curricula, in the controlling and perfecting of performance management systems, and in the drawing up of standards. Yet, in their attempts to extend 'customer' rights to citizens, employees or consumers, such 'standards' may perversely disable them, since those rights and standards have ceased to become an issue of public debate. Those who have undergone any quality assessment exercise in higher education may feel frustration as the 'value' of one's work is not perceived to be what students have or have not learnt, but on whether the learning objectives match up with the learning outcomes. The same can be said of the various research assessments that take place in higher education. The setting of distant standards means that the all-important debate about what is or is not ethically sound (that is, *why* are we doing research) gets wiped from the agenda. Competence processes, once they are drawn up in all their complexity, and by focusing on creating the 'competent manager', may deny the debate about why we need competent managers in the first place.

The more technological processes dominate processes of individual and social development, the more the moral and ethical elements of such processes are lost. Because, in the system, these processes seem to be value-free; their ideological power resides in the fact that communicative action does not take place and thus these practices cannot be questioned. In modern-day work organisations, dominated by technological systems, it becomes more and more difficult to see if and where there are any ethical concerns in decision-making. The values which create our social and economic lives are rarely open to debate. Instrumental rationality from the system world, takes over the social interaction in the lifeworld. The person whom we greet on the phone or in the 'front-line' of the customer relationship has been trained in reflecting the 'values' of the organisation. The quest for 'efficiency' and 'effectiveness' are taken for granted as being the prime aim of the worker. Social scientists help managers 'train' teams – but only teams whose prime aim is working more 'efficiently' together. Technological rationality has appropriated the language of practical rationality, and thus rendered critique impossible. The first task of critical theory then in management science is to examine the social relations and assumptions that underpin the concept of management itself, and how it constructs itself.

Management as a Source of Concern

Most mainstream management literature and practices assumes that manage-ment is a technical activity that acts in the interests of employer, employee, citizen and consumer. However, critical theory would question the assumption that management is politically neutral. While this assumption may give managers a comforting sense of their own 'impartiality', 'professionalism' and 'functional importance', critical theory would maintain that the way in which this 'management knowledge' is produced is conditioned by relations of power and domination. As Deetz (1992) points out:

The presumed neutrality [of management practices] makes understanding the political nature of organizations more difficult. Order, efficiency and effectiveness as values aid the reproduction of advantages already vested in organization form. The dream of organizational effectiveness hides the discussion of whose goals should be sought. (p.24)

Conventional approaches to management assume that established relations are already rational, and build upon creating efficiency and effectiveness within the given state. Critical theory, on the other hand, seeks to find out how the practices and institutions of management are developed and legitimised within relations of power and domination (for example, capitalism and patriarchy) and how these may be transformed. It is understood that organisational structures, communication and decision systems, technologies and work design influence the way in which certain human interests are developed. They also tend to meet some people's interests more than others. The problem is that this is unnoticed. Such an advantage is not seen as a right, as with the old owners of the past, rather it is reproduced in an unquestioned manner in the very routines and practices and language of the workplace. However, workers have interests that are only partially shared by owners and managers. The paradox of the modern workplace is not that the worker is living an illusion or failing to accomplish interests, as a Marxist might have said. If we look at these systems closely, we see the individual appears to be making a 'rational' decision – just as the choices a woman makes to move into low-paid work appears rational. However, it is in making these rational decisions that a structure of advantage is perpetuated, one that is *apparently* of advantage both to the individual and corporation. The identities and decisions structured here are not politically neutral or simply advantageous. The decisions lack an open democratic character not because someone in a position of authority is deliberately closing down a situation, but 'because the human character and needs are specified in advance' (Deetz 1992). The lack of conflict in these discussions means that there is no open discussion about what happens in the future. It is this area of critical theory that is particularly important in helping answer the question about how it is that women appear to 'choose' positions which are structurally subordinate to men. Competence approaches, specifically targeted at behaviour and which define the particular 'attributes' that organisational members should possess (or develop if they are seen not to have them), may provide such a way of defining and creating interests.

Critiques

Like any other theoretical position, critical theory is not without its flaws, and it is useful to examine some of these to help refine understanding.

For those in the positivist tradition, who believe that there is an 'objective truth' that can be seen and measured, critical theory is seen as value-laden and political. Here it would seem that there is no meeting ground. Despite the ever-growing volume of literature that questions the apparently 'objective' basis of science, there are still many who remain comforted by this world view – this is apparent both in academia and management. The explicitly political position of critical theory is challenging – both politically and existentially. All critical theory can do is to ask such sceptics to make the roots of their position clear.

A strong critique is mounted from the post-modern school who ask whether knowledge can ever be separated from power, and therefore would question the grounding on which any sort of rational claim can be made. Thus, post-modernism would challenge the assumption of an essential human core that the emphasis on the emancipatory power of reason implies. In post-modernism, subjectivity is the product of diverse and contradictory discourses through which individuals routinely come to be identified. Promoting the idea that human reason has an emancipatory potential can produce a social theory that privileges abstract theorising, thereby runs the risk that proponents of critical theory establish themselves as authorities, thus silencing a dialogue that they profess to promote. Critical theory, say the critics, is dangerous because of its lack of questioning about its own particular oppressive effects.

Critical theory has further been criticised on the intellectual grounds that, while it has emancipatory intent, critical reflection operates in the realm of ideas and has no necessary effect on broader processes of self-transformation. Fay (1987) for example, argues that the powers of critical reason are limited in the sense that we are actually bodily conditioned by our society. People become physically habituated to the world as they know it, and true transformation can only take place when these physical habits are also addressed. Because cognition is given primacy in critical theory, it cannot transform or reach these experiences of the world, and thus affect the way in which people conduct and organise themselves. The argument here is that an individual may be well-versed in the theoretical sophistication of critical theory, but this knowledge may exert little practical effect upon his or her conduct, and hence may have little 'emancipatory' consequence.

Critical theory has also been critiqued for its oblique theorising, and its tendency to think about management and corporations as though they were simply a matter of power and ideology – a tendency to ignore the fact that management has a vital role in producing goods and services for which certain well-tried technological and economic solutions may be appropriate. We cannot wholly understand 'management' if we only examine it from an ideological or cultural position. There are crucial management tasks that have to be carried out, managers in stressful situations such as the social services, or education, who are struggling with very real day-to-day situations that demand instant decisions. So often in academic conferences we hear the practitioners asking academics to 'live in the real world'. Management is a difficult and sometimes painful task that involves not only the disciplining of labour (including managerial labour) but also the production and distribution of socially useful goods and services (Alvesson and Willmott 1992). If critical theory is to be a transformative tool in organisational life, then an ideal model of critical theory must equally pay attention to the very real demands of production or service. In other words, we cannot lose sight of the fact that managers are working under very real, very intense pressures to meet certain demands, and often the 'objective' management tools are the quickest and easiest way of getting the job done. Critical theory provides a means of 'opening up' the particular political structures, but it must also provide a means of change.

Most significantly for this study, critical theory has been criticised on the grounds that, to date, it is gender blind. This attack has been mounted on two fronts: not only are there few empirical studies in this genre, but more fundamentally, from a feminist perspective, the model itself may be flawed. For example, Gilligan's work on the moral thinking of women shows that girls approach moral questions from a very different point of view than boys. Rather than applying abstract reasoning, girls ask questions of the situation and seek to find out more of the 'story' in a particular world (Gilligan 1982). Thus, Gilligan would question the validity of any universal 'ideal speech situation' which Habermas would claim could lead the way forward (Habermas 1984). Gilligan's work contests the notion of an abstract morality, showing that women tend to make moral judgements from contextualised situations. While Habermas would argue that a communicative model would mediate both between *Moralitat* and *Sittlichkeit,* that is between morality which is both abstract, and based in concrete situations, Gilligan would argue that, since the domain of morality only comes into *direct* view as subjects confront one another's claims in speech, the model begins with the experience of separation and difference rather than that of attachment and relationship. Any attempt to deepen Habermas's insights into communicative orientation must draw heavily on sources such as Gilligan which explore the social side of being human, not in terms of language terms, but in term of our character as creatures with concrete relationships rooted in our need to care for our young (White 1988).

1.3 RE-LOCATING SUBJECTIVITY: INTEGRATING THEORETICAL APPROACHES

How might we address these critiques? Following the thoughts of Craib (1992):

> To argue that because knowledge is not absolute or final there is no knowledge, only interpretations ... undermines what I still think is one of the most vital contributions of theory: it can offer a deeper understanding of what is at stake in political and social conflicts that have a very real external existence; it provides an opportunity to become what might be called 'better citizens', more aware and with a deeper understanding of what is going on around us. If it does not provide answers to problems, it enables a better understanding of their complexity and difficulty. (pp.249/50)

And in the specific context of management, along with Alvesson and Willmott (1992), I would argue that: '... in the present context of developing management studies there is less point in stressing theoretical rigour and orthodoxy than in welcoming a broad inspiration from a variety of theories and ideas that share "enough" affinities to advance or enrich critical studies of management' (p.9).

It has been suggested that a dialogue between critical theory and post-modernism (particularly the works of Foucault) may lead to less abstract understandings of management and organisation that will not only render empirical investigation more dynamic, but also make the often remote philosophical arguments of critical theory more accessible (Alvesson and Deetz 1996). Further, the critiques above point out quite clearly the omission of gender issues from the critical theory agenda. We are not concerned here with refining further 'metatheory'. We are concerned with addressing very real problems at the workplace, where, though the gains may be small, they bring possibilities of emancipation. The issue here is not which theory to choose, but the balance, choosing the right moments (Alvesson and Deetz 1996). One way of combining positions is to 'see both [critical theory and post-modernism] as metatheories useful as inspiration for reflexivity rather than as theories directly relevant for guiding and interpreting studies of substantive matters' (Alvesson and Deetz 1996).

However, the most major flaw is that critical theory is gender blind. Cohen and Arato (1992) point out: 'The largest gap in Habermas's work is his failure to consider the gendered characters of the roles of worker and client that emerged along with the differentiation of the market economy and the modern state from the lifeworld' (p.543). Thus, while reviving the 'autonomous ego' lost by Adorno and Horkheimer, Habermas retains an androcentric model of the subject – a view premised upon the abstract individual, which, has been inherently male (Marshall 1994). The end result is that Habermas is unable to break away from 'universalistic' assumptions that have plagued attempts to realise critical reason.

Through gender relations men and women struggle to recognise and emancipate themselves from the conditioning of being either male or female.

It is not enough merely to raise the issue of gender blindness in projects of modernity. Organisations comprise both women and men. Gender is a fundamental organising principle of workplace identity. Radical feminism highlights the critical importance of understanding patriarchy as a fundamental source of domination. Feminist ideas are potentially of relevance for critical theory because they open up awareness of and communication about gender-related forms of subjugation, and the ways in which they may be impacting on, and possibly exacerbating already distorted forms of communication. Habermas's insights into communicative rationality need to be strengthened by feminist work.

But which feminism? Feminist approaches vary in their theoretical orientation. Some focus on creating conditions of 'equality', and do not hold a position about the possibilities of difference (liberal feminism); others treat gender as a social construction, and examine gender as practice of power (socialist feminism, post-structuralist feminism); psychoanalytic and radical feminism focuses on the difference between men and women; Third World/(post)colonial feminism problematises the concept of gender as articulated in the West, and offers up a more pluralistic view of political engagement (Calas and Smircich 1996). These positions, too are compromised by the 'sameness/difference; debate talked about above.

Calas and Smircich (1992) aptly describe the tension:

> ... while poststructuralist feminism works expose the apparently unimpeachable structures of truth and knowledge in society, and help to debunk mythical social constructions that silence and oppress many of society's members, women's voices, on the other hand, construct new possible views. Together they stand in constant tension, because poststructuralist feminism prevents women's voices from establishing themselves as 'the last word' ... the two positions need each other for creating the space that brings society, constantly, toward a more just and moral state. This is a never-ending task given the flux in which societies exist. (p.227)

In post-structural feminism (for example, Acker 1992; Calas and Smircich 1992) the stability of such categories as gender, race, class and caste is questioned which raises questions about the significance of validation by experience. In the latter (for example, Gilligan 1982; Belenky *et al.* 1986; Marshall 1984) women's experience (and the difference between men and women) is documented and asserted to be valid knowledge in its own right.

Perhaps, rather than 'choosing' a theoretical position which may open up the problem of 'difference' we can transcend it by holding the two positions provisionally. Along with Marshall then: 'the effectiveness of our theory and our politics rests not on finding some middle ground between these two poles, but by grasping both poles simultaneously, with all their contradictions' (Marshall 1984, p.112).

To reconcile these apparently competing and conflictual positions within the context of critical theory, we need to reconceptualise a different and more provisional understanding of the 'subject' – one which can be incorporated into the 'modernist' agenda of critical theory, and yet one which also takes on board the biological and psychological reality of being born into either a male or female form. Here, gender is not only the psychic ordering of biological difference, it is the social ordering of that difference. Smith *et al.* (1988) suggests that:

> ... psychoanalytically informed explanations of the relationship between 'subject' and other cannot be taken as if they were the last word in the theorizing of subjectivity, but always brought back round to a historizising discussion of the ideologies and institutions (and thus the interests and practices) upon which subjectivity is predicated and which it serves. (p.112)

This is: 'a subjectivity that gives agency to the individual while at the same time placing her within particular "discursive configurations", and moreover conceives of consciousness as a strategy' (Alcoff 1988, p.431). The 'subjects' of my study, as we shall see, are psychologically and bodily conditioned by the fact of being born either male or female, yet also subjects conditioned by ideological forces. It is precisely this conceptualisation of the subject that addresses those critiques concerned about the 'disembodied' and purely cognitive 'subject' of critical theory (see Fay 1987), and equally the 'universalist' subject as critiqued by both post-modernist and feminist thinkers. Adopting this 'embodied' subject also opens up the theory for practical application in the workplace, and thus moves away from the 'hypercritique' for which critical theory has been rightly criticised.

Thus, I am proposing a more eclectic way of theory building, in which a range of critical thinking, including the post-modern (especially Foucauldian) emphasis on power, the textual work of deconstructionists such as Derrida, the thinking of radical feminists, and critical approaches to workplace identity can be welcomed. The turn here, however, is made by relocating a fleshed-out and embodied subject within the analytical frameworks of critical theory. Making this decision released me from the shackles of 'pure theory' and opened up newer fields of both theoretical and methodological inquiry. This decision also released me, as a woman and a gendered being, from the inevitable marginalisation that accompanies purely feminist research – a marginalisation which often leads many women to deny the notion of difference – and therefore from the pain of adopting a position which is perceived to be (and therefore, to a certain extent is) antagonistic and disempowering.

1.4 GENDER AT WORK: A CRITICAL HISTORY

While there are few examples of specifically gender-related work carried out in critical theory, a body of literature has developed drawing on Marxist, feminist and feminist/Marxist approaches which highlight the politics of gender relations, both in the workforce and more specifically in organisational contexts. These studies form the backdrop against which this research has developed, and many of the insights have been taken into the current study.

First, there is a very important body of work that focuses on the way in which gender politics can play a role in the way in which men and women's jobs have been constructed. Research has shown that the major characteristics of patterns of women's working are characterised by occupational segregation and part-time working (Rees and Brewster 1995). This has often been associated with low pay. Beechey and Perkins (1987), in their study of part-time working in the UK discovered that:

> It is invariably women's jobs which have been constructed as part-time, that part-time working is inextricably linked to the existence of occupational segregation ... gender was crucial to the ways in which managements organise their workforce. (p.167)

The crucial factor linking these aspects is that of job construction – or in other words definitions of skill and perceptions of the value of such work. With few exceptions (see below) skill has been considered unproblematic – but we must ask the question: who determines what is and is not skilful? What are the underlying criteria for allocating varying degrees of skill levels to particular jobs? In some forms of Marxism (cf. Braverman 1974) it would appear to be allocated on the division between manual and mental labour. On this basis, occupations such as nursery nurse, for example, can on one level be seen as manual rather than mental, and thus the occupation is generally considered unskilled, and calls for no special attributes. Does this mean then, that anyone can work as a nursery nurse? Could it not be argued that the mental problem-solving required in such an occupation is greater than that required for so-called skilled work, such as computer work? Skill is, then, not a 'fixed' entity – what we mean by 'skill' at any one time and place, is defined by those in positions of power in organisations and by supply and demand in the labour markets. Despite the fact that we often 'take-for-granted' what is or is not skilful, viewed through another lens, other types of occupation may be seen as more or less skilful than other. In this sense, then, skill can be seen to be a social construction (Dex 1988).

And the notion of skill permeates further than the workplace. Since managing a household, does not (apparently, by the lack of reward) require any skills, then the work that the majority of women carry out, is deemed, in capitalist terms, worthless. This notion is perpetuated on two fronts: on the one hand, anyone can and does run households; on the other, the work in the home does not contribute directly to productivity and hence capital. Furthermore, research shows that most women still carry out the major part of work in the home, and thus do not have the energy or time available to develop those 'skills' which are highly rewarded in the workplace. This attack on a double front means that the cycle of inequality is created and perpetuated in the home.

If the skills which women develop at home are consistently undervalued, then, as they enter the workplace, offering those very same skills (in, for example, the service sector), then they are already undermined and underpaid from the moment they start. This is true not just in the lower paid jobs (as manifested by occupational segregation), but also further up the hierarchy (such as women's over-representation in 'softer' areas such as personnel, training etc., as opposed to general managerial jobs).

Most of the theories relating to the labour market (human capital, labour market segmentation, reserve army) are based upon unquestioning acceptance of definitions of skill (Steiger 1993) and, due to the differing nature of women's experience, have failed to account in their entirety for women's participation and types of participation over time. Skill is not considered problematic. However, there are some exceptions.

A study by Craig *et al.* (1982) found that women who worked on hand-fed machines were considered classified as unskilled workers, while men who produced cartons on a more automated process which required less individual concentration were classified as semi-skilled. Other studies back up this finding. There are cases of sewing done by men being labelled 'skilled' and sewing done by women being labelled 'semi-skilled'. Indeed one study of the clothing industry found that men who were forced to take on machinery work usually done by women and labelled semi-skilled fought to have the work redefined as skilled. As Dex (1988) pointed out: 'It would appear to be the case that for a woman to become skilled in the clothing industry, she would have to change her sex' (p.291).

Outside the manufacturing industry, the picture is the same, though the process different. Instead of craft-based unions defining skilled areas, the idea that women's work is semi-skilled or unskilled can be built in from the start. The expansion of public sector jobs has taken place on this basis (Dex 1988). The caring occupations, childcare, nursery nurses and the whole array of social service jobs done by women (for example, home helps) are not recognised as skilled by either employers or society.

For Phillips and Taylor (1980):

> Skill definitions are saturated with sexual bias. The work of women is often deemed inferior because it is women who do it. Women workers carry into the workplace their status as subordinate individuals, and this status comes to define the value of

the work they do. Far from being an objective economic fact, skill is often an ideological category imposed on certain types of work by nature of the sex and power of the workers who perform it. (p.79)

Game and Pringle (1983) discovered the same phenomenon in their empirical work based in manufacturing, banks, retailing, computer and hospital work:

It should be pointed out that even when management consciously uses a strategy of a sexual division of labour as a means of controlling the labour process, it is not a matter of imposing it. They don't have to. It is experienced as natural, both in the workplace, and in the so-called private sphere of life ... A logic of the organisation of work did emerge; but only once we began to think in terms of the dynamics of the gender construction; how masculinity and femininity are produced in relation to each other through work. (p.23)

For example, they found the push for professionalism in nursing by which it was narrowly and technically defined led to processes of hyperskilling and deskilling. The ideological nature of the concept emerged quite clearly in their work and they conclude that: 'There may be collective struggle over skill, but it is not necessarily about skill. It is about the value of labour power and control over production' (p.121).

Coyle (1982) in her analysis of the clothing industry demonstrates that the distinction of skill in men's and women's work has much less basis in the content of jobs than in male workers' resistance to loss of control and status. Crompton, Jones and Reid (1982) show that the work women carried out in clerical work is actually skill-extensive in the technical sense of the word: 'In some cases, it seemed to us that the designation of a job as "clerical" depended not so much on the nature of the work involved (the "official" basis for calculation) as on the nature of the incumbent' (p.59).

Cockburn (1983) aptly summarised this phenomenon:

Skill is, however, not only a class political weapon. It is also a sex/gender weapon. Skill as a political concept is more far-reaching than the class relations of capitalism – it plays an important part in the power relations between men and women. (p.116)

Further, research by Horrell *et al.* (1990) showed that in a random sample of over 600 employed adults, differences were found between men and women in perceptions both of the types of skills required in their jobs, with women emphasising personal and social skills, and a significant difference was found in women part-timers who were much less likely than men to perceive their jobs as skilled, even when sharing similar perceptions of job content.

It seems from the foregoing that we can argue that skill is a political concept that may be used as a focus for collective action against women (for example, a history of trade union action against women moving into 'skilled' jobs). It is also one that may be used to help divide the workforce into class sections (for example, battles between semi-skilled and unskilled labour).

Redefinition of jobs as skilled or unskilled acts as a mechanism which subordinates women both in the wider context of the labour force, and at a more micro level in the way in which organisations structure their jobs at senior management level. The myth that occupations concerned with 'reproduction' are inherently 'unskilled' is systematically perpetuated through the separation of home from work, thus creating the assumption that actions that are more explicitly concerned with 'reproduction' do not contribute directly to the perpetuation of the capitalist ideal.

Such research then, shows how the intersection of gender and skill works to disadvantage women at the structural level of the labour markets. However, with increasing globalisation, flexibility and fragmentation of the workforce, collective definitions of 'skill' are no longer so appropriate. The growth of individualised pay schemes together with the explosion in information technology has brought with it the creation of many different types of jobs, and new ways of evaluating and rewarding such jobs. In many organisations, as we have seen, competence has replaced the notion of skill as a means of evaluating, and rewarding performance. Management in particular, is rewarded on its levels of 'competence'.

The story of management has been largely told in gender-free accounts that ignore the realities of organisational life by assuming a universal worker. In not 'naming men' we are, in fact, ignoring the categories of men and masculinities which are frequently central to the analyses (Collinson and Hearn 1994; Roper 1993). Collinson and Hearn (1994) point out:

> Within organisations, many men do not seem to recognize their actions as expressions of men's power and male identity. Where men see humour, teasing, camaraderie and strength, for example, women often perceive crude, specifically masculine aggression, competition, harassment, intimidation and misogyny. Men in organizations often seem extraordinarily unaware of, ignorant about and even antagonistic to any critical appraisal of the gendered nature of their actions and their consequences. (p.3)

But critical organisational theorists have highlighted the way that men in organisations tend to be engaged in the creation and maintenance of various identities which include the expression of power and status in the workplace that relates to gender (see, for example, Knights 1990; Collinson, Knights and Collinson 1990; Kerfoots and Knights 1996). They show how masculine identities constantly have to be constructed, negotiated and reconstructed in routine social interaction, both in the workplace and elsewhere. Studies have shown how masculine identities are threatened by social and economic forces such as new technology (Cockburn 1983) and equal opportunity initiatives (Cockburn 1991). Typically, men's gender identities are constructed, compared and evaluated according to a whole variety of criteria indicating personal success in the workplace. It is not simply these more obvious processes such as new technology, that threaten identity, attempts by men to construct secure identities may in themselves reinforce this threat as critical writers on subjectivity have emphasised (Knights 1990; Willmott 1990). In other words, attempts to secure a masculine identity are not merely material: the experience of self and other as both subject and object is a central and highly ambiguous feature of human subjectivity. Given the socially constructed, multiple and shifting character of identities, these attempts may reinforce the very uncertainty and ambiguity they are intended to overcome (Collinson and Hearn 1994). Further, in the process of construction and maintenance of masculine identities, there is evidence that feminine identities become a kind of residual.

It may be therefore that it is in the process of constructing these shifting masculine identities, that feminine identities are denied or suppressed. While there has been research into the way in which men are controlled in the workplace through identity-securing strategies (Collinson, Knights and Collinson 1990; Collinson and Knights 1986), research pointing to women using identity-securing strategies has focused only on women behaving in the dominant 'masculine' forms of behaviour; for example on all-female floors, research suggests that women often swear and participate in aggressive and sexualised forms of behaviour (Collinson and Hearn 1994). Some ethnographies have focused on how some women trade on traditional types of femininity as resistance to males. Barker and Downing (1980) illustrate an informal collective work culture which cannot be penetrated by masculine work standards. Pollert (1981) shows how women 'switched off' from their mundane work, to talk about topics such as domestic life, marriage, health etc. However, these authors recognise how such resistance reinforces gender constructs which fuel male practices of domination and discrimination. As Collinson, Knights and Collinson (1990) point out:

> Whilst this [evidence of resistance] is a valuable counter to those arguments which view women as the passive recipients of dominant ideologies and therefore as harbouring 'false consciousness', the reasons why women remain attached to specifically 'feminine' self-definitions as sources of positive personal power and security, and the consequences of so doing, remain underexplored. (p.206)

The reasons why women remain attached to specifically 'feminine' self-definitions as sources of personal power may be because they have no other choice. Given the pervasiveness of the practices of gender construction, they could not even attempt to develop 'masculine' self-definitions without encountering social rejection (since women behaving in a 'masculine' manner are perceived differently from men; Burton 1992), but if the workplace is already inimical to 'feminine' self-definition, women are left in the position either of being 'defined out' of the workplace or by adopting 'masculine' behaviours which, as Burton showed, are not perceived as effective in a woman anyway.

What is problematic, as Acker (1992) has pointed out, is the fact that while organisational realities are structured around gender among other issues, this is not made explicit and the concept of gender neutrality prevails. Over the past few years, a growing body of critical feminist literature has developed alongside mainstream management studies that explore these realities (for example, Calas and Smircich 1992; Hearn and Parkin 1992; Martin 1990; Ely 1995; Acker 1998; Rubin 1997). Such literature is beginning to explore and theorise gender relations in organisational life.

Acker (1992) suggests that gender, as patterned differences, usually involves the subordination of women, either concretely or symbolically. Power relations are closely related with processes of gender construction. These processes are concrete: what people do and say, and how they think about these activities. But this daily construction takes place within material and ideological constraints that set the limits of possibility. They are also integral to other social processes such as class and race relations. Power relations involve domination where one group has a weak bargaining position (in women's case because they care for children, the old and the sick) and this impaired bargaining position is rationalised by the dominant group as natural or divine. Acker categories processes of gender construction as:

- production of gender divisions (the gender patterning of jobs, wages and hierarchies, power and subordination
- creation of symbols, images and forms of consciousness that explicate and justify gender divisions
- interactions between individuals, women and men, women and women, men and men, in the multiplicity of forms that enact dominance and subordination and create alliances and exclusions (for example, exclusionary talk among women secretaries)
- internal mental work of individuals as they consciously construct the 'correct' gendered persona, and hide unacceptable parts of their life, such as homosexuality

Such processes, Acker argues, are built upon, and in turn help to reproduce a gendered substructure of organisation. This lies in the spatial and temporal arrangements of work, in the rules prescribing workplace behaviour, and in the relations linking workplaces to living places. These are supported by assumptions that work is separate from the rest of life and as such has first claim on the worker. So, she argues, today there are two types of worker, those, mostly men, who, it is assumed can adhere to organisation rules, and those, mostly women who cannot because of other obligations to family and reproduction. As Acker points out, organisations depend upon this division, because in a free market economy, they could not exist without some outside organisation of reproduction to take care of supplying workers (see also Webb 1997). This is recreated in ordinary organisational activities which do not appear on the surface to be gendered – and by implication are remarkably difficult to change. For Acker then, the way into underlying processes that maintain gender divisions, images, interactions and identities, is to discover which practices produce this facade of gender neutrality. These practices, she suggests, are the impersonal, objectifying practices of organising, managing and controlling large organisations. These processes are increasingly textually mediated, and are proliferating as rationalisation of management and production expands globally. Garnsey and Rees (1996) show, in their analysis of the texts surrounding 'Opportunity 2000', the neutral and scientific terms of the discourse constrain even those critics who may have found issue with some of the practices.

Thus, for Acker, ostensibly neutral everyday activities of organisation and managing large organisations reproduce the gendered substructure within the organisation itself and within wider society. As she notes, this is the most difficult part of the process to comprehend, because it is hidden within abstract, objectifying, textually mediated relations and is difficult to make visible. Acker's theory emerges from a growing corpus of critical feminist writings on organisations. These critiques are helping to create the conditions in which organisational theories can be reworked to account for the persistence of male advantage in male organisations. Because it is hidden, it is easier to deny, harder to detect, more difficult to study, more difficult to address (Martin 1990). It is in this denial of the construction of gender relations that Acker's notion of the 'gendered substructure' is perpetuated. It is as a result of this denial that this book is working on two levels: first it traces the practices which appear as objective, showing how such practices 'work' to construct a particular type of competent manager, and then it moves on to examine whether the 'competent manager' as envisioned in such practices implicitly perpetuate a 'gendered substructure' without however denying the provisional 'reality' of 'difference' in emotional and cognitive responses of men and women.

1.5   WHO IS BEING EMANCIPATED?

This chapter has mapped out the contours of a theoretical journey taken in an attempt to overcome the problem of 'difference' which as we have seen is open to political contestation. In so doing it seeks not to polarise theoretical positions, but to draw on theory and empirical research in such a way that a further mirror on the gendered organisation may be held up. It is not an attempt at universalisation – but accepts that gender is a constructed phenomenon, open to contestation. It argues for a theoretical plurality that enables one, while upholding a provisional notion of difference, to uncover practices which further build upon that difference in order to perpetuate advantage for some men.

There is a final consideration about critical theory that needs to be taken seriously and practised. Part of the spirit of critical theory implies self-transformation of the researcher. How might this take place? A major critique is launched at critical theory in terms of the lack of empirical studies, and the unbalanced emphasis on oblique conceptualisations. Self-transformation does not take place in the dusty and sterile ivory tower or research institute. In order for critical theory to be emancipatory, it would be incumbent upon each and everyone of us involved in such a critique to attempt, as far as possible to free ourselves from our own constrictions and habitual self-views. Not only would this imply a greater focus on empirical work, which is sadly lacking in critical theory, but also it would imply that researchers are actively engaged in the place of observation: either the university or the workplace. It also implies a personal practice of self-examination, both in relation to oneself and in relation to other. How many studies show this process?

Despite insightful work on how practices can constrain and restrict choice and action, and how the self is constructed around these practices, writers and theoreticians in this school rarely provide a story about their own practice. For critical theory, any lasting and substantial form of emancipatory change must involve a continuing process of critical self-reflection and associated self-transformation on behalf of the researcher.

However, this self-transformation is not easy, and to undertake this as a researcher does not just involve telling a tale but it means participating in a struggle, a human struggle, one of creating meaning in our lives. See, for example, Van Maanen (1988). Whilst critical theory writers may be aware of, and indeed represent how difficult this struggle is for employees, there are few accounts of the painful existential and emancipatory process for the researcher herself. But knowing oneself is a crucial part of this process – and this means knowing oneself as an embodied being, as well as someone who makes 'rational choices'. If critical theory is to be truly emancipatory, it will require these painful processes of self-exploration to take place while carrying out research, before any meaningful social emancipation can ensue.

The story of how this research was carried out and how it evolved, from its genesis in a highly respected business school through to one of the most prestigious academic institutes in the UK, and the battles which I have had to fight both as a woman and academic, have created a sense of personal transformation in keeping with the emancipatory intent of critical theory. The process has been one of internal liberation, but this is still an on-going struggle, to which I return at the end of this book. It is from the pain of this struggle that creative approaches can emerge. It is only by questioning, struggling against the discourses that hold us back as individuals that truly free thinking can develop and a fruitful dialogue open up.

We can only escape the discourses that frame our own thinking by constant self-questioning, which may in itself require putting ourselves in situations where we do not 'know' ourselves – or into the dynamics of relationships where we feel uncomfortable. For critical theory to be truly transformative, requires a mutual opening out between researcher and researched. The role of the researcher here would be to aid 'subjects' in viewing their situation from a number of different perspectives, and opening up the possibilities of more conscious choices. It is only in recent years that I have come to understand what this demands of the researcher. While the bulk of the empirical work does not necessarily carry the depth of this insight, I hope that I have become more conscious of why I choose particular theoretical positions, and have not allowed 'self-interest' or 'self-comfort' unconsciously to return to 'safer' areas of investigation, such as elaborating theoretical positions without reference to the reality of practice.

2. A gendered sense of self

Gender construction is an on-going process built into the way in which society organises itself, and the way in which organisations organise themselves. The process is continual, and involves a continuous renegotiation of the relationship between ourselves and others. The way in which we relate through gender is one of the most important ways in which we build up our sense of ourselves, our 'identity' – the process begins at birth and is continually on-going. This, in its turn, is mediated through our relationship to our bodies and yet it is mostly hidden, or banished to the 'edges' of our consciousness. And so, too, it is banished to the edge of a collective consciousness – or only referred to public life when considered politically relevant. Because our gender conditioning starts so early, most of us have an armoury of largely unconscious views about ourselves and others in relation to gender that rarely see the light of day. To do so challenges our very sense of ourselves. The process may well provoke a sense of fear or anger. A gendered identity is thus an interpreted identity, mediated through social systems and indeed textual relations, and also by the relationship with the body.

In this chapter, ideas from radical feminism and psychoanalytical feminism are brought in to enhance critical theory, and to adopt a 'fleshed' out biological and psychological subject, the target of intersecting discourses, but capable of transcending these through a strategy of increasing consciousness. To do so we first need to theorise gender relationships.

The problem with theorising relationships of gender is that, as Connell (1985) points out, the social categories (men and women) used to define these relations, are, unlike other social categories such as class, different in that they are: '... firmly and visibly connected to biological difference and function in a biological process. It is therefore tempting and easy to fall back on biological explanations of any gender pattern' (p.266).

In his practice-based theory of gender, Connell argues that the social practices that construct gender relations transform the original underlying biological difference: 'This practical transformation is a continuing historical process. Its materials are the social as well as the biological products of previous practice – new situations and new people. The practices of sexual reproduction are often quite remote aspects of the social encounters in which gender is constructed and sustained' (1987, p.79).

Thus masculine and feminine behaviours can be constructed and reconstructed so that new forms become dominant. They vary over time and space. It is even possible for a whole new category to be constructed – as with the emergence of the 'homosexual' in the late nineteenth century. Thus there is a logic to grossly exaggerating difference through social practices such as dress since, as Connell argues: 'They are part of the continuing effort to sustain the social definition of gender, an effort that is necessary precisely *because the biological logic*, and the inert practice that responds to it *cannot sustain the gender categories*' (his italics, p.87).

Over time, according to Connell, any original biological reason for difference becomes so distanced from social behaviour that a cycle of expectations sets in which is so deeply ingrained and culturally reinforced that the probable, though unobservable, biological causes of difference are overlaid by demonstrable social causes. I think this misses the point, and reflects the way in which, theoretically, the denial of our relationship to our bodies means that a whole aspect of our experience is not theoretically encapsulated. To assert the remoteness of the biological logic may be to deny part of the reality of being human.

The feminist idea of a 'gender order' is helpful here to address this problem. Marshall (1994) notes that: 'A gender order begins with embodiment – the existence of males and females as inhabitants of different bodies and their self-awareness of such – and is elaborated through the historical construction of biological differences into essential psychological and social differences between women and men' (p.116). This means understanding that there is a sense of being a 'man' or 'woman' that has its roots in biology but that is subject to historical change. Alcoff (1988) suggests that we need 'to construe a gendered subjectivity in relation to concrete habits, practices and discourses while at the same time recognizing the fluidity of these' (p.431). Thus, gender can be considered to be both 'different', and also socially constructed. What is at issue here is how these biological differences are constructed, and in particular, how these are reconstructed in the workplace.

2.1 EARLY ELABORATION OF DIFFERENCE: THE REPRODUCTION OF MOTHERING

The work of Chodorow still provides unequalled explanations for how differences come to be elaborated and inscribed in social practices. In her seminal work *The Reproduction of Mothering* (1978), Chodorow showed how the structure of the family and family practices reproduce in women, at a psychoanalytical level, the need to mother. This has implications for the psychological development of women and men, and may provide one explanation for 'difference' as it is manifest in empirical studies of children and adults.

She begins by noting how, historically, women's emotional role in the family and their psychological mothering role grew just as their economic and biological role decreased. In the early 1800s, women bore children at the same time as carrying out a range of other productive work. Children were integrated early into the world of work and men took responsibility for the training of boys once they reached a certain age. Nowadays, children spend longer at home and, mothering, as a task, has become an object of cultural and media interest.

Women, as mothers, produce daughters with mothering capacities and the desire to mother. The mother–daughter relationship itself builds up these capacities and needs. By contrast, the mother–son relationship tends to systematically curtail and repress the nurturing capacities and needs of the sons. In such a way, men are prepared for a more distant family role, and to become the primary breadwinner in the impersonal world of work and public life. She shows how the way in which sexual and family relationships are structured leads to girls being involved in more interpersonal, affective relationships than men, and a subsequent division of psychological capacities which leads them to reproduce this sexual and familial division of labour. In other words, the social relation of mothering is enacted at a psychological level of expectations and norms.

Through psychoanalytic methods, which provide an empirical vehicle for a systemic and structural account of socialisation and social reproduction, she goes on to show how the structural effects of women mothering, create personality types in both women and men. She draws on culture and personality theory to demonstrate that early experiences common to members of a particular society contribute to the formation of typical personalities organised around and preoccupied with certain relational issues:

> To the extent that females and males experience different interpersonal environments as they grow up, feminine and masculine personality will develop differently and be preoccupied with different issues. The structure of the family and family practices create certain differential relational needs and capacities in men and women that contribute to the reproduction of women as mothers. (p.51)

Drawing on clinical and academic evidence, Chodorow shows how women's mothering produces asymmetries in the relational experiences of girls and boys as they grow up. They grow up with personalities affected by different boundary experiences with a differently constructed inner world. Thus girls, by a longer retention of a pre-oedipal relationship come to define and experience themselves as continuous with others, and their experience of self contains more flexible ego boundaries, while boys come to define themselves as more separate and distinct with rigid ego boundaries. When the Oedipus complex is resolved, woman's inner world becomes more complex in the relational sense and there remains a preoccupation with relational issues. Men's inner world tends to be more fixed and simple, and relational issues tend to be more repressed. Relationship abilities and preoccupations are extended in girls' development and curtailed in boys. Boys and girls then experience and internalise different kinds of relationships; they experience conflict, develop defences and understand the effects of these relationships differently.

The understanding of self in relationship to others then produces, in girls, capacities appropriate to mothering (and indeed appropriate to the increasing number of service jobs in the labour market). The early experience of being cared for by a woman produces a set of expectations in women and men that mothers are expected to show selfless concern for their children. Daughters grow up identifying with these mothers, about whom they have such expectations. This set of expectations is generalised to the assumption that women naturally take care of children of all ages and the belief that women's 'maternal qualities' can and should be extended to the non-mothering work that they do. In this sense, reproducing the theory of gender. As Chodorow concludes:

> The reproduction of women's mothering is the basis for the reproduction of women's location and responsibilities in the domestic sphere. This mothering, and its generalization to women's structural location in the domestic sphere, links the contemporary social organization of gender and social organisation of production and contributes to the reproduction of each. It is basic to the sexual division of labour and generates a psychology and ideology of male dominance as well as an ideology about women's capacities and nature. Women, as wives and mothers, contribute as well to the daily and generational reproduction, both physical and psychological, of male workers and thus to the reproduction of capitalist production. Women's mothering also reproduces the family as it is constituted in male-dominant society. The sexual and familial division of labour in which women mother creates a sexual division of psychic organization and orientation. (p.208)

Critics have argued (Connell 1987) that such a theory is ahistoric, and essentialist – however, change is possible within such a theory. Parenting qualities are created in women through specific social and psychological processes. By implication these qualities could be created in men if men and women parented more equally.

It is not because fathers are incompetent or insensitive parents that they are less important attachment figures than their mothers, but because in most cultures they interact less (Bowlby 1988). Lamb (1986) points out that parenting skills are usually acquired 'on the job' by both mothers and fathers, but because most mothers are 'on the job' more frequently than fathers, it is not surprising that mothers become more experienced and sensitive and fathers less so, and that differences between mothers and fathers become more extreme. Not only are fathers less available, but when they are at home they interact less with their infants and are less likely to provide basic care. Men are more prone to engage in the recreational aspects of childcare, playing with their children, rather than providing practical care (Lamb 1977). In childhood and adolescence, mothers still interact more frequently with their children and are more involved in caregiving and fathers are more likely to engage in play (Collins and Russell 1991). Even when both the father and mother are employed, fathers spend considerably less time with their children than mothers and assume less responsibility for their care (Lamb 1977; Lamb and Oppenheim 1989).

It is important to acknowledge, however, that all women do not mother or want to mother, and all women are not 'maternal' or 'nurturing'. Some men are far more nurturing than some women, some women more distant than men.

Clearly, this material would suggest that identity construction in the workplace is likely to be far more complex than merely a scramble for status, or power. It would seem from this analysis that for many women, the need to relate could be of far greater importance than the need to be separated out in hierarchical positioning.

A Different Understanding of Self

Chodorow's work has been reinforced by one of the most influential works of the last 25 years – Gilligan on conceptions of the self (1982). In this work, based on three studies encompassing all age groups, she explores conceptions of self and morality, and experiences of conflict and choice. She finds that:

> ... the relationship between self and the other is exposed. ... From the different dynamics of separation and attachment in their gender identity formation through the divergence of identity and intimacy that marks their experience in the adolescent years, male and female voices typically speak of the importance of different truths, the former of the role of separation as it defines and empowers the self, the latter as the ongoing process of attachment that creates and sustains the human community. (p.156)

By illuminating life as a web rather than a succession of relationships, women portray autonomy rather than attachment as the illusory and dangerous quest: 'In this way women's development points towards a different history of human attachment, stressing continuity and change in configuration, rather than replacement and separation, elucidating a different response to loss, and changing the metaphor of growth' (p.48). Gilligan shows that it is this dialectic from which the tension of human development arises, and that the former silence of women in the narrative of adult development distorts the conception of its stages and sequence.

Gilligan's work shows that females seem to have a different moral orientation than males. Both males and females use care and justice-based reasoning in discussing moral problems, although females seem to use more care-based reasoning than do males. When asked to discuss personal moral dilemmas, females focus on interpersonal dilemmas and use care-based moral reasoning, whereas males focus on abstract, impersonal problems and use justice-based moral reasoning.

The work of Belenky *et al.* (1986) makes audible 'hidden' voices in their exploration of women's ways of knowing, and reinforces Gilligan's findings. By listening to the voices of women they show how the sense of connectedness deepens with maturity. They further hypothesise causal factors later in the life cycle such as being a mother as reinforcing the sense of connectedness. This would suggest that the sense of gender identity is likely to be constructed not only in historically specific time (that is, the meaning of being a woman varies across time) but that on-going development and growth, different life experiences, that may or may not be biologically based, will have an effect on the way in which men and women construct themselves over their lifetimes in relation to gender.

2.2   EMPIRICAL EVIDENCE FOR DIFFERENCE

There have been numerous studies that show consistently that there are behavioural differences between men and women. These studies run through from early childhood to adolescence and adulthood.

Difference in Early Childhood and Adolescence

There is a substantial body of literature which provides evidence for difference at a behavioural level. Leaper (1991) observed girls' tendency to adapt to boys' styles in his study of 138 children playing in pairs at the ages of five and seven. Although 'collaborative' speech accounted for the majority of all the children's speech, there were differences in degree. Collaborative and co-operative exchanges were more frequent when girls played with girls, and controlling and domineering exchanges more frequent when boys played with boys. When girls played with boys, they used more controlling speech than when they played with girls. Maccoby and Jacklin (1987) found in their study of children whose ages averaged 33 months, that, when children played in pairs, when girls told boys to stop doing something, the boys just kept on doing it, but boys did respond to the verbal protests of other boys. Girls, in contrast, responded to the verbal protests of both boys and girls. In a further study of children playing in pairs, girls were not more passive when they played one-to-one with another girl; they observed more passive behaviour in boy–boy pairs. But when girls and boys played together in pairs, girls often stood aside while the boys played with the toys. This has been found also by Sadker and Sadker (1994) over and over again in their lifelong study of schools. Madhok (1992) compared 23 small groups of students working on a science problem. When a group was made up of three girls and a boy, the girls deferred to the boy, who ended up speaking twice as much as all the girls together. When a group was composed of three boys and a girl, the boys ignored and insulted the girl. Girls, then, find it hard to influence boys.

In conversation, girls have stronger conventions for turn-taking than do boys and they are more likely to reach consensus through discussion than through dominance. In general, boys use language to assert, to boast, and to take the floor; girls use language to create and maintain relationships and to express agreement (see, for example, Lever 1976; Maccoby and Jacklin 1987; Sheldon 1993).

Boys and girls also resolve conflicts in different ways. Boys initiate more conflict than girls. Girls tend to use conflict mitigation tactics, such as compromise, changing the topic, or clarifying another's feelings in order to resolve a conflict (Miller, Danahar and Forbes 1980). Sheldon (1993) examined spontaneously occurring conflicts in the play corner of a pre-school. When three-year-old girls enter a conflict situation, they try to resolve it through compromise and clarification. Boys in contrast use a good deal of physical threat and appeal to higher order rules to get their own way.

These differences are reinforced and constructed through patterns of play and friendships. Lever (1976) examined various aspects of school-aged children's friendship and play patterns. During the early years, children are quite gender-segregated in their friendships. School-age girls are much more likely to have a single best friend. They spend a lot of time talking to each other, sharing secrets and discussing mutual interests. Although girls do play games, these seem to be secondary to the relationship itself. Boys play in groups and tend not to have a special friend. Their activities revolve around rule-governed games, especially team sports, and when conflicts arise, they are negotiated and settled in order to keep the game going. They tend not to enter into long or intimate conversations with their friends. Examination of the content of conversations between female and male friends provides further evidence of gender differences. Tannen (1990) analysed video-tapes of same-gender best friends conversing. Female best friends aged eight were already engaging in long, intimate conversations about personally significant events in their lives. Boys of the same age found little to talk about, and displayed discomfort in the situation. Two years later, these differences were becoming less; boys shared problems with their male friends, but between males one friend tended to downplay or dismiss the other's problems whereas between females, each friend provided support and understanding.

During adolescence, girls and boys bring, as we might expect, different skills and expectations about friendship and play. Females tend to have deeper, more intimate friendships involving more discussion of personal problems. Males develop friendships over shared interests (e.g. sport) and spend much of their time on these activities. Females stress the importance of emotion in their friendships, while males tend to converse about current events, sports and personalities rather than about their own beliefs, values and feelings (Golombok and Fivush 1994).

Girls' emphasis on the importance of connectedness and relatedness is borne out by research on leadership carried out by Lyons *et al.* (1990). This work was part of a major study carried out in collaboration with Gilligan and colleagues to assess differences in adolescent girls' ways of thinking. The purpose of the study was to identify how a sample of adolescent girls think about and act as leaders. Following the methodology used by Boyatzis (1982) to draw up competences, a set of ideas emerged around two different modes of leadership in an analysis of the responses of adolescent girls in leadership positions, to questions about leadership. Each mode points to a different set of values and assumptions about leadership. Table 2.1 highlights the sets of indicators derived from this research. The study showed that the interdependent mode was the predominant mode in the Emma Willard School.

Manifestation of Difference in Adult Life

There is evidence for difference in adult life, but care needs to be taken in the selection and use of such evidence, particularly when the evidence is based in organisational literature, since often the measurements for difference are already set out in gendered constructs, such as power, leadership, motivation and so on, which do not take into account women's different life experiences (for example, Ragins 1989; Donnell and Hall 1980). Evidence from psychologists and linguists which reflect behavioural differences is, however, useful, and is not predicated upon assumptions about 'best ways' of managing. Many studies have shown how women constantly present themselves more modestly than males in achievement situations. Heatherington *et al.* (1993) for example, in their study of 'female modesty' show that, contrary to recent studies which suggest that girls and women provide lower estimates of themselves due to a

Table 2.1 Model of leadership related to priority competences: goals, processes and skills (Lyons 1990)

Leadership mode	Goals/vision	Interpersonal skills	Decision-making; leader makes decision	Related skills
1 Interdependent-in-relation-to-others	Goals/plans derived from listening to people, being open to new ideas, and then making a plan from people's suggestions in order to get things done. Although leader enters her own ideas, acts more as idea synthesiser.	Listening to other, synthesising ideas, facilitating interactions. Worst thing a leader can do is make a separation between self and others. Motivation for people to work together comes from people who know each other and get along.	Takes into account all things people have said and then decides. Considers individuals in their contexts and situations. Tests a reading of conflicts with those involved.	Listening; eliciting ideas and information from others; being patient. Synthesising, conceptualising, idea synthesiser, creativity is in integration
2 Autonomous-in-relation-to-others	Goals/plans come from leader using her own judgement. As representative of others, leader puts forth a plan in order to get something done to solve problem. Although leader will modify her ideas for others, acts as idea generator.	Developing and presenting people with ideas/plans. Worst thing a leader can do is be ineffective or misuse power, that is, go beyond what the group or structure allows. Motivation for people to work together comes from structure/organisation and efficiency of leader – being on time, getting things done, having agendas and so on.	Leader makes decision – even if everyone has not always been heard – in order to move forward. Uses standards, principles as guides in decision-making.	Being organised, being efficient, being persuasive, conceptualising, idea generator, creativity is in development of new/different ideas.

lack of self-confidence, that this lower estimation of their performance may be due to the fact that the self-esteem of female subjects rested more on the quality of their interpersonal relationships. In other words, they suggest that a woman may be motivated to downplay her ability because of her concern for the other person. Thus the context in which women and men evaluate their achievements and abilities is critical in what they report, because of concerns of how they present themselves, and not from an inherent lack of confidence. Tracy and Eisenberg (1990/91) showed how, when giving criticism, men showed more concern for the feelings of the person they were criticising when they were role-playing a person in the subordinate role, while women showed a great deal more concern about the other person's feelings when they were playing the role of a superior. Women, it seems were aware of the power inherent in their authority and expended effort to avoid wielding it carelessly. Holmes (1991) showed how women apologise far more frequently than men, and offer compliments more readily. In their review of gender differences in amount of talk, James and Drakich (1990) show that of 56 studies the majority show that males talk more than females. However, there were significant variations. They suggest that these variations are due to the variations in the social structure of the interaction and to differing expectations and consequently behaviour in these differing environments. They suggest that gender differences in amount of talk may be due to the fact that men and women are socialised into having different goals in interactions and to use talk in different ways to achieve these aims. Spender (1992) basing her argument on 20 years of research claims that:

> Women in general, from a variety of backgrounds, know more about what is going on in conversation and have much more experience in managing them than is the case with men (no matter what sort of label you give this form of behaviour – nurturant, expressive, empathetic, etc. and no matter what context is specified – for example, in the home, at the workplace, in the classroom) ... women are ordinarily more aware of the layers of meaning, the ironies, ambiguities and even contradictions in a conversation. (p.549)

Tannen's work (1994), set in the workplace, cites various aspects of conversational styles (or rituals) that characterise feminine and masculine behaviour. Drawing on the body of literature that highlights differences, and on her own research, she suggests that the types of behaviours, apparent in the workplace, but with its roots in behaviours observed between boys and girls is that of (in females):

- emphasis of equality of relationship
- taking into account the effect of the exchange on the other person
- asking questions and for information

while men and boys show different behaviours such as:

- joking and teasing (banter)
- playful put-down
- expending effort to avoid a disadvantageous position

By not blowing their own trumpets, not making an effort to hide errors, engaging in rituals where one seems to take the blame even when it is not deserved, women find themselves in situations where these types of behaviours all work against them when others are not observing the same rituals. For example, Nadler and Nadler (1987) demonstrated significant gender-related differences between males and females in negotiating pay, resulting in greater asymmetries.

Thus, the set of behaviours that a woman takes into the workplace are likely to put her in an asymmetric power relation where, if the organisation is dominated by hierarchical thinking, they are less likely to make progress than their male counterparts. Machung (1992) in her study of secretaries shows how organisational hierarchies are set up such that these types of behaviours become associated with, and expected of those in the clerical hierarchies. Since these differences in behaviour are often tacit and unspoken, they are opaque to members of the opposite hierarchy – the managerial or professional hierarchy – and they help maintain the subordinate position of women at the bottom of organisational hierarchies. Given the language styles identified, one can predict a certain set of behaviours that more women than men are likely to use. These behaviours reflect the more 'connected' world as identified by Chodorow, and not the rational 'achievement-orientated' and 'directive' world of corporate life.

Summarising the evidence from Tannen's and other work, we can draw up a typology of behaviours that we might expect more women to display:

- asking for information
- apologising
- taking blame
- thanking
- praising
- complimenting
- masking abilities so that the other person appears in an advantageous position
- listening
- not boasting
- downplaying authority
- supporting others' remarks
- linking and connecting one set of comments to another

Differences in Modes of Cognition

Alongside differences in ways of perceiving and presenting in the world, the discipline of cognitive psychology has discovered different ways of looking at the world. Bruner (1986, 1990), has identified two modes of cognition. He termed these paradigmatic and narrative. In the paradigmatic mode, cognition is viewed as an information processing phenomenon in which concepts are coded in memory and manipulated by cognitive operators. Situations are represented as concepts to be 'solved' by rational analytic thinking procedures, making computations, comparisons and substitutions in a form of scientific reasoning. This model dominates cognitive psychology, as it dominates other cognitive sciences and the other social sciences, and indeed our everyday understanding of cognition (Boland and Schultze 1996).

Despite contributing to the establishment of this mode in his own discipline of cognitive psychology, Bruner (1986, 1990) has now suggested that this has suppressed the recognition of another, more powerful and universal mode of the cognition: the narrative mode. Here events are selectively isolated in experience, events populated with actors with their own histories and motivation, and stories are told by setting the actors and events in a meaningful sequence. This mode, Bruner argues, as a means of making sense of ourselves and the world we live in, is ubiquitous but consistently ignored.

The narrative mode is also used to forge a link between the ordinary and the exceptional. Bruner (1990) gives the example of children who cannot create a narrative about why a girl should be happy at her party, but they can construct elaborate stories as to why she should be sad. A further characteristic of the narrative mode is that the narrator has her own voice. Narrative is not therefore distant and voiceless like the paradigmatic mode of cognition (Boland and Schultze 1996).

The major difference between the two modes is the organising principle: the narrative mode is organised on time; the paradigmatic on space. In the paradigmatic mode a problem space is reduced to a set of variables which can be organised into classified and commutated space. Boland shows how a chart of accounts represents this mode of cognition: a hierarchical categorisation scheme is used to classify and record officially recognised events: accounting periods are metered out into standardised variables. In the narrative mode, time is imposed as boundaries at the beginning, middle and end on a set of events. These depend on the situation in which the narrativised events have occurred. The significance of individual actions and events are attributed based on their contribution to the plot. In this whole accountability is assessed. Time may be a 'moment' lasting the entire narrative, or a long period in which nothing happens.

These different ways of using time and space in cognition are significant to the construction of self through accountability (Boland and Schultze 1996). However, the paradigmatic view: 'synonymous with an abstract theoretical view of the world, is taken to be *the* mode of cognition not only in science and technology, but in all forms of human reasoning' (p.9, authors' italics).

A probable reason for the predominance of the paradigmatic mode of cognition lies in the actual interrelationship of the two modes. As Lyotard (1984) has highlighted, scientific practice does not recognise narrative knowledge as valid, even though the paradigmatic mode itself relies on the narrative mode to justify and legitimate its claims. The narrative mode, built as it is on a meaningful reconstruction of the world cannot be proved by analytic or cumulative logic. According to science 'narratives are fables, myths, legends, fit only for women and children' (Lyotard 1984, p.27).

It is only when the 'masculine bias' in accepted psychological categories such as 'identity' and 'morality' came to be recognised that important concepts such as relationships, intimacy and so on, began to emerge in the discipline of cognitive psychology. For example, in the work we looked at earlier, Lyons (1990) shows how adolescent girls, rather than using an abstract conceptualisation such as justice for analysing a situation, may resolve a moral problem by stepping into – not back from – the situation and by acting to restore relationships or to address needs (p.42). She puts forward a dual model for making decisions based on a care/justice dichotomy which may well reflect the paradigmatic/narrative dichotomy. Gilligan (1982) shows how one adolescent girl, rated on Kohlberg's measurement instrument for moral development, was unable to reply in the paradigmatic mode within which it was constructed, but in what was a sophisticated contextualisation of the problem in narrative form, was rated below others who showed more paradigmatic moral reasoning. In this way, important concepts come to be excluded from the agenda.

While neither of these writers suggest that girls and boys use different models exclusively, the fact that the recognition of the narrative mode has emerged following on from this earlier research might suggest that girls are more likely to use the narrative mode more frequently. It certainly could be inferred from the ways in which girls and women perceive themselves, and also from Chodorow's theory about the reproduction of mothering. The distancing process that boys go through when disidentifying from the mother is more likely to lead to the paradigmatic self 'characterized by separation from others, segmentation and calculation' (Boland and Schultze 1996). The narrative self, acting out situations, taking into account relationships with others, building beginnings, middle and ends, does bear a greater resemblance to women's psychological development as explored above.

These ideas may help us understand the processes through which the original biological difference is built upon cognitively. This may provide some explanations for how the gender substructure can be perpetuated unconsciously in the workplace. Men and women are likely to respond to organisational practices in different ways, and this may create the imbalances in the workplace.

The 'nurturing/directive' continuum

For the purposes of empirical investigation differences in behavioural and perceptual are characterised along a 'nurturing' and 'directive' continuum. This is not to say that difference is in any way fixed. We have seen that gender is not simply something that is imposed on children and adults; at all points of development, children and adults are actively constructing for themselves what it means to be male or female. Changes in the system of mothering could well lead to changes in the psychological and behavioural differences between men and women. Indeed, due to the increased divorce rate, growth in single-parent families will almost certainly lead to different constructions of what it means to be male or female. However, I have shown how the patterns that construct these differences are developmental and thus also generational, so change will be slow. Further, of course, this set of differences has been drawn from literature in the UK and USA, and is therefore specific geographically.

This chapter has explored an understanding of gender and introduced the idea of an embodied subject. This takes into account the concrete practices that provide definitions of 'masculinity' and 'femininity' yet which also recognises the biological logic on which these differences are elaborated. This 'being' is subject to historical discourses, yet also capable of raising awareness of his or her own conditioning, and therefore of self-transcendence. At every front, we are all engaged in gender processes, habitually reinforcing our ways of relating to ourselves and to others, yet with every opportunity to reflect upon and exchange experience of what it means to be born in a male or female body. Thus, while we may feel the pull of the 'conditioned', we can transcend it. To do so requires a compassionate language in which we explore what is or is not useful in our experience: it is not the processes of gender construction themselves that cause suffering, it is the fact that they are often caught up in and create 'fixed' and hidden ways of dependence where what we can offer is no longer freely given. It is taken as a conditioned part of the system.

3.   Interpreting organisational life

In keeping with the spirit of critical theory, and the eclectic way of theory building, this chapter focuses on the different 'interpretive' lenses through which the research was conducted. According to Alvesson and Deetz, the interpretive repertoire is made up of the paradigmatic, theoretical and methodological qualifications and restrictions of the research work. It is made up of 'theories, basic assumptions, commitments, metaphors, vocabularies and knowledge' (Alvesson and Deetz 2000, p.184). The analytical tools and methodological considerations that have guided the study are spelt out here.

3.1   LANGUAGE AS A PRODUCER OF IDENTITY: DISCOURSE AND DISCURSIVE PRACTICES

Critical theory, post-modern and feminist work all emphasise in different ways the importance of language in shaping the reality in which we live. The origins of a 'discursive' understanding of language began with the work of the French linguist, Saussure. In his semiotic of language, he emphasised two properties of language that are of crucial significance in how we come to know ourselves (our subjectivity) and how we tend to construct ourselves (our identity). First, he saw that the linguistic sign was arbitrary – in other words there is no natural connection between the sound image (signifier) and the concept it identifies (signified). Second, he emphasised that the sign is differential, part of a system of meaning where words acquire significance only by reference to what they are not.

The conception of language that Saussure develops is thus one of a social phenomenon and although the arbitrary and differential qualities of language are claimed by Saussure as 'a priori' (Dant 1991, p.101) they need not appear so to the user. For the user, language is a tool that expresses meaning. However, for Saussure, once meaning is located in the language itself between signifier and signified, it is seen as single or 'fixed'. Signs are fixed as positive facts that are the product of the conventions of a 'speech community'.

The problem with this is that it does not account for plurality in meaning, or changes over time. It cannot, for example, account for why the signifier 'woman' can have many conflicting meanings which change over time. The philosopher of language, Derrida, moved this understanding of language on and claimed that: 'the signified is not in fixed relationship with the signifier, but the signified is only a moment in a never-ending process of signification. There is no rest ... it always signifies again and differs' (Derrida 1973, p.58).

In other words, meaning is never stable, it is constantly in a state of negotiation and renegotiation within time and space. Language, far from reflecting an already given social reality, constitutes reality for us. Thus, for example, femininity and masculinity mean different things in different cultures; what is termed work in one environment (the home) may not be termed work (the workplace) in another; what is determined as a 'skilled job' in one organisation may not be termed so in another. Meaning varies between discourses (for example between feminist or management discourses) and is subject to historical change. A job description, for example, far from reflecting the nature of the job, actually constitutes the job. What is termed 'the job' at one particular moment in time may mean something completely different in later months, or in other parts of the organisation. However, the job description, as a determining factor of how the job is viewed by others, stays the same until it is contested. In other words, the job description has classified knowledge in such a way that it becomes a 'taken-for-granted' reality.

Language, then, as an ideological practice mediates between individuals and the conditions of their existence. This mediation is not between pre-formed individuals and objective conditions but it is the means by which the individual becomes a subject. This process has been called 'interpellation'. As Weedon points out:

> The crucial point is that in taking on a subject position, the individual assumes that she is the author of the ideology or discourse which she is speaking. She speaks or thinks as if she were in control of meaning ... it is the imaginary quality of the individual's identification with a subject position which gives it so much psychological and emotional force. (1987, p.31)

Thus, if an individual can make meaning out of her situation, then she feels she is in relative control of her place in the universe (that is, her identity is secure); to allow in the possibilities of other meanings poses a threat to this identity. In this way, the individual closes down other possibilities and thus rejects the possibility of greater expansiveness. She is both forming and formed by the discourse with which she is engaging. Thus:

> Systems of thought, expression and communication media contain embedded values that constitute a particular experience through the making of distinction and relations through perception. The very ordinariness of common sense hides the implicit valuational structure of perceptual experience. Each discourse and attendant technology constitute ways of knowing the world, privileges certain notions of what is real, and posits personal identities. (Deetz 1992, p.32)

But discourse is not only part of the 'text' we use to construct our world, it is also constituted in a discursive context, and thereby constituted through discursive practices. Discourse can be considered as a group of statements which provide a language for talking about a topic and a way of producing a particular kind of knowledge about that topic (Du Gay 1996). In other words: 'The truth, factual or otherwise, about the meaning of objects is always constituted within a particular discursive context, and the idea of a truth outside of that context is nonsensical' (Du Gay 1996, p.43).

Institutions as Producers of Subjectivity

Just as language produces subjects, so too do the discursive practices that constitute institutions. Routines, practices, procedures each implement values and establish a subject's point of view. For example, Deetz (1992) shows how the change of banking from a single site to home-like dispersed branches changes images and needs. The subject becomes a consumer of money. The 'old' subject in the new configuration becomes absent and difficult to produce. It is not just that attitudes to money have changed, but the institution, the way of saving is changed. It would no longer be possible, for example, for someone whose identity, and sense of well-being was constructed through the relationship he had with the bank manager to continue with that construction. This is why change of any sort can be so difficult. However, the person is not merely a user of banks. She is a home owner, a product consumer, a parent, a sportsperson. The relations between institutions produces a complete person, a subject with many different identities. The individual is subject to a range of discourses, some of which conflict. Here the psychological subject is not an originator of meaning, but as the subject moves about the world, reading books, watching television, attending parents' evenings, it takes on the subjects of these contexts as their own (Deetz 1992). It is precisely this 'freedom' to identify with these contents that conceals the processes of construction, leaving the subject unaware of multiple systems of control.

Further, because these systems of control are multiple they are difficult to detect. Gramsci's notion of hegemony showed how common sense was engineered through everyday institutional activities and experiences, dominated by 'organic intellectuals' (teachers, writers) whose world view appears as 'normal'. Deetz (1992) suggests that modern managers, technical experts and consultants may become the 'organic intellectuals' of our own time. This is not to suggest a new type of 'class', but it is clear that those who produce the systems and control the discourses (for example, designers of performance management systems) have the means to produce order by systems which are 'taken-for-granted', yet which also produce dependency. Because they are 'taken-for-granted', they are rarely challenged. Yet how is it that the subject's world is produced? What are the systems of representation that make it appear necessary and unproblematic, and who is gaining and losing from this representation? In terms of management, we need to reproblematize the obvious. This means asking the self-evident questions: Why does management control rather than co-ordinate? Why do women choose to work with women? Why are some jobs 'more' skilful than others? Why are some behaviours deemed to create 'effective performance', and thus provide benchmarks for management behaviour? Why is the more competent manager more likely to be male?

We must not forget that, whilst critical theory posits a subjectivity that is subject to multiple, often conflicting discourses, our feminist position suggests that interweaved in this range of discourses are gendered patterns, rooted in biological logic. Here, the strategy at an individual level, as I have argued, could be consciousness itself, that is a drive towards greater understanding of what are the underlying structures and reasons for making what seem 'obvious' choices? At a systemic level, we need to look again at what we consider 'obvious' – we need to identify the conflict that does not happen by examining whether and which practices block value discussion and close the exploration of differences – to do this we need a framework by which we can trace the workings of power.

An Understanding of Power

Most conceptions of power in organisations have been derived from political scientists. Such conceptions appear to suggest that ideology is produced by agents who are somehow outside of it, constructed by some identifiable material interests. In organisational theory, this has been expressed in classic terms of control and resistance (as formulated in the labour process debate, in the legitimation of power as a form of domination, see Pfeffer 1981) or, in Lukes's groundbreaking work *Power: A Radical View* (1974), which first began to unravel the complexities of 'meaning-making' in relation to power.

In critical theory, power differences are equated with domination and held to be in opposition to reason. Subjects are either in open conflict, deluded by false consciousness into colluding into practices, or being removed unknowingly from decision-making which may put them at a disadvantage. Thus disadvantaged groups (workers, women, non-experts) are deluded into accepting their position in the hierarchy, except when the veil of false consciousness falls and open conflict breaks out. However, if we assume that this is a monolithic ideology, then by implication, there are hidden real interests, or if only we all got round the table, then a power-free rational discussion could solve the question. This is not in keeping with our revised version of the subject, rooted in biological and psychological history, interpreted and mediated through the body. To help us, we can turn to Foucault's notion of power which implies a free-floating set of conflicts yet which still produce asymmetries. Foucault (1980) has demonstrated that it is often *because* our discussion of power is dominated by an apparent monolithic tension between freedom and power that we have failed to understand its presence or manner of its deployment. We need to understand the nature of power as having both an enabling and constraining capacity.

Foucault's notion of disciplinary power resides in every perception, every judgement we make, every act. It acts on the body and the mind. It has both positive and negative sides. In its positive sense, it can enable, but in its negative sense it can exclude and marginalise. It manifests itself through the way in which people conform, the way things become 'common sense' and through 'proper behaviour'. It has been present in corporations from the outset, but it would seem that over time, perhaps with the increase in textually mediated relations, overt forms of control have become more hidden, more taken-for-granted. With the growth of individualised reward systems, disciplinary power of the Foucauldian type is growing in organisational life.

While new forms of resistance are made possible, they are made less likely by complicity and new forms of surveillance. It is the truth and naturalness of this domination that make it so powerful. Team-building approaches can be seen as an extension of this complicity, as employees enquire into whether they are the 'plant', the 'shaker' or the 'mover' that we find in classifications made by psychologists such as Belbin. All such approaches draw more of the employee's identity into the organisation. It may be that competence approaches represent a further step forward in this transformation. By yoking the individual's sense of self into the organisation's aims, individuals are 'empowered' to dream up their own form of surveillance by talking about how they can promote their self-development to meet organisational objectives.

Disciplinary power draws attention to the fundamental role that knowledge plays in making aspects of existence thinkable and calculable and therefore the object of conscious action. 'Power and knowledge directly imply each other; ... there is no power relation without the correlative constitution of a field of knowledge, nor any knowledge that does not presuppose and constitute at the same time power relations' (Foucault 1977, p.27).

Thus, power works through the multiplicity of ways in which knowledge is classified, codified, recorded and inscribed. Foucault's notion of governance emphasises regulatory processes and methods of thinking about or perceiving a domain. He identified three primary methods or 'dividing practices' which make it possible to manage people en masse: enclosure (the creation of a space which includes others); partitioning (each individual has her own place and each place an individual; and ranking (the hierarchical ordering of individuals). Dividing practices are carried out on the space which individuals occupy (work space), on the individual's body (the way he or she is expected to comport herself), and in terms of a division of the working week into hours and quarters (allocated schedules) (Foucault 1977).

However, governance is not simply about the ordering of activities and processes, but acts on agents as subjects. Within dividing practices lie further disciplining processes which alternatively 'objectify' and 'subjectify' the individual. These Foucault called 'examination' and 'confession'. The *examination* provides a mechanism by which individuals can be measured, codified and classified within these procedures. This constant visibility keeps individuals 'arranged' like objects. This has two consequences; the constitution of the individual as a 'knowable', describable object, and the possibility of the building up of records to arrive at generalisations, about populations, averages, norms and so on.

Just as examination objectifies individuals, so the process of 'confession' subjectifies them: '*L'homme, en Occident, est devenue une bete d'aveu*' (Foucault 1976, p.80). Although superficially, the capacity to 'know oneself' through confession appears to promise liberation, Foucault believes this is an illusion: confession draws more of the person into the domain of power. Confession has a special capacity to change the person who confesses.

One of the major advantages of Foucault's disciplinary practices is that it shows how organisation exists in a constantly shifting dynamic. It can allow a view of power that avoids reducing the chaotic and often paradoxical qualities of management and organisation to a product of some single unified power (such as capitalism, technocracy, top management, patriarchy). In the modern context, disciplinary power exists in the social technologies of control. These include experts and specialists of various sorts who create or build upon normalised knowledge, ways of going on (for example, organisational culture), modes of inquiry (for example the scientific method), and thereby cut out any possibility of alternative discourses. For example, the way in which school curricula in the UK are now developed tends to organise knowledge in such a way that it would sometimes be difficult to trace an epistemological centre – information is derived from the Internet, from modular books, and the explicit authority of the teacher as a holder of knowledge has been decentred. Whilst in the past the teacher had authority as the holder of a particular knowledge (that is a discipline with some traditional epistemological basis) this 'authority relationship' with the teacher is now mediated through a fragmented modular way of gathering information, rather than conceptual systems of thinking. When the system of thinking is explicit, then it is open to contestation, when it is implicit (or not even present) then what remains is the power relation. It would be an interesting piece of research to see what effect this has on our children and young adults, and indeed on teachers themselves.

Following Foucault, to understand modern forms of rule, then involves not only analysing political activity, but analysing the 'apparently humble mechanisms which appear to make it possible to govern: techniques of notation, computation and calculation; procedures of examination and assessment; the invention of devices such as surveys and presentational forms such as tables; the standardization of systems for training and the inculcation of habits; the inauguration of professional specialisms and vocabularies' (Miller and Rose 1990, p.8).

Yet Foucault does not dissolve all forms of structure into an endless one of meaning making. He attempts to grasp what form of regularities, relations, continuities and totalities do exist. All discourses are produced by power, but they are not wholly subservient to it and can be used as 'a point of resistance and a starting point for an opposing strategy' (Foucault 1980).

As such, this conception of power can be used alongside the emancipatory goal of critical theory. Indeed, in his later work Foucault's notion of the subject changed. The subject is still discursively and socially conditioned, and still situated between power relations, but now he sees that individuals 'have the power to define their own identity, to master their bodies and desires, and to forge a practice of freedom through techniques of the self' (Best and Kellner 1991, p.65). Foucault now suggests a dialectic between an active and creative agent, and a constraining social field where freedom is achieved to the extent that one can overcome socially imposed limitations and attain self-mastery. At this point in his thinking there is an interesting mutation in his conceptualisation of power, and one which is critical to the theoretical position suggested here. Now he distinguishes between power and domination, seeing 'domination as the solidification of power relations such that they become relatively fixed in asymmetrical forms and the spaces of liberty and resistance thus become limited' (Best and Kellner 1991, p.65).

Despite the earlier, 'free-floating' conceptualisation, here we have a conceptualisation that can embrace emancipation that would be acceptable to critical theorists and feminists. For Habermas, communication becomes distorted when there are 'relations of dependence' and for Foucault domination occurs when power relations become 'solid' or 'fixed'. If we can allow a notion of power that is both enabling and constraining, and yet also potentially dominating, or 'fixed', then that leaves the door open for an investigation into where these power relations have become solidified. Where inequalities are constantly reproduced as the employment figures for women in management show, then we can infer that power relations have become solidified. Yet with our revised version of the subject, it would seem that the road to liberation lies in the practice of 'self-mastery', not as a Greco-Roman project as Foucault would have it, but initiated and learnt through bringing awareness constantly to the relationship between mind and body. Where power has become fixed in gender relations, it is often in the denial of the importance of the feminine. By holding a subjectivity that has at once agency, yet which is also subject to discursive figurations, our framework of enquiry opens up the possibilities for individual and collective emancipation, theorised within an understanding of the constraining and enabling potential of power.

3.2 THE STUDY

This study sets out to explore the discourse of competence as it is implemented and perceived by senior and junior managers in six different organisations using an understanding of the relationship between language, discursive practice and power to provide a critical and interpretive framework. I will be particularly looking out for ways in which gender relations become subsumed into the presumed objectivity of managerial practices. The competence framework may create a 'taken-for-granted' picture of ways of being that become naturalised for leaders and managers. Competence frameworks make an explicit connection between 'best performance' and 'managerial behaviours' thus constructing a picture of what a successful 'competent manager' would look and behave like. Does this hide latent conflict and create asymmetrical relations of power?

In the light of competence frameworks, this will mean asking such questions as: What do competence frameworks look like? How are these frameworks derived? Are the competence frameworks likely to play a part in the perception of self? Do competence frameworks differ between organisations? What are the implications of these differences? What are the assumptions made in the discourse of competence? What is the likely impact of these competence frameworks on the different types of manager in the workforce (that is, men and women)?

The implementation of competence frameworks is examined in six organisations of different sizes and in different sectors. In the first stages, the language of competence frameworks and the implementation of competence practices, how they are perceived, and the degree to which open consensus is reached about their implementation are examined. Competence is reconsidered in the light of disciplinary practices. Secondly it moves on to examine the implications of these frameworks for women managers. Finally, it draws upon a case study where there was more open consensus and an understanding that competence frameworks are not necessarily objective. While still retaining the critical approach, I undertook more research in this organisation since I felt there were here real possibilities of opening up consensus around competence frameworks. These frameworks were compared with those in other organisations. In so doing I hoped that the study could provide some indications of how competence frameworks could be implemented without necessarily being subject to disciplinary practices. This meant maintaining a 'bilingual' position – keeping the critical dimensions in mind, but finding ways of working within and beyond the competence frameworks to expand their usefulness (Alvesson and Deetz 2000).

Throughout the research, which operated on several levels of interpretations, I kept at the back of my mind the question:

> Do competence strategies reinforce the existing gender substructure by masking ongoing processes of gender construction and if so, how?

Along with Acker (1992), my feeling was that a gender substructure was perpetuated by the way in which organisational practices banish gender, sexuality, reproduction and emotion to the outside of organisational boundaries. In this particular case, as in most critical research, I was not primarily concerned with the way experience and meaning of the subjects were expressed. Rather the focus was on the social and linguistic processes producing the kind of subjectivity 'behind' or at least constructing an integral part of these experiences and meanings. While this does not mean that experience and expressed (espoused) meanings are disregarded: 'The ideal must be to pay attention to experiences and meanings as well as discursive and other processes of an ideological and material nature that may constitute experiences and prescribe meaning' (Alvesson and Deetz 2000, p.141).

This was carried out using a combination of textual analysis and ethnographic techniques.

3.3   RESEARCH DESIGN AND METHODS

The implementation of competence frameworks in a number of different contexts, and in different 'moments' of their implementation formed the focus of the study. This required a spread of cases across different sectors and organisation size. This 'spread' was to be, as far as access issues allowed, across organisations in different operating environments, with different business imperatives.

Company documentation and interviews with those responsible for implementation (senior managers/consultants/chief executives) were used to gain this information. This was to determine whether the context affected the type of implementation both in terms of the practices of the competence frameworks, and in terms of the subjects' perceptions of what was going on, and what they expected from the competence strategies.

From this initial comparison across cases, three were selected for more in-depth analysis in order to gain a sense of how the process operated across time through observation and continuing engagement with the organisations. Of these, the third differed in such a radical way from the other organisations that it offered a way of testing an established way of implementing competence strategies, and a possibility of challenging some of the assumptions in the competence framework, and thus of creating some useful policy guidelines.

Identification of Research Sites

The organisational research was carried out from June 1994 to December 1995. The initial plan was in two stages.

Stage 1: Broad overview and contextualisation
This was to consist of open-ended interviews with the initial contact in each of the organisations. These interviews generally lasted from one to two hours, and provided the basis for the material in Chapter 7. The material was backed by company reports, documentation, and sometimes follow-up telephone calls.

The following organisations and people were interviewed in this stage:

Organisation A   A University that was the instigator of 'open learning' techniques in the early 1970s (Head of Human Resources)

Organisation B   A major multinational in the oil industry (Head of Leadership Programmes)

Organisation C   A multinational construction company (Head of Human Resources)

Organisation D   A semi-privatised national utility (Head of Human Resources and Head of Training – two people)

Organisation E   A Health and Social Services Trust based in Northern Ireland (Consultant responsible for competence programme)

Organisation F   Beauty and Cosmetics Retailer and Manufacturer (Performance Improvement Manager)

Stage 2: In-depth case studies
Stage 2 consisted of case studies at the beauty cosmetics and manufacturer, the University and the Trust. These took place from December 1994 to October 1995. Because of the 'organic' nature of the implementation process, the

research schedule also 'evolved'. This stage consisted of interviews, observation and participation in workshops. Apart from a couple of mishaps with the tape recorder, all the interviews and workshops were taped and transcribed.

Stage 3: Continuing ethnographic engagement with the beauty and cosmetics manufacturer and retailer

Appendix 1 lists the number and type of interviews and the questions asked. The field work yielded over 50 hours of taped transcripts plus extensive documentary evidence.

Ethnographic Material

Interviews

Although the interviews were primarily non-directive, there was a complete list of issues to cover. These are listed in the appendix. These 'questions' kept the interpretive repertoire alive, and the connection between the local and the more general characteristics of management and organisations. This was the way in which I worked from 'insight' to 'critique' and back again. Most cases started with the 'harder' issues to elicit the overall competence 'framework' and to provide some historical grounding. Then there were more 'subjective' understandings of the competence initiative, although generally, once respondents had begun to 'tell their story' the majority of these issues were covered with little prompting.

Participant observation

In two of the organisations I was able to undertake some participant observation. In these cases, I either was invited to sit in on workshops where competence methods were being introduced to employees, or at the beauty and cosmetics retailer, I was invited to participate while I was an 'observer'. In one instance, this involved helping with the clustering of the competences at the early stages of identification.

Textual analysis

Part of the analysis consisted of a more in-depth analysis of a sample of texts relating to competence. To aid me in this exercise, I drew on the insights of discourse analysts, cultural analysts, and deconstructionists, to 'deconstruct' the language of competence as it was disseminated through a corpus of management material, through company documentation, and through the lists of competences themselves.[1] In order to do this, I used and built upon a set of analytical tools first published in Garnsey and Rees (1996). These are listed in Appendix 2.

3.4   THE INTERPRETIVE REPERTOIRE

Critical management research calls for an approach that is at once interpretive, open, language sensitive, identity-conscious, historical, political, local, non-authoritative and one which has a textually aware understanding of research (Alvesson and Deetz 2000). This is a reflexive methodology that does not advocate the following of specific procedures or techniques. On the contrary, it views such focus as dangerous as it draws attention away from many of the most crucial aspects of research and tends to give priority to accurately processed data. The general rule in carrying out this type of research is to try and maintain an awareness of the interpretive repertoire, and be ready to build and develop parts of this repertoire when necessary. This requires a constant iteration between critical position, theory and empirical material.

The interpretive repertoire guides the work, the choice of empirical sites, the decisions taken at those sites, how and where to continue the research. Certain lines of interpretation are given priority, others are possible but not prioritised, while others never appear possible. A narrow repertoire has narrow possibilities. An economist will not necessarily see relationships as being important. A Foucauldian may only see the inner 'psychic' prison. In good research, the researcher will always be willing to develop theory by developing his or her repertoire. This requires creativy, theoretical sophistication, breadth and variation (Alvesson and Deetz 2002, p.186). Furthermore, powerful ideas and concepts of critical theory need to be open to non-critical, or calls to other metaphors. This calls for an 'empirically grounded' imagination, the seeing of possibilities that did not exist before, making connections that have not been made before, leading to a multiple interpretation.

As a woman, with a background in editing management journals and working for management consultants, and with experience in academic institutions, my interpretive repertoire has its own story. I might not concentrate so fully on the theoretical repertoire. Such abstractions may not tell such an interesting story for me. From one woman's perspective, I might see the ability to 'relate' as being of prime importance in this repertoire. In this case, the 'empirically grounded imagination' relies not only on the breadth of theory and ability to see various aspects, but perhaps there is a different type of 'relational' imagination that comes from an ability to empathise, to retain connectedness. This way, further insights may be gained into people's lives and processes of identity construction.

Thus the reflexive approach means viewing the implementation of competence through my own sociological knowledge, through my own leanings towards the powerful tools of critical theory, through my own experience of being a woman in different organisations as employee and supplier, yet constantly retaining awareness, as far as possible, of the lenses through which I am looking. Consequently, I am including my own responses to the organisations and the people working within them, as part of the 'research data'. This, I believe gives the research an innovative strength in that, to a certain extent, it transcends the dominant scientific paradigm which may constrain voices, in particular women's voices, from theory-making.

ENDNOTE

1. There are two critical strands of textual analysis which have emerged over the past decade. Discourse as a focus for analysis has emerged in several disciplines, though its roots can be traced back, if not to Aristotle, then certainly to the philosophers of the Enlightenment (Van Dijk 1993).
    Three (neo) Marxist approaches can be identified: in members of the Frankfurt school; in Gramsci and his followers in France and the UK such as Hall and the members of the Centre for Contemporary Cultural Studies; and finally yet another approach can be traced through the (neo) Marxist approach of Althusser through to Foucault and Pecheux. Although often dealing with language, these approaches do not explicitly and systematically deal with discourse structures of language. Such contributions have come from critical linguistics and social semiotics, though they often do not provide sophisticated socio-political analyses (see Van Dijk 1993 for a summary and full references).
    A second tradition can be identified emerging within psychology and social psychology – and that is of non-critical discourse analysis (Fairclough 1992). This includes the work of ethnomethodologists who attempt a general descriptive system for analysing discourse, of conversational analysts and psycholinguists and the use of discourse analysis in social psychology. (For a fuller discussion of these approaches, see Fairclough 1992.)
    The second major school of textual analysis is that of deconstruction which draws on the work of philosophers and literary critics. In particular that of Derrida. The methods have been used in particular by feminists, since, it exposes, in a systematic way, multiple ways a text can be interpreted (Martin 1990). It is a particularly useful approach to studying suppressed gender construction/conflict in organisations. As Martin points out: 'Women's interests ... often appear as contradictions, disjunctions, disruptions, and silences of suppressed conflict (Martin 1990, p.341). However, the epistemological basis of deconstruction begs questions about the paradox of theory building and research in any field.
    I shall therefore be using insights and techniques from both schools of thought, since, as I argued in the conceptual framework, my position implies that, whilst ultimately all systems change, some are more enduring than others, and here vested interests may be lodged. I therefore have no qualms about using insights from both discourse analysts and deconstructionists where appropriate.

4. The birth of the competent manager

In the 1980s a number of reports stressed that British companies were in danger of losing out to foreign competition because there was not sufficient stock of managers necessary to meet the exigencies of the changing environment (Barham and Conway 1988; Constable and McCormick 1987; Handy *et al.* 1987). The notion of competence emerged from a plethora of discourses of work reform as a means of training and building such a stock of UK managers.[1] In this same era, the notion of the 'enterprising organisation' strongly emerged, with its advocacy of such measures as individualised pay schemes, appraisal systems, and individual and group incentives. The intention was to persuade workers of the advantages of managing themselves and their work, not only to develop better as skilled workers but also to meet organisational objectives (Keat and Abercrombie 1991). Near-simultaneous initiatives such as 'Excellence', 'Total Quality Management', 'Culture Change Programmes', 'Teamworking' and 'Business Process Re-engineering' tended to focus upon relations with customers, where the sovereign consumer (whether internal or external to the organisation) dominated the design of organisational processes.

This panoply of notions and initiatives in the 1980s generally emphasised the establishment of 'organic' or flexible organisational forms which were expected to overcome the perceived stasis and inefficiency of rigid 'bureaucratic' structures and practices (Du Gay and Salaman 1992). Managers were charged with the pivotal role of securing change through the fostering of 'entrepreneurial values', first within themselves and then within their subordinates (Du Gay, Salaman and Rees 1996). The notion of competence referred to those areas and aspects of an individual's behaviour, attributes, skills or knowledge which could be used by the organisation in order to meet its strategic objectives. The 'competence framework' described how such areas and aspects could be marshalled, clustered and organised to assist the development both of the individual and the organisation (for example Boyatzis 1982). Competence did not arise in a vacuum, but was one of several initiatives that formed a general move towards the creation of the 'enterprising' organisation. Before looking at competence approaches, let us first examine in more detail the conditions in which the idea of management has evolved.

4.1 MANAGEMENT AND ITS MEASUREMENT

'Management' as a concept is both relatively new and also very old. In the sense that it has its own body of theory and literature, it only emerged in the second half of the twentieth century. Prior to the Second World War management literature was limited to probably less than 100 texts (Williams *et al*. 1995) with few managers of the day realising that they were practising management as we would know it today. Management was embedded in the disciplines of accounting, banking and finance.[2]

Perhaps the greatest influence on modern-day organisation was one of the foremost exponents of 'scientific management', F. Taylor. The foundation of his notion was to use 'scientific' methods to determine the most efficient way that a task could be carried out, and to redesign jobs accordingly. These methods aimed to achieve the best technical way of organising work in the best physical environment. 'Time and motion' was central to this approach, and jobs were broken down into component elements which were timed and the information used to plan workflows. Decision-making was transferred from workers to management, leaving workers with routine repetitive tasks which were paid on the basis of their allotted time (Beynon and Blackburn 1991). The Human Relations approach which developed in the 1930s at Harvard under the direction of Elton Mayo took things a step further in its attempt to recognise and incorporate the social relations between workers in its planning.

It was only post-war that management or organisational studies as a body of literature and theory developed. Such studies have concentrated on structures of organisations, management and decision-making within it, and managerial behaviour and decision-making (Pugh, Hickson and Hinings 1988). The last 15 years have witnessed increasing globalisation and internationalisation of markets leading to a burgeoning literature on international and cross-cultural management (for example, Hofstede 1991; Brewster and Hegewisch 1994; Trompenaars 1993).

At the same time, the 'measurement' of management in terms of managerial performance has been notoriously difficult. One of the major problems in evaluating managerial behaviour lies in defining the role of the manager with any precision, since this differs between industries, organisations and functions. Some management positions are mainly administrative, with a heavy load of paper work, other positions require a large amount of personal contact to co-ordinate the work of subordinates. Different organisational or environmental demands are placed on managers at different times, which render the measurement task even more difficult.

The first real attempts at measuring management performance and behaviour drew their inspiration from military assessment programmes.

Among the first of these were those used for selection of army, air force and naval officers by German military psychologists in the early part of the century. The British War Office Selection Boards developed methods to assess leadership qualities during the Second World War, which were refined for the British Civil Service Selection Board. In the USA, work carried out in the Office of Strategic Services was particularly influential, as were the studies later undertaken by the US Veterans Administration (Thornton and Byham 1982).

Early research on non-supervisory levels leading to the growing use of more systematic selection and appraisal procedures (Townley 1993b), was later adapted for use at managerial levels. Such techniques focus on the attitudinal and behavioural characteristics of employees, which lend themselves to monitoring through selection and performance review. This includes techniques such as personality and psychometric tests, biodata and performance appraisal reviews. As early as 1985, appraisals in the UK were extended to 78 per cent of first-line supervisors, 66 per cent for clerical and secretarial and 24 per cent for skilled and semi-skilled employees (Long 1986). In the USA figures had reached 91 per cent of first-line employees, 88 per cent office and clerical and 63 per cent skilled manual workers by 1982 (Bureau of National Affairs 1983). These approaches were not new. Child points out the early interest in behavioural and attitudinal aspects shown by Quaker employers (Child 1964). However, the changing nature of production requirements, with a move away from direct supervision of work, has created an increase in systematic selection and appraisal procedures (Townley 1993b). Competence approaches were seen as a new and 'objective' way into developing and measuring the performance of managers in the UK.

4.2 THE EMERGENT BACKGROUND: THE DEVELOPMENT OF THE 'ENTERPRISING' ORGANISATION

These more systematic techniques of measurement have contributed to, and emerged from the reconceptualisation of the organisation and its members as 'enterprising'. These are perpetuated by and reflected in the numerous 'change programmes' and work reforms such as 'Excellence', 'Total Quality Management', 'Just-in-Time', 'Culture Change Programmes', 'Teamworking' or 'Business Process Re-engineering'. These approaches place emphasis on the development of more 'organic' and 'flexible' organisational forms and practices. The early bureaucratic and hierarchical structures could no longer cope with the flexibility required to meet the constantly changing customer demand. Here, it appears, the customers, not management, exert control over employees. Employees need to act in subtle and 'branded' ways to deliver what customers define as 'quality service' and this cannot be achieved through the alienating control of the bureaucrat. In order to encourage this type of behaviour, organisations are required to develop more sophisticated ways of 'changing culture' by, for example, analysing behaviour, values and attitudes of employees, and measuring such change through customer feedback.

In organisations dominated by this view of the customer, the traditional view which espoused the merits of 'bureaucratic' structures has been torn down and replaced by so-called customer-facing structures. In order to compete successfully, and to achieve adequate profit margins, organisations must be able to satisfy customers. And in order to do this, internal organisational relations must resemble, even become, market relations (Du Gay and Salaman 1992). Indeed, employees are encouraged to treat each other as their own 'internal' customers.

While each of the new discourses of work reform have abundant literatures, and each proclaims its logical superiority over the other (Flood 1993), what is interesting about these latest discourses of work reform is the rapidity with which they are displaced by other discourses, and the minimal differences that there are between each. Hill (1991) for example, basing his understanding on the works of the American quality gurus Deming, Juran and the Japanese Ishikawa defines TQM as:

> a business discipline and philosophy of management which institutionalises planned and continuous business improvement: indeed many people prefer to talk of managing for continuous improvement rather than for quality, which has a product-centred connotation.

Some basic principles appear in most TQM systems (Hill 1991):

1. Quality is defined as conformance to the requirements of the customer.
2. There are internal as well as external customers.
3. Appropriate performance measures are used routinely to assess quality of design and conformance and initiate corrective action when performance is below standard.
4. New organisational arrangements are required.
5. Wider participation in decision-making is essential.
6. An appropriate culture is required if everyone in the organisation is to endorse the objectives and routinely follow the procedures of quality management.
7. The quality of the final product or service results from every single activity in an organisation.

If we set this against the school of Excellence as propounded by the guru Peters (1987), we find little difference in meaning:

1. Prescriptions for a world turned upside down.
2. Creating total customer responsiveness.
3. Pursuing fast-paced innovation.
4. Achieving flexibility by empowering people.
5. Learning to love change: a new view of leadership at all levels.
6. Building systems for a world turned upside down (Peters, chapter headings, 1987).

Business process re-engineering has been defined as: '... the notion of discontinuous thinking – of recognising and breaking away from the outdated rules and fundamental assumptions that underlie operations. Unless we change these rules, we are merely rearranging the deck chairs on the Titanic' (Hammer 1990, p.107).

Hammer's basic principles of BPR are:

1. Organise around outcomes, not tasks.
2. Have those who use the output of the process perform the process.
3. Subsume information-processing work into the real work that produces this information.
4. Treat geographically dispersed resources as though they were centralised.
5. Link parallel activities instead of integrating their results.
6. Put the decision point where the work is performed and build control into the process.
7. Capture information once and at the same source.

Though written in different styles, and being from different management movements, such approaches have much in common. All are customer-focused, all aim at restructuring the present ways of delivering product, while both TQM and Excellence stress the importance of the culture. Such initiatives then, form part of the same managerial discourse.

Such approaches have arisen in response to a number of conditions within the environment of the organisation. These have been variously detailed as competitive pressures from Pacific rim countries with low labour costs and high productivity, new generations of IT and other technologies creating a need for fast-responding organisations, demographic conditions creating problems of supply in the labour markets, and a changing occupational profile of the workforce with a resultant growth in the number of managers, plus the effects of recession (IPM Report 1994).

4.3   MANAGING PEOPLE: FROM PERSONNEL TO HUMAN RESOURCE MANAGEMENT

Against and within this background, ways of managing 'people' have undergone considerable change. This can be seen in the many and varied changes undergone in the personnel and human resource management functions. The accepted view about the emergence of human resource management has been predicated upon the differences between an individualist and collectivist model. The industrial conflict that characterised much of the 1970s business environment, with its emphasis on collective bargaining has, it is argued, been overtaken by a focus on human resource management with its perceived emphasis on individualist approaches. The former was focused on trade unions, collective bargaining and the handling of collective grievances and disputes, and its centre was seen as the 'personnel department', acting as gatekeeper between unions and management; while the latter, with its emphasis on the individual employee, is focused on matters of recruitment and selection, appraisal, reward and training, and its centre is seen as the Human Resource Department.

In the individualist model, management aims to speak directly to its employees through employee communications rather than through the mediation of the trade unions, occupational psychologists are employed to measure the competences of employees, and ensure that they are properly motivated to be working towards the organisation's main goals. At the heart of many of these approaches is the appraisal system, which attempts to measure and control the individual's output over the year. Such a tool is seen as key not only to managing by objectives, but also to setting and measuring conformance to behavioural norms (Storey and Sisson 1993, p.3).

However, we need to be somewhat cautious about these espoused differences in managing people. The above models are based upon normative descriptions that emerge from management literature. Legge (1989) draws a useful distinction between the normative models, showing how each, in practice, is conceptualised differently. One of the major differences she notes is that personnel management is conceived as an activity which is largely aimed at non-managers, that is, it is something carried out on subordinates, while HRM not only emphasises the importance of employee development, but focuses particularly on the development of the management team. While both personnel and HRM highlight the role of line management, the former emphasises personnel management on the line as an additional responsibility for line managers, while the latter highlight HRM as an integral part of a 'business manager's' role including the management of other resources – it should be an integral part of the line manager's strategy. Finally, some HRM models emphasise the role of the management of the organisation's culture as integral to senior management's role. In this sense, these three differences point to HRM, in theory, being essentially a more central strategic management task in that: 'It is experienced by managers as the most valued company resource to be managed, it concerns them in the achievement of business goals and it expresses senior management's preferred organisational values' (Legge 1989, p.28).

The reality of the workplace does, however, belie even these distinctions. Storey and Sisson (1993) show how, despite the claim that the HRM model is essentially unitarist (that is it has supposedly little tolerance for the multiple interest groups and the multiple expression of interests) the take-up of HR strategies as an integrated programme in the UK's large mainstream organisations has been fragmentary. Through a survey, they note how the way in which the organisations were operating might: '... indicate the true nature of the HRM phenomenon – that is, that it is in reality a symbolic label behind which lurk multifarious practices, many of which are not mutually dependent on one another' (Storey and Sisson 1993, p.23).

However, their research does back up Legge's emphasis on the emergence of line managers as general business managers. Further, there was evidence for increased employee communication and an all-round acknowledgement of the importance of managing culture. Cressey and Jones (1992) show also in their study of a British bank and an Italian car manufacturer that there are unforeseen and concrete difficulties in integrating HRM into the broader business strategy. They conclude that the integration of policies and business functions that characterise HRM is, paradoxically, what limits the practical implementation of HRM reforms.

The reason that HR initiatives are not taken up wholesale as predicated in the normative models is probably due to an internal contradiction in the model itself. In drawing together what are perceived as the predominant characteristics of HRM Legge (1989) notes :

> ... that human resources policies should be integrated with strategic business planning and used to reinforce an appropriate (or change an inappropriate) organisational culture, that human resources are valuable and a source of competitive advantage, that they may be tapped most effectively by mutually consistent policies that promote commitment and which, as a consequence, foster a willingness in employees to act flexibly in the interests of the adaptive organisation's pursuit of excellence. (p.25)

The internal contradiction here, according to Legge, lies in the words 'mutually consistent policies that promote commitment'. Matching HRM policies to business goals calls for minimising labour costs, which will not necessarily be policies that promote commitment. The rhetoric adopted to attempt to mediate this contradiction is that of 'tough love' as characterised by the Peters and Waterman approach (1982). If an individual's abilities and performance are inappropriate to the company, then the person must be redefined as no longer an employee, and a tough decision may have to be made for the greater good of the company and the other employees (Legge 1989). In other models, a distinction is made between 'hard' and 'soft' HRM models, where the former concentrates on the quantitative, calculative and business strategic aspects of managing the headcount resources in as 'rational' a way as for any other factor and the latter emphasises 'communication, motivation and leadership' (Storey 1989).

Given the reality of the workplace and the inherent contradictions within normative HRM models, Legge (1989) asks how it is that the language of HRM has gained its present currency. She suggests that the dual usage (passive and proactive) of the term 'resource' and the 'hard' and 'soft' models is very useful. The language and policies of the 'hard' model can be used on employees peripheral to the organisation while the 'softer' versions can be used on employees whom the organisation wish to retain. As she notes: 'Ironically, it is the contradictions embedded in HRM that have facilitated the development of this rhetoric even if they simultaneously render strategic action problematic.'

The contradiction shows no sign of abating. HR has always had a dual responsibility. On the one hand it must work in the interests of the company. It needs to hold a line on salaries, negotiate with the unions and author policies that protect the company from litigation. On the other hand, due to its emergence from the 'welfare' role of personnel, it must represent the interests of employees, even though this may appear to go against the best interests of the company. What is clear though is that in some companies, the human resource function has become 'big business' (Pasmore 1999). Pasmore notes that as the corporate political battles of the 1980s and 1990s unfolded, information technology and human resource professionals elbowed their way into the inner circle of decision-making. Organization restructuring often took place under the banner of HR and change management, along with an increased lip service to 'diversity' issues.

It is in this inevitable tension between managing people as a resource to further the ends of the organisation, and in seeking the commitment and motivation of employees that 'government' takes place. The competence-based organisation may represent a further step in attempting to 'govern' individuals so that they are moving collectively towards the organisation's aims. And it is in the rhetoric of the enterprising, change management model of HRM that competence-based initiatives in the UK have emerged.

4.4 THE ORIGINS OF COMPETENCE[3]

The term 'competence' has its origins in the research of the McBer Consultancy in the late 1970s in the USA as part of the initiative by the American Management Association to identify the characteristics which distinguish superior from average managerial performance (Iles 1993). The work was encapsulated in the seminal book *The Competent Manager* (Boyatzis 1982). This has spawned a mass of literature and initiatives in organisational attempts to identify and construct the 'competent' manager.

However, the term and its related concepts have become problematic as they have been taken and adapted to different environments. It has been used from the training of a select group of managers, to total change of an entire organisation, to the growth of a system of national vocational training. How have so many different interpretations arisen? The major reason lies in the ambiguity of the term. It has been taken up by academics, consultants, management, psychologists, trainers, and educationalists who in their turn have used it to focus at national, organisational and individual level.

The Start of the Confusion: Definitions of Competence

There is no agreed definition about the meaning of the word 'competence'. Boyatzis (1982) defined the term as: 'an underlying characteristic of a person'. It could be a motive, trait, skill, aspect of one's self-image or social role, or a body of knowledge which he or she uses. However, as Woodruffe (1993) has pointed out, there is a mass of literature attempting to define the terms 'motive, trait, skill etc.' This again opens up the term to a multitude of interpretations. Woodruffe (1993) for example, defines 'competency' as: 'a set of behaviour patterns that the incumbent needs to bring to a position in order to perform its tasks and functions with competence'.

Others have used the term skill and competence interchangeably: 'Perhaps the most fundamental implication of moving to a skill- or competency-based approach to management concerns the area of work design' (Lawler 1994). For Rhinesmith: 'If mindsets and personal characteristics are the "being" side of global management, then competences are the "doing" side' (Rhinesmith 1992). While Kanungo and Misra (1992) view: 'skills and competences as two distinct constructs of managerial ability', and examine them along several dimensions such as specific/generic, task-driven/person-driven and nontransferable/transferable. In this framework managerial abilities are stratified as those that are needed for specific routine tasks (skills) and those needed for all non-routine tasks (competences). In an attempt to find a way out of the confusion, Brown (1993) has coined the term 'meta-competences' which are: 'the higher order abilities which have to do with being able to learn, adapt, anticipate and create, rather than with being able to demonstrate that one has the ability to do'.

Finally, some have used the term so loosely that it is difficult to see any connection with Boyatzis's original idea: 'The functions that Jung puts forward are only the beginnings of his development model since expanded by many others. Simply stated, his view is that we all develop high levels of competences in certain preferred functions which we try to use to the exclusion of others' (Lewis 1993, p.29).

Despite the enormous diversity of interpretation, attempts at encapsulating the history of the word and its developments have been limited if not inaccurate. For example, Iles (1993) identifies differences in methodologies between US and UK work. He argues that in the USA the dominant approach is a person-oriented job analysis (for example, behavioural event interviewing) to identify those characteristics which distinguish successful role incumbents, while in the UK a task-oriented job analysis technique called functional analysis is used to identify the necessary roles, tasks and duties of the occupation. In fact, in the literature I have examined, and in the case study organisations presented here in the UK, the approach has been predominantly the former. Functional analysis has been reserved for the NVQ approach, which, as I shall argue later, is somewhat different. Further, commentators disagree as to whether functional analysis is a job analysis technique, or whether it has the capacity to take into account the wider context in which it is situated. (See, for example, Mansfield 1993; Stewart and Hamlin 1992a, b, 1993, 1994.)

The extent of the ambiguity of the meaning may be seen in the fact that, at various times, all these terms have been identified as 'competences' (in Stewart and Hamlin 1992b, p.23). Bearing this unresolved ambiguity in mind, let us now examine different competence frameworks.

4.5   DIFFERING MODELS OF COMPETENCE

It is important to differentiate between generic or organisationally-specific models. Some of the literature, derived directly from Boyatzis, concentrates on attempting to define generic lists of management competences that can be universally applied in organisations. Other writers and commentators claim that each organisation needs a specific list of competences aligned to the business plan. Two distinctive fields tend to emerge from this differentiation. On the one hand, the generic school of thought has created, in the UK, a network of managerial qualifications based on generic competences, and locked in to the NVQ system of qualifications. At the same time hosts of management trainers and developers have used such competences as the basis for management training – at varying levels of the organisation. On the other hand there are those who subscribe to the organisationally-derived models.

The Generic School

The generic school generally accepts that there are universal management competences that are applicable in all contexts. There is debate about the level of competence required in any particular situation. Boyatzis, for example, proposed 'threshold' and 'performance' competences. Threshold competences are those requirements necessary to carry out the job, while performance competences actually differentiate between levels of performance. Jacobs (1989) made a distinction between hard and soft competences, where soft competences are personal qualities such as creativity which lie behind behaviour. Thornton and Byham (1982) generated a list aimed at encompassing all the competences relevant to 'top management'. Schroder (1989) builds on the Boyatzis model to develop eleven high performer competences. Dulewicz (1989) focused on middle management research, in which he identified 'supra competences'.

Further, many such lists have been generated for international managers. With an increasing emphasis on globalisation, attempts are being made at identifying particular skills that are required of the global manager. For example:

> Global competences are the centrepiece of the HR strategy … They're grounded in business needs. Armed with competences that are tiered throughout the organisation, we can target our efforts and be much more effective in bringing the best talent to Colgate … These competences have first a technical/functional focus, then a managerial planning focus, and then a leadership focus. (Solomon 1994, p.98)

While Wills and Barham (1994) claim that in international management it is misleading totally to attribute success to specific behaviour competences or skill. In addition to these, they argue, such people appear to be operating from 'a deeper, core competence which is essentially holistic in nature. These are described as 'cognitive complexity, emotional energy and psychological maturity'. Rhinesmith (1992) identifies six development clusters that should characterise the 'mindset' of the global manager. In addition, some writers have drawn up generic team competences (Alderson 1993).

The Management Charter Initiative and NVQs

The aim of the Management Charter Initiative (MCI) established in 1988 was to increase the quality and professionalism of managers at all levels throughout the economy. The MCI is being developed by the National Forum for Management Education and Development (NFMED), formed jointly by the CBI, the Institute of Management (IM) and the Foundation for Management Education. This has been set in place among the NVQ initiative, which aimed to have occupational standards for all occupations. based on competence frameworks, with a national system for accreditation. NVQs are a set of occupational standards which set out clearly what employees need to be able to do in order to perform effectively in their jobs. NVQs are obtained by a variety of routes including mixing on- and off-the-job training and accumulating credits towards a qualification over a period of time. Three awarding bodies, the Business and Technology Education Council (BTEC) the Royal Society of Arts (RSA) and the IM, have now received NCVQ accreditation for certification in management based on the MCI standards. It seems as though it is building a large ground swell of support among British organisations (that is, it now has a membership of almost 1000 employers, representing 25 per cent of the UK workforce).

The approach in drawing up the management standards was so-called 'functional analysis', that is a top-down approach to identifying what people need to be able to do in the workplace. It takes the various job functions and breaks them down into a series of units and elements. To establish the competences, a group of industry representatives are asked to identify the industry's key purpose and are then asked to identify what needs to happen in order for this to be achieved. By repeating this process iteratively one arrives at a point at which individual units are described (the level at which an individual rather than a team is responsible for the work) followed by elements, and ultimately, performance criteria. The performance criteria describe the standard of performance which is expected of an employee, but do not prescribe the techniques, routes or processes by which he/she should attain that outcome.

The parallel development of the MCI initiative alongside companies developing organisation-specific competences has brought with it fierce debate. For example, in a series of articles in the *Journal of European Industrial Training*, Stewart and Hamlin (1992a, b, 1993, 1994) argue that the competence movement is not, as is claimed employer-led: that the meaning and definition of competence is misleading; that there are problems in applying generic competences to specific situations; that there will never be as much objectivity in assessment as required; that it is costly to administrate; that competence standards are not written in output terms (that is, they identify procedural steps that should be taken); and that functional analysis, as a major analytical tool only identifies what is to be done – not how or the knowledge and skills required to perform it. They argue for the use of existing methodologies such as job or task analysis to draw up competences.

Burgoyne (1989) amongst other criticisms pointed out that competence is a complex whole which cannot be split up and represented in separate parts, while Wills (1993) in defence pointed out that the standards can be used as flexible tools and are not to be set up as panacea. Finally Kilcourse (1994) questions the value of academic qualifications in developing managers for a turbulent future. While recognising what the MCI has achieved in pushing the question of competency to centre stage, he argues that NVQs at the management level are too often academically driven, largely managed and awarded through academic establishments with accreditation resigning more on rigour and method in assessment than on relevance of the job.

The debate has continued over the years.What is clear, however, from this research, is that organisations are not swayed by such arguments – those who have adopted the MCI approach have used it in association with their own strategies, while others have proceeded on entirely different, but parallel trajectories.

Organisation-specific Models

In organisations, there are two distinct stages in the competency approach: in the first stage competences are identified; and the second focuses on extent, and way in which the competence framework is implemented in the organisation.

Identifying the competences

There is an on-going debate over the meaning of the term 'competence' which obviously has repercussions on the way in which competences are identified within an organisation or generically (Spencer and Spencer 1993; Fletcher 1992; Schroder 1989). However, although there are innumerable variants and debates over ways of identification, the core process for identification can be summarised as follows:

Stage 1: Select level of analysis (management strata, specialist functions, whole organisation).
Stage 2: Conduct behavioural event interviews across selected sample.
Stage 3: Analyse interviews, cluster characteristics of competences.
Stage 4: Feedback competences to relevant personnel.
Stage 5: Draw up model of competences to characterise behaviour required across the management strata, function or organisation.

Central to this model (and indeed any model for generating competences) is the behavioural event, or critical incident interview. In this type of interviewing, job holders, and 'significant others' who regularly see a person perform a job, are interviewed to generate accounts of observed behaviour or activity that can be shown to be crucial to effective or less effective performance of the job in question. To qualify for a 'behavioural event' two criteria must be satisfied. First, the event has to be observable in some way and, second, there should be little doubt concerning its relevance to effective or less effective performance. The process elicits a list of behavioural characteristics that can then be translated – through the medium of a variety of techniques, both quantitative and qualitative – into competency clusters of critical behaviours underlying the effective performance of the job. The difference between this and traditional methods of job specification are twofold: first, the interview focuses on the 'behaviour' needed to carry out the specific task and not the task itself; and second, the 'behaviour' is elicited from the individuals themselves.

4.6   ASSOCIATED COMPETENCE TECHNOLOGIES

The competence movement is associated with a raft of human resource technologies which help validate, measure and implement the competence framework. The critical underpinning of the competence framework is the notion of appraisal. On-going assessment and appraisal are key to success in monitoring whether the competence programme is working. With fewer management layers and more direct reports to each manager, increased use of matrix or project management and greater geographical spread of staff, the old principle of the immediate boss carrying out the appraisal becomes unworkable in many instances. There have been a variety of responses to this problem. One is to increase the use of self-appraisal, and the combination of self and superior appraisal is still the most common approach. The competence approach itself implies a greater level of self-management, and most of the more comprehensive competence programmes have workshops built in so that managers are trained in profiling people against jobs. There has also been a growing use of 360 degree feedback, or upward appraisal (Fletcher 1993; Novack 1993; Moravec *et al.* 1993; Bicknell and Frances 1998). 360 degree assessment is a process whereby feedback is collected 'all around' an employee, from his or her supervisors, subordinates, peers and customers. It provides a comprehensive summary of an employee's skills, abilities, styles and job-related competences. These, it is claimed, are challenging the traditional command and control and performance management systems (Moravec *et al.* 1993). Competence frameworks can provide the bedrock on which such structures operate, since they provide a measuring tool.

Other techniques include:

- the selection interview
- ability tests and personality scales
- the assessment/development centre

Despite its renowned reputation for poor reliability and validity, the selection interview remains the commonly used procedure in most organisations. The 1995 Price Waterhouse Cranfield survey on international HRM, found that one-to-one interviews were used for 40 per cent of all appointments in the organisations surveyed in the UK. Some organisations recognise the problems endemic to the selection interview and have introduced more standardised information for their selection decisions. Such information may be collected from ability tests and personality scales, and psychometric testing (Alimo-Metcalfe 1994). Competences can provide a framework against which potential performance can be assessed.

Growing in importance, and particularly associated with competences is the assessment centre. An assessment centre is a procedure that uses multiple assessment techniques to evaluate employees for a variety of manpower purposes and decisions (Thornton and Byham 1982; Gammie 1997). It will use techniques such as paper and pencil tests, questionnaires, and the use of background information. However, what is particularly important is the focus on relevant behaviours displayed by the assessee in simulations (Seegers 1987). It aims to gather information in a standardised and controlled way on behaviour that is representative for future job behaviour. It can be used for performance appraisal, achievement evaluation or potential evaluation.

While most commentators seem to feel that assessment centres offer a more accurate and comprehensive appraisal of an individual's potential and development needs than traditional methods (Dulewicz 1989; Shuttleworth and Prescott 1991; Seegers 1987), they can suffer from design inadequacies (Dulewicz 1991). Despite the problems however, there seems to be agreement, that, even if costly, assessment centres are currently among the best of the methods of assessment and selection available to personnel managers.

In addition to literature on assessment centres, there is a burgeoning literature relating to psychological methods of assessing competence. Kinder and Robertson (1994) for example focus on the relationships between personality and a range of competences that are deemed to be important in successful leadership and management. Lewis (1993) attempts to examine how Jung's theory of psychological types could be related to competences. Robertson and Kinder (1993) show how The Occupational Personality Questionnaire may be appropriate for predicting job-relevant behaviour, while

Arnold and Davey (1992) show, through a large statistical study, how self-rating and supervisor ratings of competences can vary.

Competence-based Pay Systems

The fullest type of competence framework is that which includes pay systems. As Nemerov (1994) points out: 'Implementing a competency-based program requires considerably upfront measurement, the courage to disengage from traditional pay systems that no longer add value, and the willingness to manage the effect on the company's workforce' (p.53). Where these have been successfully integrated, commentators seem to agree that the systems build in to the organisation the capacity for change – the capacity that will generate competitive advantage (Reagan 1994; Cofsky 1993; Hofrichter 1993).

Like all human resource technologies, there are a host of variables, but some commonalties can be identified. First, a competence-based system is people-based, not job-based. Pay distinctions are determined on the basis of individual differences, as measured by the level of demonstrated competence, not job responsibilities. If the competence models are created correctly, more complex responsibilities will be linked to higher levels of competence.

A fairly simple model reflects how the system may work:

1. Distinguish levels of competence.
2. Assess the competence of job incumbents.
3. Review incumbent's job placement.
4. Create pay bands.
5. Develop a pay delivery system.

In a competence-based system, pay bands replace salary grades. Pay bands will reflect the level, the breadth and the depth of each competence. The bands may be constructed on the basis of an increasing number of competences, increasing levels of proficiency, or a combination of both. Usually pay band values are market-based. The compensation professional usually measures pay distributions across several benchmark jobs to create the requisite continuum of pay increments based on increased levels of competence (Nemerov 1994).

4.7   CONCLUSIONS

Competence as a way of appraisal and reward is of growing importance in organisations for 'maximising the value of their human resources'. Indeed, even where there are no formal competence frameworks, people often talk of the 'competence' of their employees, as opposed to their skills or performance. Despite the burgeoning literature, there is little to distinguish the various approaches, though the extent and depth to which competence frameworks are connected with human resource strategies does vary. Competences, in whatever form, it seems, are here to stay. Further, with few exceptions (Townley 1990), in the literature, the relationship between gender and competence goes unremarked.

Are these frameworks however, as helpful as the literature claims? Do they actually conceal, or, in their very act of concealing, even construct different realities that become 'taken-for-granted' in organisational life?

ENDNOTES

1. Throughout this book, unless quoting from others, I shall refer to 'competence' and 'competences'. Other commentators may use the spelling 'competency' and 'competencies'. Whilst there have been some crude attempts at relating different meanings to these different spellings, the parallel existence of the two forms is merely an indication of the confusion surrounding the terms, not of any deeper meaning.
2. Note that the analysis here is concerned explicitly with 'discourses of work reform' as they have emerged over the twentieth century. That is to say that it focuses on approaches that have the increase of productivity and profit as their implicit or explicit goal. (It does not include more sociological approaches such as that of interactionism, neo-marxist analyses of the labour process or feminist contributions.) Discourses of work reform tend to provide prescriptive ways of working for enhanced efficiency, even if they come from an espoused academic and theoretical base. Having to point this out reflects an inherent ambiguity that has developed with the burgeoning growth of business schools: there is rarely clarity about whether such research is analytical or prescriptive.
3. I am distinguishing here 'competences' from 'core competences' as defined by Prahalad and Hamel (1990). For Prahalad and Hamel core competences represent the collective learning of the organisation and consist of the co-ordination of diverse production skills and multiple streams of technologies. It refers to communication, involvement and a deep commitment to working across organisational boundaries. The competence approach I am referring to here is specifically initiatives aimed at improving the 'competence' of the workforce, usually initiated from the human resource department, and not the 'core competences' which refers more to a specific articulation between product and human resources.

5. Competent organisations

Why do organisations choose to adopt competence approaches, how are they introduced and what do senior management hope and expect from the competence frameworks? How do the models match up to those examined in the last chapter? What do people think of them? This chapter presents the espoused expectations and hopes as they were presented by those who initiated and/or implemented these schemes.

5.1   WHY AND HOW IMPLEMENTATION TOOK PLACE

Organisation A: Higher Education Institute

This particular institution had been the first to provide distance learning at graduate level. As higher education was changing, the University recognised that it would have to adapt to a new environment. The university was currently undergoing a major Plans for Change, 1994–2004 project which was the organisation's first strategic development plan, laying out the direction in which the University would have to move to face the challenges of an expanding and increasingly competitive market.

The University management structure was divided into three: academic/administrative/regional to reflect the fact that the courses are developed and written centrally, but delivered regionally through a country-wide tutorial system. The impetus for introducing competences came from the HR department who felt that the ways of working and communicating needed to change. It was expected that this would provide better information and increase the speed of response throughout the organisation and a perceived need to reduce unit costs and become 'more businesslike'.

There was equally a recognition that senior staff should play a key role in deciding the future of the organisation. Some senior staff had become increasingly dissatisfied with senior management training courses whose content was felt to be 'rubbish'. At the same time, the University was seeking to be awarded Investors in People initiative. Competences were seen as a way of combining effective HRM with strategic business plans. Further, many heads of academic units were being asked to take on more and more managerial roles, and since these heads are elected members, competences were considered a way of helping these academics learn the skills of people management.

Thus the initiative was driven by the HR department who were looking for some way of delivering 'skills, knowledge, and the appropriate behaviours' to meet the strategy of the organisation.

Identifying competences

The HR Director first of all identified a management consultancy that had expertise in competences. The consultant carried out eight telephone interviews with senior staff at the University using a semi-structured questionnaire. These senior staff were selected because they had objected most to the content of the existing training programmes. The objective of these interviews was to discuss the implications of the changes taking place at the University for the individuals concerned. In the following month, the consultant held a further eight face-to-face interviews in which these issues were further clarified. Also interviewees were asked to specify positive and negative behaviours associated with competences they had identified over the phone and to 'paint a picture' of the University as they would like to see it develop over the next ten years.

The consultant then held an interview with the Vice Chancellor in order to attain a view of the strategic plans of the University. This information was compiled by the consultancy and competences were drawn up for senior managers within the organisation. A 'competence steering committee' was set up of senior managers from all different areas and a workshop was held in which these competences were discussed and amended. Prior to this, work had been carried out in the regions where a different set of competences had been identified.

Uses of competences at time of interview

The next stage, once the competences had been drawn up, was for a group from the steering committee including the Vice Chancellor to undergo a pilot appraisal scheme with 360 degree feedback. Eventually, the hoped-for outcome was for competences to be used as an integrating mechanism for recruitment, selection and appraisal, and performance management techniques. There were plans for the competences to be extended to include secretarial and clerical jobs. It was not expected that competences would form the basis for pay.

Use of national standards

In a separate initiative, the University was also using NVQs for technical and administrative staff.

Timing and levels of implementation

Although the scheme was yet in its infancy (one year in), due to the amorphous nature of the organisation, the HR Director thought timing would be a problem. It had taken a year to reach the stage they were at the time of interview. For example, a separate initiative was already underway in the regions, and there were differences both in the way competences had been gathered and in the definitions of competence (that is, the regional ones were more 'outcome-orientated'). Because of a series of initiatives happening across the University (Investors in People, Plans for Change) there was concern that this would not happen in an integrated way. The HR Director also thought there might be problems with acceptance by the academic staff.

Organisation B: A Major Multinational Oil Company

Competences were first introduced in 1989 when the organisation went through a major culture change exercise called 'Project 90'. This was designed to change the whole way the company was organised, and change the culture to make it better able to face the challenges ahead. This was to be done through developing the following four aspects: Open Thinking, Personal Impact, Empowerment, and Networking. This was accompanied by considerable downsizing (100000 to 50000 employees) and an increasing emphasis on teamworking. During this time the Chairman left, and profits were at their lowest in 1992.

This therefore created pressure for everyone to 'look internally at how everyone should behave'. The competence initiative started with the identification and development of leadership competences, since it was felt to be important that the organisation recognised the type of leader they needed and how they should be developed.

Identifying competences

The initiative was begun by the Head of Leadership Programmes in the company. The first stage consisted of stepping back and taking a strategic look at where the company was going. This was gained through talking to the various businesses and the corporate centre to decide what type of approach would be appropriate. This was not strictly speaking tied into the business plan, focusing not specifically on brands, but more with which markets to concentrate upon, and how to exploit the margins of the markets.

With the help of a consultancy, the Head of Leadership Programmes and his team sent a questionnaire to all top senior management (100) focusing on the culture and style of the team. From the questionnaire, they identified 15 top performers and 15 ordinary performers. Using critical incident techniques, these 30 were interviewed in order to identify the types of behaviours used by top performers.

There then followed a period (18 months) when the interviews were analysed both from the point of view of the strategy, and from external benchmarking of what competitors were doing. In addition to input from external consultants, the model had to be sanctioned by each of the managements of the different businesses. Further, the executive members of the main board used the competences to assess their own performance against profiles of their jobs. The results of this exercise were used as a tool to talk about how they worked, and who their successors were likely to be. The three business heads then went through a process of 360 degree feedback to assess their own performance. This exercise was considered critical to ensure that the rest of the company took competences seriously.

Once the Board had undergone the competence exercise, the competences were introduced to the next level down. Rather than communicating this universally through the internal communications system, the Board decided the best way would be to introduce them as one of the key aims of the training programme for senior managers. The Head of Leadership programmes began by reworking the initial questionnaire so that managers could profile themselves against the competences as part of a training programme. These people then took their questionnaires to their bosses and underwent 360 degree feedback.

After the process had gained acceptance, the top 100 managers went through the same process. Each manager was sent a questionnaire and instructed to select four subordinates, a boss and a peer with whom they could discuss their competence profile. This was followed by a counselling session with an external consultant, and then final results were presented back to the main Board. The process provided a summarised competence profile of the top 100 managers with their development plans which was then integrated with formal succession planning processes. The process went on to be duplicated lower down the organisation.

The competence profile is not matched rigorously against the job profile. As the Head of Leadership Programmes noted:

> I think they have to be aware of the job so we can then match it up with the originals. One of the dangers in my experience is that people change their jobs anyway. We can put somebody new in the job and very suddenly get a very different flavour, apart from the fact that jobs change.

Uses of competences at time of interview
The programme was initially conceived very much as part of an organisational change programme, but actually introduced first of all as management development for the top 100 managers. Once these were identified and

cascaded down the competences form part of the management development architecture.

Competences were built into the assessment processes used to select and promote people moving from junior to middle management posts. The competences had not yet been introduced at the entrance to the high flier scheme, at least not formally. The very senior managers were assessors on that programme but there were plans that the competences would soon be incorporated here. The leadership competences were informally aligned with recruitment processes and the HR department were making sure that the graduate competences reflected early indications of the leadership competences.

Competences were not yet being used on appraisal. At the time of interview (November 1994) appraisal was viewed as assessing whether the 'deliverables' had been met in terms of operating targets. Competences, on the other hand looked at 'how' targets are met, and formed the basis for discussion. Competences had not yet been introduced into the reward system.

Use of national standards
Some parts of the business in the UK had taken an interest in MCI standards but these were not considered useful at an international level.

Timing and levels
The competences were introduced in a fluid way, 'almost through the back door of management development'. In the Head of Leadership Programme's words:

> It's a gradual transition and as the processes become aligned around competences then that becomes reinforced ... there is hesitation at first but let's push this thing further and further out ... It's, you know, a gradual inclusive kind of approach we take.

The identification of competences, and the internal process of checking it 'seemed to go on forever'. This was exacerbated by the loss of the Chairman, but the process was deemed to be useful since it allowed those who were implementing it time to check what they were doing.

Organisation C: A National Construction Company

The construction group consisted of a head office, with eight regional centres. These were run as a matrix style of management, each led by a regional management director and management board, underpinned by eight functional groups in each region: line management, estimating, purchasing, quality surveying, planning, engineering, accounts and personnel. Each of these regions were in the business of 'winning work, doing the job, and getting paid' and are based around major towns.

Since 1992, the building trade had been severely affected by recession. A particular problem in this business is that, in recession, tenders are offered at low prices, and at the time, as the country was emerging from recession, these tenders had to be implemented at below cost prices. Working on negative margins meant that there was less depth of cover. Partly in response to these pressures, in 1992, the then 12 regional centres were reduced to eight, creating new management structures with a need for different types of management skills. Because of their greater geographical area, the businesses had become more complex, creating even greater demand on managers to manage resources effectively. As the market place changed the business became broader, with more necessity to build relationships with clients and their organisations.

The company no longer 'owns labour' in the sense that it used to run training apprenticeships. The company employed directly hourly-paid workers through sub-contractors. This meant that time-served craftsmen were difficult to find, and that graduate managers lacked the trade knowledge required on site. This was the reason that competences were developed. Competences, then, were introduced not so much as a competency-based programme, but as part of the on-going need for effective general managers who could combine generalist with technical skills.

Identifying competences
Although not explicitly labelled a competence process, the beginning of the process took place with the running of development centres in late 1990. The company felt they wanted some measure of objective testing, and sent employees off for psychometric testing. The HR department however, did not find this information company-specific enough.

To develop the idea, with the help of an outside consultancy and internal facilitators, a meeting was set up with senior managers. The Head of HR was responsible for introducing the initiative. Using critical incident interviewing as a starting point, they earmarked different 'top' behaviours. Because the company had a long-established tradition of employees working 'from cradle to grave', most people knew each other well so, during this process, there was an 'internal knowledge-based dynamic'. There were no 'huge surprises' about the competences that did emerge.

Use of competences at time of interview
Competences were not used in a totally formal manner but more as 'guidance for development'. They were used in staff development, appraisal (as guidelines only) and for recruitment and selection guidance. The HR

department set up development centres in which six staff undertake a number of work-related exercises, and the information from these is reviewed in relation to a set of criteria (competences). Participants are asked to measure themselves against these criteria before attending. The information gained from the centre is then used for 'one-to-one' meetings with immediate supervisors and at the annual performance review. The company provided management development and personal skills courses that managers could attend as a result of identifying gaps in their development.

Timing and levels

The process was still in its early days but it was perceived as one which would evolve over a number of years (5–10 years). The HR director believed they were'laying the bricks for the future', not simply implementing something 'just to bring about a sea change'. Competences here were seen very much as a long-term project.

Organisation D: Semi-privatised National Utility

This organisation comprised two companies, one UK-based and the other international. These were underpinned by three corporate divisions: Technology (research engineering); Finance division (shareholders); Group corporate services.

Since the product supplied by this organisation cannot change (being a natural product), the perceived way to differentiate from competition was by cost. The competences were introduced as part of a major cost reduction programme. This was manifest in terms of reduction in staff (17 500 to 5500 in three years) aided by the introduction of new technology. At the same time there was need to grow by diversifying into international markets. The long-term targets were to invest £2 billion internationally by building power stations abroad, for example in the USA, Portugal and Pakistan.

This had been accompanied by pressures from having to invest in new technology, both to increase productivity which had increased to 86 per cent and by the aim to be 'the world's best practising power station'. For example, the company had succeeded in running power stations efficiently with 25 rather than the former 250 employees. This had brought with it a need for new skills such as company secretarial work, knowledge of investment and different taxation practices, managing contracts, cultural awareness and appraisal techniques. The flatter organisational structures, reflected overall in a reduction of reporting lines from 12 to three or four throughout the business, had created a need for a new type of management style.

The numbers of staff had been reduced at the centre, so many of the corporate/specialist skills such as drawing up contracts, or managing human resources had created extensive training needs. There was also a need for developing skills in acquisition, mergers, market opportunities, languages and cultural awareness.

Identifying competences

The project was initially set up by a well-known consultancy firm. Unlike some of the other organisations the process of identifying the competences was not claimed to be 'scientific'. As the Head of Human Resources noted:

> Like a lot of in-house competence development, a lot of people have a rough idea what they are looking for and they have a pretty picture and as you work towards it you tend to sort of say 'Well it's not that, it's not that', until you get something that you know you are after. It was a really lengthy process, we had a few false starts, but that helped us find out what we didn't want.

Once the competences were identified, assessment centres were run for the top 600 managers over 6 weeks, at 4 hours per manager. This comprised interviews, assessment of performance, psychometric tests, and measuring each manager against each competence.

Use of competences at time of interview

Competences were used for appraisal, selection and recruitment. For each job specification there was a person specification which was based on competences, not as a rule but as 'good practice'. The HR and Training Department also ran assessment and development centres based on competences. These were used for identifying training and development needs of individual managers. In this process managers were measured against the competences. The appraisal and performance-related pay were built on competences. Competences were also used as a tool for identifying outside providers.

National standards

These were used where appropriate for training and development. They were currently used for purchasing, and there were plans in hand to use them for personnel and IT.

Timing and levels

One thing the company had underestimated was the pace of change. Once they had drawn up strategies: 'We saw through the mist there was another course line altogether.' Although they can see a plan now, 'one is painting a grand design in hindsight'. There was an acknowledgement that whatever was done would only be fit for its purpose for a limited period of time.

Organisation E: Health and Social Services Trust based in Northern Ireland

Like all organisations in the National Health Service, this Trust was under considerable pressure to change and respond to market forces. Government reform had brought with it the need for organisational change. Devolved budgets meant that more control and management skills were needed down the line. At ground level, workers (nurses, social workers, health visitors) were being formed into independent multi-disciplinary teams in order to strengthen the domiciliary service and bring care back into the community. Such a process meant strengthening the autonomy of line managers, meaning that professions such as social workers would possibly report both to a professional boss and a line manager. In terms of the previous nursing arrangements the health visitor, district nurse and district midwife would combine as a community support worker.

Three years previous to the time of research, a new chief executive from the private sector arrived at the 'sleepy hollow' with 1800 employees. He had a mission to develop the Trust from a sleepy culture to one where people could respond to customer demand and where they 'moved a lot faster, were a lot more flexible and a lot less expensive'. Further, although the social services and health services had been amalgamated since 1973, there was little communication between the two.

Through the competence approach, the Chief Executive hoped to break down the traditional demarcations by challenging practices and changing perceptions so that people 'think differently and form the right sort of alliances with key bodies'. This would entail 'liberation from the bureaucracy' so that other aspects and other abilities may flourish. The Chief Executive firmly believed that culture change could only come about with behavioural change. Ultimately the process should drive selection, recruitment and potentially, even pay. With its emphasis on change of behaviour, the competence approach provided a means whereby 'ingrained and embedded cultural patterns' could be challenged. Here, it was claimed, competences were being used as a major tool for organisational change.

Identifying competences
The Chief Executive, knowing that the competence approach could only be driven from the top, had as a first task to convince the board of directors that this would be the best approach. Second was to bring in specialist consultants with experience in developing competency models. Two consultants (occupational psychologists) were used who had been involved in developing the 'ground-breaking' competence model used at a major

building society. During 1994 the consultants carried out over 600 organisation-wide interviews to identify the competences that characterised top performance. Critical incident interviews were used. These were clustered together and crystallised into 34 different competences at six different levels. These 34 competences represented the types of behaviours deemed to be critical to organisational success. This was completed at the end of November 1994.

Then the competence framework was fed back to the board of directors, and amendments made where appropriate. The eight directors and Chief Executive were then themselves profiled against the competence framework. A series of two workshops was set up to inform and train all 90 managers in the competence framework. In the first (awareness raising), participants were introduced to the process and practice of profiling an individual and role against the competence framework. In the second set, participants brought along their own individual profile, and then conducted practice 'appraisal' interviews with each other. The whole process was then rolled out throughout the organisation. In the meantime, the consultants had produced an in-depth manual that indicated how development 'gaps' could be met – using a process of open learning, knowledge gaining etc. General awareness raising sessions were used to introduce the process to the entire work-force.

The Human Resource department acted as a pivotal role, scrutinising all personal development plans (PDPs) and identifying gaps or inconsistencies. It would also be able to identify organisation-wide development needs and draw up strategic training plans. The trades unions were informed of the initiative once it was ready to roll out.

Uses of competences at time of interview
Competences were being used extensively for company-wide performance improvement. At the time, role specifications for promotion and recruitment were being drawn up in the 'language of competence'. The former 150 grades were being rationalised. The consultants were still acting as external evaluators, checking that the process was understood and correctly implemented throughout the organisation.

Timing and levels
The competence approach in this organisation was extremely rigorous. Great care had been taken throughout the process to ensure that everyone had been informed of what was happening. This has been due to the fact that it was anticipated that the process was likely to cause 'pain and challenge' (consultants' words) to some individuals.

5.2   DIFFERENCES AND SIMILARITIES IN FRAMEWORKS

While the theory of initiating and implementing a competence framework is fairly standard, in practice there were many differences in implementation. These seem to depend on a variety of different factors. As Table 5.1 shows, in all five organisations, one of the major reasons for implementing competences was the 'need to face up to change'. In the case of the multinational and the semi-privatised industry, this was also associated with 'downsizing' on a large scale. In all cases apart from the construction company it was claimed that there was a need for 'culture change'. In these cases, the initiative had come down from the chief executive, and had been tested out on senior managers first.

The extent and way in which competences were incorporated in the central tasks of the human resource function (recruitment, selection, appraisal, management development and pay) varied from company to company. In organisation D they were incorporated not as a 'rule' but as 'good practice'. This company also had extensive and glossy documentation drawn up based on the competences. In company B competences were used for selection of high fliers, and there are long-term plans for their inclusion on graduate selection. In companies C and A, where the implementation was not so far ahead, there were plans for their use in recruitment and selection, but they were being used primarily at the time as a tool for senior management development. In the Trust, they were introduced as a comprehensive performance improvement system, and plans were laid for their use in selection, recruitment and eventually, pay.

Overall, despite the apparent cohesiveness of the competence approach, different organisations have very different experiences of its implementation. The extent to which it is embedded in the HR technologies in terms of a tight relationship with selection, recruitment and promotion varied. Thus in companies A and C competences were still in their infancy, and the process was being introduced in a comparatively leisurely manner, however in organisations B, D and E the relationship with selection, recruitment was much tighter and there had been and is a sense of urgency about introducing the initiative. All three of these organisations were undergoing considerable change (downsizing, need to respond rapidly to market forces) and hence were open to more resistance and industrial relations problems.

From the foregoing, three types of expectations about the competence frameworks in practice can be identified. Companies either used competences simply as a training and development tool, as a tool for performance management, and/or for organisational restructuring. All five identified competences as a major tool for training and development, while three

Table 5.1 Competence frameworks

Organisation	Reasons for implementation	Type of architecture (recruitment, selection, appraisal)	Organisational use (Training and development, organisational restructuring, performance management)	Time scales
A: University	Change in higher education. Need for academics to be managers	Hopes to use it for recruitment and selection. Bringing in 360° appraisal	Training and development	2 years (still on-going)
B: Multinational oil company	Need for culture change. Downsizing	Not formally but recruitment models aligned with selection at lower levels. 360° appraisal	Training and development, performance management	4 years (still on-going)
C: Multinational construction company	Recession created need for new management skills	As guidelines. Assessment and development centres	Training and development	2 years
D: Semi-privatised national utility	Privatisation, downsizing, flatter organisation, change in culture	Recruitment, selection, appraisal	Training and development, organisational restructuring, performance management	4 years
E: National Health and Social Services Trust	Break down 'traditional demarcation' between social services and national health, create market-driven culture	Recruitment, selection, appraisal	Training and development, organisational restructuring, performance management	3 years (still on-going)

companies (B, D and E) used them as a tool for performance management, while companies D and E also used them as a tool for organisational restructuring (associated in both cases with downsizing).

It seems that from the fairly standard model that I identified earlier in the literature, in practice, competence frameworks can vary enormously in terms of the depth in which they penetrate the organisation, depending on the expectations of those responsible for the implementation, the type of organisation and the pressures it is responding to, and most importantly, as we shall see, on the history of the organisation.

5.3   THE PERCEPTIONS OF COMPETENCE FRAMEWORKS

As the research progressed, four understandings and expectations of the competence approach emerged as common to all organisations. These were:

- the approach could and would bring about culture change
- the process was objective
- change would bring about creation of 'enterprising and empowered' new managers
- the approach was underpinned by a common 'shared' language that needed to be learnt before it could be used.

I arrived at these categories through a thorough analysis of the transcriptions. At no time in the interviews did I myself use these terms. Respondents themselves offered them up quite naturally. While the objectivity and the importance of language were not surprising (although the extent of the importance respondents attached to language was unexpected) I had not anticipated culture change or the concept of the 'enterprising manager' to be so dominant, or perhaps unquestioned.

Culture Change

In all five companies there was, to a greater or lesser extent, an expectation that competences would provide a means of changing the culture in order to meet the demands of the consumer and so meet the environmental pressures. Although 'culture' was not a word which I had used in the interview, it was invariably used by respondents. Here, the term 'culture' was used by the respondents loosely in the sense that it encompassed both 'thinking' and 'doing', and referred to organisational and/or individual 'ways of being'. Respondents used the term 'culture' in the sense of: 'this is how we are, this is how we do things and this is how we think about things'. The academic debates going back over the past decades which attempt to characterise and define 'culture' (for example, Deal and Kennedy 1982; Schein 1985; Morgan 1986) for example were of little direct relevance in this context. Thus, although respondents used the term 'culture', what they meant was that they intended to 'change' from the current way of doing things, to a different way imposed by the perceived demands of competition.

In organisation A there was a long-term hope that competences would eventually help in changing the culture to a more 'externally aware' organisation. As the Vice Chancellor pointed out:

> It is embedded in a whole process of change, where things are building on each other, and gradually making the whole thing more systematic, and rational and describable.

In organisation B where competences were incorporated into senior management development, competences were viewed as a means of breaking down organisational structures and had been associated with downsizing. And, while not explicitly defined as a culture change initiative:

> Clearly it is the attitude of the people and competences are very powerful in describing what you want people to do, and also to get the right individuals in the right positions to change things, so in that sense, you can call it a driver of change, or supporter of change ... I think quite clearly people have got to be comfortable or have got to be able to live with change. I think above all whether that is flexibility, adaptability, or whatever I mean we have got to be able to manage change and to live with change, you have got to see change out, you have got to be expecting it and anticipating it. (Head of Leadership Programmes)

In organisation C, the process was associated with moving from a culture of a 'family firm' to one in which the increasing pressures of the 'market' could be met. In organisation D the competence process was introduced almost directly as a need for culture change. After the company was privatised in 1990 the then Chief Executive wrote:

> It is talking about teamwork and it is talking about not writing letters to everybody, calling them by their first names ... and not keeping lots of files and things like that, it is about being informal and giving people responsibility and about taking risk. It is about being understanding and forgiving about mistakes.

The original style was a heavily unionised traditional command and control, 'very structured and very status conscious and all letters and memos addressed to Mr. so and so'. Because of the downsizing, responsibility had devolved downwards bringing with it an espoused need for a change in management style. As a result of the competence initiative:

> Managers, when you are talking to them about their staff, will talk much more in terms of the behavioural side of people's activities and people's deliveries ... one thing all of us have got to keep reminding ourselves is how we've achieved the changes over the past three years, and although we haven't got it right, but if we could change pace at the same pace for the next three years, by God we will have cracked a lot. (Head of Human Resources)

In organisation E competences were introduced specifically so that the organisation would become more 'client-orientated' which would entail 'liberation from bureaucracy'. This was to be achieved by changing behaviour. As the Chief Executive noted:

> I would be expecting to find an understanding of the organisation's purpose and goals very much deeper down into the organisation ... it [competence approach] is about more people on board looking for a better way of doing things, not only open to change, but in fact themselves wanting to change things ... I will expect to see a reinforcement of some of the views that I have ...

In most cases, then, the perceived culture change was also associated with organisational restructuring. In every case, the move to competences was closely associated with structural efforts to make the organisation more competitive, more efficient, more market-focused. Competences were seen as critical to helping organisations describe and achieve the new managerial qualities required by structural and cultural changes. This was largely to be achieved through developing the enterprising manager, and to be built upon a new, common language of competence.

Objectivity

A further expectation about the competence approach was its objectivity. Thus the focus in most organisations lay in the 'technical' issues of identification and application rather than in questioning the validity and strategy of the competence initiative itself. This emphasis on 'objectivity' was stressed by all senior management respondents. The competence approach 'unearths' and 'discovers' the qualities underlying successful incumbency of the management role under changed conditions: it, apparently, does not construct them, nor does it question the underlying change in strategy or structure. In the interviews, competence programmes were largely viewed as objective: managers rarely seriously questioned the basis of the competences, or disagreed with their intentions. Indeed, they were positively vaunted for their objective nature. As the Head of Human Resources at the University pointed out:

> It is clearing up their blind spots, and people will do objective assessing.

In the Trust in Northern Ireland, the objective nature of the competence process was stressed, and also the tightness of the equal opportunity system. As one of the project implementors noted:

> I would say our system is so stringent that there really is no discrimination.

The feeling that because the actual competences had been derived from people interviewed and were therefore 'neutral' was also considered of great importance. At the Trust again:

> Basically the competence framework is the words of the staff ... a framework that has not been imposed from the outside, in fact it is our own framework.

Further, because the competences were apparently derived in this objective manner, there was an underlying, but unstated assumption that they were gender-free. When asked, all respondents considered that then the competence approach would provide an excellent system to make sure that equal opportunity issues were fully addressed. The HR Director at organisation C explained how they gave: 'higher levels of accuracy than more traditional methods of assessment'.

Empowerment and the Enterprising Manager

The way in which culture change was to be achieved through the competence programme was through the construction of the new or 'enterprising' manager. These managers would be 'empowered' to make changes, take responsibility. Such managers were similar to the 'enterprising individuals' as described by Keat and Abercrombie (1991) who are self-reliant and independent, who can make their own decision and take responsibility for their own lives. Their activities are directed to achievable goals and objectives and they are concerned to evaluate their progress in pursuit of these aims. If they cannot achieve these aims as they are, then they are motivated to gain sufficient skills through training. They show high levels of energy, optimism and initiative and are keen to partake of the fruits of commercial activity (p.6).

This was not always received positively, as we shall see in the following chapter. Thus, in organisation A, the Dean of Social Science viewed the competence initiative as:

> ... an attempt to get rid of the academic manager, as somebody who is somehow representative of his or her academic area, professional area, and rather to make them part of an overarching schemes ... with loyalty towards management ... rather than to professional routes.

When asked what he felt the 'new manager' would look like, the Head of Leadership Programmes at organisation B offered the following:

> You have got to be able to understand, motivate, coach, counsel, provoke, agitate, whatever is necessary, and I think it comes from understanding, you have got to be able to understand the needs of each individual and treat them differently. I think you need to be ... able to handle and live with contradictions, tensions, be active.

This organisation is aiming to be peopled by 'enterprising selves' who are 'active', who can 'coach, counsel, motivate and agitate'. Parts of the statement read like the introduction to some of the more proselytising books on management.

In organisation C, which is a traditional, family-based firm, there is a feeling that, because people are taken on as school leavers and trained there throughout their career, this creates a set of 'introverted managers' based on a very strict hierarchy. It was hoped that the competence initiative would begin to break this down. Further, it was recognised that new managers will need a 'more sophisticated set of techniques' and will need credibility both in technical and generalist fields. The old-style managers had technical bias but showed lack of confidence and sophistication. The old manager was not interested in the client and saw them as 'more of an irritant than asset'. This was no longer tenable. Because the clients were becoming more demanding, managers needed to show more 'sophistication, self-confidence, and ability to say "no"'. They also needed to be capable of building relationships, with good personal qualities and be given more autonomy and accountability.

In organisation D the new style of management was seen to be moving away from the:

> traditional command and control, to a power-devolved, team-working, more informal style, walking the job, even things like making it company policy to call each other by their Christian names.

In organisation E, since the competence approach breaks down embedded ways of doing things, it would provide a means of creating the 'new breed of fluid manager'. The Chief Executive also saw it as a 'lever' that could be used to break down professionalism and create more realism necessary in an enterprise culture. For the Head of Human Resources in this organisation, the new manager:

- is dedicated to achieving delivery services
- must have leadership qualities
- is restless with failure to deliver
- has a repertoire of approaches with people

- is 'entrepreneurial'
- is well-grasped in opportunism

There was an expectation, then, in all these organisations, that somehow, the competence methodology would help create these 'empowered' and 'enterprising' individuals. With few exceptions (see Ch. 8) this was assumed to be a 'good thing'.

The Language of Competence

It was through the development of a common language that such change was to be introduced and understood. Every person that I interviewed pointed out, unbidden, the importance of understanding the new language of competence. For example, in organisation A:

> It is actually quite interesting to have something that through a shared emphasis you come out with shared understandings. (Dean of Social Science)

> And I think they (competence consultants) have produced something, discovering a new language. (Head of Human Resources)

> I think it is developing a language, that helps people interpret and function in your new world, and therefore relates to what they are doing at every level. (Operations Director)

In organisation B:

> I think one of the great things which proved that it is a language that you can use to talk about, or to describe things like succession climbing, in a way that has some commonalty. (Head of Leadership Programme)

And in organisation D:

> We went down the competency route, and the language was professional language ... most people to whom you want to deliver, don't understand what the hell you are looking for. (Head of Human Resources)

In organisation E:

> I can remember that for the first month my greatest thing was actually understanding the language, and once I understood the language then I understood the concepts. (Project implementor)

What was intriguing about this understanding of the importance of language, was the lack of questioning about whether and how the language actually shaped the way the competence approach was perceived. In other words, respondents were drawn into implementing and working with the competence agenda through the constraints of the language itself. Language played a fundamental part in ensuring that the competence approach gained currency.

5.4   RESISTANCE

There was certainly evidence of some resistance to the introduction of competence frameworks. However, this was not surprising. Management initiatives are rarely if ever implemented unscathed. Unplanned outcomes nearly always emerge from the unexpected consequences of putting them to work (Du Gay, Salaman and Rees 1996).

This is because (it has been persuasively argued) every discourse arises and exists within a framework of perception and is dependent upon certain conditions (Fairclough 1992; Astroff and Nyberg 1992). For Fairclough (1991, p.55; 1992, p.103) a discourse is conditional upon relations of power, and its continuance is both encouraged and constrained by the other discourses within which (and besides which) it operates. Fairclough (1992) notes that 'meaning' is a site of struggle, and organisational discourse is inherently unstable, always open to strategic transformations. Du Gay (1996) emphasises the importance and role of instability since discourses of work reform arise primarily in response to specific political contexts. It can therefore be suggested that a dominant organisational discourse is dependent upon relations of power, but that it may be challenged, competed, or supported by other discourses within a context of uncertainty and change. All the organisations adopted the competence frameworks in response to the changing nature of the environment.

Resistance is here highlighted rather to show the *effectiveness* of the implementation process rather than its failure. In attempting to redress anomalies in the situation, more techniques may be added to the armoury of the competence practitioners. Further, the attention paid to addressing resistance at this overt level may well detract from inequalities that may be embedded in the successful parts of the implementation process.

Despite the language of competence which is continuously upbeat and manifest both in the documentation and the language and perceptions of those responsible for implementation, there was resistance to the approach. Some of the following comments pick up fears and anxieties. In all organisations there were varying degrees of acceptance of the competence frameworks, and any actual or anticipated resistances tended to vary, depending on the different power groupings within the organisation. Though there was evidence of individual resistance, the capacity for collective resistance had been severely curtailed by the individualising nature of the competence process. The only possibility of collective resistance appeared to be in the University where the cynicism with which some academics were receiving the administration's communications about the approach suggested that a collective passive resistance would be possible. Whether this is due to the fact that academics may be more aware of ideological manipulation, or whether they are less at risk if they do not co-operate would require further investigation.

With one exception, the initiative was introduced by the HR department, and in most cases it was introduced with the direct support of the Chief Executive. There was, with few exceptions, which I will mention below, little reference to the potential of industrial relations conflict, and in most cases the HR department became the centre of information on competences – although there were in two cases specific attempts made to deny the fact that the structures were being imposed from this function.

In organisation A, because of the differing nature of the workforce (academics, administrators, technical people) there was a fear that nobody would take 'Plans for Change' seriously. At the steering committee when the competences were being fed back, there was a 'great deal of pain' and initially 'people fought like mad against the whole idea'. As the Dean of Social Science comments:

> I am not convinced that there is actually something here which is going to change the way in which the institution works ... I suppose I question, however powerful it is, whether it is actually substantially going to shift some of the underlying systems in the institution.

Some of the senior managers – who were academics – had doubts about the validity of the competence approach. Some doubted whether competences could change culture; others questioned whether culture change was necessary or desirable. Academic members of staff felt the competences were possibly an attack on professional standards and knowledge and an attempt to refocus the loyalty of the manager towards management rather than professional routes. It was noted that the competence project assumed a certain implicit view of the organisation's structure, functioning, objectives and values. In some cases, concern was voiced about the definition and allocation of behaviours labelled negative and positive to competences. The imposition of competences from above was seen by some as an attempt to gain control of the organisation. It was noted that competences constituted an attempt to impose a different vision of what the organisation is and does. In the words Dean of Social Science again:

> Competences could be a threat to ... professional people... I suppose, I mean I don't feel the professional side of what I do is being undermined by competences, but in principle it could be.

In company B, because of the many HR changes and programmes that had taken place, care had to be taken in introducing the notion:

> Well obviously the selling-in process is part of the introducing, the difficulty with that is that you seem to spend an awful lot of time in intellectual debate and ... What we did was we clearly created this process, and had people debating and arguing, and talking about the relevance of using these ... but there are some people who would say well we have got competency fever ...

From these comments, we can see that there was extensive debate and frustration in attempting to implement the framework.

In organisation C acceptance had not so far been seen as a problem. The HR director felt it had been well-received, even though there was a small audience. In organisation D, despite the fact that the initiative had come down from the Chief Executive, there had been problems in acceptance. The HR director commented:

> I think it is in the nature of the process ... it is too complicated and bureaucratic, and maybe too long-sighted.

However, efforts were made to ensure that the initiative was not seen to emanate from the HR department:

> As a company the question of whether it is accepted shouldn't be an issue for personnel ... the idea was that it wasn't something introduced by personnel, it was something introduced by themselves.

In the Trust implementation took a great deal of time. Progress was slow and constantly behind target. The competences required a huge amount of administration, each job profiled, continuously; each employee profiled, development plans written up, policed and implemented. Some of the professionals saw competences as a threat to their authority and values, and resisted or subverted the approach. Here the introduction of competences was 'painful and challenging'. The consultant responsible constantly used these words in her description of the processes. They were however:

> ... very careful so far in their implementation that it is not seen as a personnel driven process, that it is a line management driven process.

As one of the people responsible for the implementation noted:

> And I think it is people's terror of what people really mean ... will I be out of a job because I am not at my present competency for my role, will I actually be developed, or will they use this as a management tool to whip me with. I think these are the types of fears that people actually have until they start to understand what is happening in terms of the process.

Like the respondent whose comments I described earlier, these comments reflect a rationalisation of what they perceive as discipline in the first instance. As soon as respondents begin to use the language of competence however, there seems to be a sea change in the acceptance of the process. It seems that identification with the process takes place when the language is conquered, and respondents can then derive their sense of self from understanding and knowing how the process works. It was, in this organisation particularly, almost as if respondents went on to 'automatic pilot' when asked to talk about the competence project. There had been here an extensive, selling-in period over two years, with considerable attention paid to timing etc. It was as though people were drawn, one by one, despite themselves, into the objectives of the competence agenda. The unions had in the past wielded a fair amount of power. As the Chief Executive noted:

> [In the past] They were terrified of the Union, nobody would support anybody trying to take disciplinary action, but that has changed.

Although there was anticipated resistance, the unions were only told about the competences when all the work had been carried out, top and senior managers already, as they called it, 'BARred' (Behaviorally-Anchored Rating) and the communications exercise effectively carried out. Unions were presented with a 'fait accompli'. Issues of professionalism were also paramount in this organisation. Of the 34 competences identified in this Trust, only one related directly to professionalism. As the head of HR pointed out, the competences could be seen by the process as diluting their authority so that their 'dignity is leeching away'.

As the Chief Executive noted:

> There are the professional barriers so this will help people to think about their roles and how they go about the work in a very, very different way, in a professional manner, by identifying the competences rather than the qualifications.

He commented that, for example, the social work style and culture was: 'totally resistant to change, like dinosaurs, left-wing and elitist'. He was hoping that with the new organisational structures (multi-disciplinary teams) that the 'demarcation is slowly blurring', and they are having to 'challenge their own practices'. So despite the rhetoric, and the apparent empowering nature of competences, management were well aware of the potential conflict that might arise as a result of competences.

Such resistance was manifest also in the difficulties of implementation in terms of planning and action. In all organisations it was done 'when the time was right'. As the HR Director in organisation D pointed out:

> But those strategies weren't going to last for very long, because suddenly we saw through the mist there was another course line altogether, and also another thing we had underestimated was the pace of change. I mean as soon as you were creating solutions to problems, the problems had gone. Em, so it wasn't all carefully planned. We had a vision and it was a vision that kept changing.

In all the organisations the implementation process could be described as 'organic', and while all concerned with the implementation process were convinced of the potential power of the competence approach once established, they were realistic about time scales and potential difficulties. This was particularly so as concerns linking competence to pay, where all organisations certainly felt it a possibility – but were realistic about how difficult it would be to implement.

Thus there was some indication of resistance, and this was apparent both at an individual level, and at the level of resistance by members of groups of workers who felt their position may be threatened by the competence project. These were, notably, professionals, autonomous business managers who may have perceived the project as a way of the HR departments exercising power, and academics, who resisted taking on board the managerial rhetoric of the competence approach.

5.5 HISTORY AND COMPETENCE

This initial comparison showed how competence frameworks varied in their depth and rigour, depending on the environment in which the company was operating, the 'way of being' of the company and the reasons for introducing competences in the first place.

For example in the semi-privatised utility, where there were fewer competing groups of workers, the competence project had taken firm hold, and was used as the basis of recruitment and selection. However, where there were more diverse groups of workers, such as the academics in the University, the competence framework was less tightly constructed and did not run throughout the organisation, though there were plans for this to happen. In the Trust, where one might have expected professionals to have resisted as they saw their traditional power base disappearing, the methods of implementation were implemented in rigorous Taylorist fashion and thus using implicit control to drive the implementation through. Implementation then was not a unilinear process: it depended on the 'structured expectations' built up through the organisation's past 'ways of being' and it depended on the diversity of the particular groups affected by the competences. Thus the semi-privatised utility, multinational oil company, and construction company implemented the framework, to a greater or lesser extent, in a rigorous and mechanical fashion, while the University implemented in a rather ad hoc fashion. The Trust implemented in a rigorous, Taylorist manner due to the stringent imperatives of the context in which the Trust was operating (need to respond to market forces), the need to oppose the possible resistance of 'professionals' and the zeal with which the initiative was introduced and driven through by the Chief Executive and his consultants. In a way, culture change here was a possibility since the Chief Executive had been brought in to wipe the slate clean, and therefore was not prepared to contend with any past history.

Thus, while the language and frameworks appear to be the same, when implemented a competence framework can look very different. It will depend upon the organisation's history, the enthusiasm and motives of the people who are implementing, and the particular context in which an organisation is implementing. The competence models as drawn up in the literature emerge in reality as new and different beasts.

6. Competence as discipline

In the last chapter, most respondents saw good reasons for introducing competences, felt that they were helpful in changing culture and in developing enterprising managers, and further, they were generally enthusiastic about the 'objectivity' of the frameworks. Were there however some different readings other than those 'instrumental' reasons for competence frameworks? Using a more critical lens, were there other interpretations that suggested that constraint was operating? To what extent did the competence frameworks shut down consensus? Was there any discussion about the values of competence frameworks? Whose voices were being privileged by these frameworks? These questions, in the spirit of critical theory, pay attention to the relation between the exercise of power and the linguistic representations of reality. Are the frameworks in fact 'fixing' relations of dependence? How much room for manoeuvre and discussion was there in the frameworks, and what was the role of language in 'creating' a particular type of meaning? Do the constructions of 'how we do things around here' privilege certain workers over others?

This chapter is concerned with analysing the discourse of competence as both discursive practice and text. To recall, discourse means a way of speaking, operating, conceptualising, communicating, and describing. Discourse involves a community of action and talk: 'speaking and writing subjects and ... readers or listeners' (Eagleton 1983, p.115). Meaning, of both language and practice, is not stable, and is constantly negotiated and renegotiated through space and time (Saussure 1968; Derrida 1973). And so, far from reflecting a 'given' social reality, discourse constitutes reality for us and may even be seen as an ideological practice which mediates between individuals and the conditions of their existence.

6.1 CULTURE CHANGE

The culture change to which most of the organisations hoped to move was that of the more 'enterprising', 'market-driven' culture to which many popular and proselytising management texts refer (for example, Peters and Waterman 1982). However, from the responses of interviewees, and from an analysis of the documentation, the hoped-for culture change tended to be somewhat superficial, and any changes wrought through the competence approach reflected as much the organisation's past as its future. Thus, in organisation A, competences were being introduced in a rather ad hoc, cautious manner. The competences had been drawn up from eight interviews, and were part of a larger 'Plans for Change' programme. However, the University's Plans for Change had had 'a bad birth, lots of revisions and drafts, incredibly bland'. As the Dean of Social Science noted:

> I am not convinced that there is actually something here which is going to change the way the institution works ... I mean these people are not going to be able to do it.

This institution was characterised by being very bureaucratic and bulky, with an enormously complicated system of administration spread at many different levels throughout the country. Despite the expectations and language used by the Head of Human Resources and Vice Chancellor, many of the respondents felt that it would take a very long time before the institution became a commercially-oriented organisation.

In organisation C, the implementation reflected the rather staid 'family firm' approach from which this company had grown. There was an expectation that any change with the competences would develop over a period of 5–10 years, and the competences themselves were used more as guidelines than as drivers for change.

In organisation D, the introduction had been associated with an enormous downsizing exercise (from 17 500 employees to 5500 in 3 years). Responsibility was being devolved down the line, and there was more managerial responsibility with line managers who were having to learn different skills. While there had been a change from the use of the formal surname to christian names, the change in terms of culture was not as extensive as the respondents suggested. For example, the way in which the respondents talked about the changes, and the difficulties I had in gaining access suggested that these changes may have been superficial. When I first entered the offices here, I was aggressively addressed as though I were touting for consultancy business. 'What could I offer' was the question that I was asked by both interviewees. For example, when talking about the implementation process the Head of Human Resources noted:

> I mean there have been massive changes, and the managers are struggling to change. Some were able to make the change quite quickly, some are finding it more difficult. We have reduced the number of managers and hopefully the ones that are left won't find it too difficult.

Despite the avowed culture change, here the change was more being forced upon managers as a result of downsizing. Managers were not expected to operate in a more 'empowered' manner: rather they were struggling with massive structural changes that were forcing them to become more competitive. The change here was actually to do with moving to a tighter, and possibly more disciplined, operating schedule. The HR and Training Directors noted with pride that they could now reduce their staff in a plant from 250 to 25. The message was very much: 'Be competent as we see it, or be dismissed.' The tight way in which competences were tied in to formal systems of appraisal, selection and promotion adds strength to this view.

In organisation E, there had been a concerted effort to move the culture to a more 'market-driven' culture, so that it would have the 'cutting edge' so that 'people realise it is a business' as the Head of Personnel noted:

> Whereas before the culture would have been one of service, now it is going out and looking what service the customer requires, and marketing these things and meeting these needs.

However, the way in which the competences were introduced, as we shall see later, reflected very much a disciplinary method, where culture change would not be that of the 'enterprising' culture, but more one where behaviour would be carefully marshalled. For example, when asked how the Behaviourally Anchored Rating Scales (BARS) which were derived to measure competence (appraisees are rated on a 1–5 scale) would be an improvement on what went before, the social work manager said:

> We were doing it before, but it was never written down and quantified in that way. It is a very structured and systematic way of appraising staff, and evaluating members of staff.

Managers had been persuaded of the importance of changing the culture to meet market demands, as the same respondent above noted about change:

> Well the nature of the change is, that if we don't as an organisation continually get better, and we don't clearly develop out staff, and improve ourselves, then as an organisation we will eventually lose contracts, we have to be good, we have to be good staff, and we have to improve staff.

There was an acknowledgement of the underlying potential of the BARS to be used as a source of discipline, in the words of the same respondent:

> If it is not handled correctly, and it is handled insensitively, it could be seen as Big Brother looking at them very critically, and it … could be seen as another weapon to be used as terms for disciplinary type hearings: I mean it wouldn't necessarily bother me, but it would bother some of the staff … well I have been given an assurance that they won't be used in a negative way …

There are some interesting points about the way this person deals with the potentially disciplinary nature of the BARS. First, he detaches himself from the process by referring to 'them'. There is clear indication that he has been worried about the nature of the BARS, but has decided that they will not affect him negatively. This respondent has not yet been 'done' as the terminology of undergoing the assessment had become known in the organisation:

It is too serious, I haven't yet come round to it, the boss hasn't called me.

Again the language of this comment is very much that of a 'command and control' structure – the detachment from authority by use of the words 'the boss' and the unusual choice of the word 'called' suggesting a clear power-based hierarchy. Thus the change in this organisation does not seem to match up to the claims. The competences have been implemented in a thorough manner, as a quasi-scientific exercise. Though the organisation may be moving to become a 'market-driven' one, this is not to be achieved through 'empowering' the workers. Quite the opposite. Perhaps the culture here is reflected more in the view of management as quoted by the Human Resource Director as being 'a mailed fist in a kid glove'.

Despite the beliefs of those implementing the competence strategies that they would bring about culture change, there was evidence that this might not be the case. In most organisations the competences and their method of implementation reflected the organisation's past as much as the future. The one exception to this was the Trust, which was driving for a real change from service to that of market. Here the competences had been introduced in a thoroughly systematic way, imposed by the new Chief Executive who had been brought in from the private sector to effect such a change. The rigour and depth of the competence framework in the Trust was more extensive than in any of the other organisations. However, as with the semi-nationalised utility, the culture change was not to the espoused one of 'enterprising and empowered' managers; the overly-systematised competence framework created little room for any manoeuvre. Former professionals, such as social workers, who carried a certain amount of autonomy and authority, were being forced into routes of behaviour that may have been incompatible with their ethos.

6.2   OBJECTIVITY

Despite claims of objectivity, both in the literature and in the words of the respondents, I found that there were several key parts of the 'technical process' where subjectivity crept in through the back door. One of the most important areas where this took place was at the point at which competences were clustered when interviews with staff had taken place.

First, there was variation as to how many, and who were interviewed; second, and more importantly, when the results of the interviews were gathered together and clustered into competences, changes were made to the competences as they were drawn up. In the Trust, for example, which made the greatest claim to objectivity, and despite an extensive period of critical incident interviewing (over the period of a year and a half), it was the consultant who examined, clustered and drew up the 34 competences at six levels. Here, it would seem the process is vaunted as totally scientific, and claimed to be written in the words of the interviewees, at the critical point of clustering, the objectivity claims fall down. It is here that the voices of the employees are subtly removed from the agenda. This is not to say that there was any conspiracy in this. The consultants themselves were convinced that they were operating a rational and highly sophisticated system.

In the multinational oil company, where top and poor performers were identified, discussion took place later and changes made in the competences as the framework was developed. In the University, where the competences were derived by a consultant from eight interviewees, the Dean of Social Science noted that:

> From the initial interviews we ended up with however many headings there were. Now, I don't remember suggesting any of these headings, I may have mentioned some, I don't remember ... For a social scientist it really drives you mad, because you think this is so unscientific in a any basic way ... but to actually draw that conclusion [about some of competences] is completely misleading.

Further, there was a lack of clarity in most organisations about what 'competences' really are which was not surprising given the lack of clarity in the literature noted in Chapter 4. There was a conceptual confusion about what was 'behaviour', 'trait' or simply 'outlook' and 'attitude'. Indeed, many of the people asked had not even thought about what a 'competence' was. This does beg the question of the objectivity of the measurement of competence.

Organisations then used critical incident interviewing techniques so that the competences use the views of the employees which are then carefully analysed, and incorporated into lists of behaviours that are 'observable' and hence 'measurable' and quantifiable. However, as Checkland and Scholes (1990) have shown, despite the prestige of quantification and prior specification of objectives, these hard methods may be inappropriate where there is persisting diversity of objectives among the various participants. They do not work in a straightforward manner where there are interconnecting systems, disparity of perspectives, diverse and vested interests and where only ambiguous measurements are available. These are precisely the conditions which prevailed here. Since the competence framework is usually applied to entire organisations, there are often several sets of relations at play. For example, the framework may cut across several different organisational functions, across different hierarchies, and across different cultures. Further, the 'hardness' of the methods proposed is actually spurious. Without clear and unambiguous understanding of 'competence', the aims of measuring such behaviour scientifically and objectively is unrealistic. What is happening here, it seems, is that despite the attempts at rendering the competence process objective, the competences reflect constructs and categories that are *already defined* within the minds of senior managers or consultants. In other words, as the discussion about language showed, unless there is a great deal of awareness, people are constrained within the frameworks (including structures and language) of the process itself. Here, the objectivity was taken as 'normal' and 'unproblematic'. In critical theory terms, discussion about the values of setting up these competence frameworks had not taken place.

Deetz (1992) identifies accepted notions of 'common sense' in an organisation as indicative of a dominant organisational discourse: '... [The] very ordinariness [of such notions of common sense] hides the implicit valuational structure of perceptual experience. Each discourse and attendant technology constitutes ways of knowing the world, privileges certain notions of what is real, and posits personal identities' (Deetz 1992, p.32).

According to Deetz (1992), people's conviction of what is obvious or an incontrovertible truth is nothing other than the expression of a set of dominant perceptions. Both Deetz (1992) and Rees and Garnsey (2003) propose that the discourse used by employees in organisations can be analysed for evidence of how their organisational experience is ordered. Organisational discourse will inevitably incorporate 'embedded values' and a hierarchical ordering of structures of thought, language and experience. In this way, 'common sense' is perpetuated, and underlying systems and frameworks persist, despite, and indeed perhaps because, of these claims to objectivity. It is no surprise then, that the hoped-for culture change, in the line of 'enterprising and empowered' managers did not appear to take place.

The second major claim to objectivity that frames the competence process is the perceived advantage of the processes of assessment and appraisal. Clearly, respondents felt that the emphasis on appraisal that forms part of the competence process leads to greater objectivity in promotion and selection. This, however, is to ignore the past decade of research into the process of assessment which shows that appraisal is not the straightforward tool that people imagine (Alimo-Metcalfe 1994; Rubin 1999). The organisations here showed little awareness of this potential problem. Given that, in the competence process, more and more responsibility is devolved to line managers to assess their subordinates, this was a surprising omission. Only one organisation, the Trust, actually ran a workshop to familiarise managers with appraisal techniques. Here, the appraisal process was so rigid that any notion of the appraisee as a human being seemed to be lost. It seemed that organisations had simply not taken this into account when introducing their competence programmes. When, for example, I mentioned to the Operations Director at the University the fact that the Trust had run workshops in appraisal, he realised that there was an omission in their competence programme. I shall return to this point later since not only does it have implications for the workforce in general, but it has even greater implications for the employment of women.

6.3   EMPOWERMENT AND THE CREATION OF THE ENTERPRISING MANAGER

The 'enterprising manager' was to be created, in the words of some of the respondents, through 'flattening hierarchies' 'devolving responsibility down the line', and 'involving individuals in their own development'. This was to be achieved, in the words of the head of Leadership programmes at the multinational oil company through understanding the needs of each individual and treating them differently. According to him: 'I think you need to be ... able to handle and live with contradictions, tensions, be active'. Did the new enterprising managers look like this? If we re-examine the implementation process in the light of the notion of 'disciplinary practices' as outlined by Foucault (1977), a different picture emerges.

Competence as Discipline

Foucault identified three primary methods through which people are managed en masse: enclosure (the creation of a space closed in upon itself); partitioning (each individual has her own place and each place an individual); and ranking (the hierarchical ordering of individuals) (see Ch. 3). To what extent does the competence approach reflect these 'dividing practices' and to what extent is it supported by disciplinary techniques of examination and confession?

Enclosure

At a broad level, the embedded assumptions about a divide between work and home life work as an 'enclosing' principle. Thus, some experiences from the home are made inappropriate for the workplace. Such a state of affairs is achieved through the development and use of a language that would be inappropriate in the home environment. Thus for example, women, in their domestic roles may actually be meeting the requirements of the competences – for example a mother providing extra help in the nursery, may well demonstrate the behaviours associated with a commonly found competence of being 'externally aware'. However, if she is not familiar with this language, she may not recognise that she has the skills an organisation needs. Nor is the organisation likely to recognise these skills.

At another level, the failure to take into account structural conditions under which women labour acts as another exclusionary factor. And finally, the failure to take into account other ways of working or ways of being, such as allowing the more 'relational' aspects of behaviour a role, furthers the work/home divide, thereby excluding those (a majority of women) who prefer one mode of behaviour over another. I shall explore the mechanisms by which this happens later.

Partitioning

Within the sphere of the workplace, the competence approach works at several levels in 'partitioning' individuals. At a fundamental level, the initial critical incident methodology serves to isolate those who are perceived to behave in 'effective' ways. Inevitably, those 'effective' ways will reflect current ways of working, current paradigms, and thus will serve to reinforce these ways of behaviour.

Splitting up these behaviours into measurable parts further renders the individual 'knowable', and 'measurable' both in temporal and physical dimensions. For example, the following is an example of one of the competences from organisation A:

Table 6.1   Example of competences from organisation A

Positive behaviours	Negative behaviours
• communicates easily with people at levels of the organisation • listens and encourages others, pays attention, shows individuals that they are valued • displays openness – to information, values and ideas proposed by others • displays a variety of ways of involving others • organises time effectively	• spends time on detail • is rigid, hierarchical or rules bound • spends a significant amount of time fire-fighting • concerned with the present • aggressive or confrontational • displays intellectual arrogance • criticises colleagues

Positive behaviours

- delegates well and encourages
  another level of delegation
- not bound by hierarchy
- is friendly and displays
  considerable interpersonal skills

These behaviours were 'categorised' from a series of interviews carried out with a cross-section of senior managers in this organisation. Here there is the attempt to 'identify' particular types of individuals who are deemed to be suitable to 'lead' this organisation. The individual specified here, is the 'enterprising' 'open' individual we saw identified earlier, open to challenge, and who listens to subordinates. The 'negative' behaviours are those associated with the rather more traditional and pen-pushing individuals required in a 'bureaucratic' way of working. Yet there are significant inconsistencies here. It is possible to see business conditions where these so-called 'negative' behaviours would be more appropriate. For example, there are certain cases where 'spending time on detail' and 'concerned with the present' would be absolutely crucial – and can be important for the 'long-term view'. There may also be times when 'criticising colleagues' is necessary, though there are obviously effective or ineffective ways of criticising colleagues. In the same way, in the 'positive behaviours' someone who 'delegates well and encourages another level of delegation' could well be someone who is 'bound by hierarchy'. That is to say that each 'behaviour' is contextual – depending on the individual and the particular problem.

Most of the competences from the organisations could be criticised in this way. Perhaps more importantly, the method of breaking down and identifying different aspects of behaviour as 'effective', and then reconstructing these into a 'perfect individual' loses the very notion of being human. One particular human being may behave one way in one context, and another way in a different context. Different behaviours will be triggered by different sets of conditions. There is no 'perfect individual' as no set of conditions is ever the same. As one interviewee noted:

> it is only too easy to look at the competences for a particular job and think 'I can never be like that'.

This may well produce symptoms of anxiety for many employees. Certainly, the competences set up a system of 'ideals' to which employees can only aspire, thus creating an implicit authority relationship. Control here is the order of the day rather than empowerment. If individuals do not match this profile, then they will either have to change, or will be 'ranked' lower than their counterparts. At worst, they will have to leave the organisation.

Ranking

The HR strategies associated to varying degrees with these competences serve to reinforce the partitioning and will bring in ranking processes. Some organisations had incorporated competences either formally or informally into recruitment, selection and promotion purposes. All were using them as methods of training and developing senior managers, and expecting at some time to cascade these down the organisations.

Ranking can happen at two levels. Either different competences can be developed for different tiers of the organisation as happened in organisations A and C, or they can be developed at the top level, and then ranked according to the different level of jobs for which they are required as evidenced in companies B and D. The ranking in the Trust was particularly striking. Here 34 competences were identified at six different levels, resulting in a highly complex grid, from which, once classified, there is very little room for manoeuvre.

Appraisal: Examination and Confession?

One of the key practices associated with competence is that of appraisal or review. This resonates with Foucault's notions of examination and confession. The examination provides a mechanism by which individuals can be measured, codified and classified within these procedures. This constant visibility keeps the individual subjected and 'arranged' like objects. Confession, however, although it may be a route to 'knowing oneself' draws more of the person into the domain of power (Fairclough 1992). The confession is characterised first by the topic – in this case the speaking subject, and second by the power relations implied by the confessional relationship, where the interlocutor acts as judge, forgiver, counsellor. Confession has a special quality in that the act of doing it changes the person who does it. It exonerates and purifies her. The value of the confession is increased by the obstacles and resistance one has to overcome to make it (Fairclough 1992).

In appraisal, the individual is examined as to how she matches up to the competences required by the job. If she fails to come up to scratch, then she needs to 'confess' these failings to the appraiser, and together they can draw up a personal development plan. Such a process is designed to encourage the individual to 'internalise' the types of behaviours required to make the organisation more effective. It is through individuals mastering these competences that the organisation reaches its goals and purposes. The degree to which behaviours are internalised depends on the depth and purpose of the appraisal system.

The type, frequency and depth of the appraisal system differed from organisation to organisation. In organisation A, for example, at senior management level, while forms for appraisal were available, appraisal itself was not a common part of organisational life, particularly for the academics. The organisation had plans to make it part of this, but this is a longer-term aim. In organisation D, although the competence framework was considered to be a 'guide rather than a rule' there was extensive documentation to help managers appraise their subordinates.

Some interesting points emerge from this documentation. The first is the extensive amount of documentation itself, reflecting the disciplinary technique of codifying and classifying. The information was backed up by 'psychometric indicators' which serve to reinforce the scientific basis of the competence profile. Though, as it says on the appraisal documentation, there is 'as yet no empirical link between these scales; they should be viewed cautiously', the scientific presentation (tabulated columns), the fact that it is printed on expensive company paper, would certainly not discourage people from making these links. In assessing the management potential of each appraisee, appraisers are requested to encircle either:

EAR (too early to assess potential)
CHA (fully challenged by present job)
LAT (potential for lateral movement)
POT (potential for further progression)
HIG (high potential (Guide: Top 5–10 per cent))

Such a way provides a good example of rendering individuals 'knowable' and hence 'calculable'. Channels for any other type of assessment are effectively closed down both in terms of the documentation and in the language itself of the documentation. Individuals in this company become known by their potential in the 'competency bank'.

The form overleaf is that used for the appraisal of a GP receptionist in organisation E. This was used as an examplar for managers when attending a workshop on appraisal. I was present when managers were assessing this person's appraisal. In the discussion, any notion of the individual as a complete human being was lost. The managers went point by point through each of the competences, working out the 'developmental gaps', then proceeded to go to the relevant place in the open learning manual to see what that individual should do to improve himself. There was no attempt at holistically assessing the person, so that the possibility that a combination of particular behaviours bringing particular benefits was lost. This eased the difficulties of the assessment, but also fragmented the person into separate parts, in much the same way as the conveyor belt broke down craft skills.

INDIVIDUAL MATCH TO ROLE

COMPETENCY	Role requirements	Individual competency
MARKETING CLUSTER		
1 Living the Aims and Values	D (I) M L H S	(D) I M L H S
2 Commercial Awareness and Drive	D (I) M L H S	(D) I M L H S
3 Building and Maintaining Relationships	D I (M) L H S	D I (M) L H S
4 Building Credibility	D I (M) L H S	D (I) M L H S
5 Understanding and Agreeing Requirements	D (I) M L H S	D (I) M L H S
6 Optimising the Use of Resources	D (I) M L H S	(D) I M L H S
7 Meeting Agreed Service Requirements	D I (M) L H S	D I (M) L H S
8 Measuring Performance	D (I) M L H S	D (I) M L H S
9 Continuous Improvement	D I (M) L H S	D I (M) L H S
TEAM EFFECTIVENESS CLUSTER		
10 Providing Direction	D (I) M L H S	(D) I M L H S
11 Ensuring Understanding	D I (M) L H S	D I (M) L H S
12 Agreeing Required Contribution	D (I) M L H S	D I (M) L H S
13 Building the Team	D I (M) L H S	D I (M) L H S
14 Resolving Issues	D (I) M L H S	D I (M) L H S
15 Encouraging and Motivating	D (I) M L H S	D I (M) L H S
16 Giving and Receiving Feedback	D (I) M L H S	D I (M) L H S
17 Recognising the Contribution of Others	D (I) M L H S	(D) I M L H S
18 Developing Self and Others	D (I) M L H S	D (I) M L H S
PERSONAL EFFECTIVENESS CLUSTER		
19 Delivery Orientation	D I (M) L H S	D I (M) L H S
20 Taking Responsibility	D (I) M L H S	D I (M) L H S
21 Change Orientation	D (I) M L H S	D (I) M L H S
22 Creativity and Innovation	D (I) M L H S	D (I) M L H S
23 Openness and Challenge	D I (M) L H S	D I (M) L H S
24 Self Discipline and Maturity	D I (M) L H S	D I (M) L H S
25 Tenacity and Resilience	D I (M) L H S	D (I) M L H S
SERVICE IMPLEMENTATION CLUSTER		
26 Planning *N/A*	D I M L H S	D I M L H S
27 Caring in the Community	D (I) M L H S	D (I) M L H S
28 Providing a Personal Service	D (I) M L H S	D (I) M L H S
29 Providing a Professional Service	D (I) M L H S	D (I) M L H S
30 Supporting Service Delivery *N/A*	D I M L H S	D I M L H S
31 Meeting Legal and Regulatory Requirements	D (I) M L H S	(D) I M L H S
32 Financial Management	D (I) M L H S	(D) I M L H S
33 Optimising the Use of Technology	D (I) M L H S	D (I) M L H S
34 Making Presentations	D (I) M L H S	D (I) M L H S

Note Date of profiling: February 1995.

Figure 6.1 Copy of mock-up form used in appraisal workshop

A further manifestation of examination is the setting up of assessment and development centres. Interestingly, there is some confusion over the terminology between 'assessment' and 'development'. Although 'assessment' is the one most frequently used, with its more overt message of examination, the term 'development' may well be used in its place. For example, organisation C uses this terminology, although as the in-house brochure for these centres says:

> They are designed to evaluate management skills and aptitudes in a systematic and objective manner. The data which the centres generate assists in the formulation of more focused development plans for individuals.

and later:

> It is intended the information derived from the Development Centres will be used in conjunction with our existing arrangements such as one-to-one meetings with immediate supervisors and the annual performance review.

Thus even though, in this organisation, competences are not formally acknowledged to be linked to HR structures, informally this is taking place. Note also the reification of the notion of 'centre' when in actual fact it is a process rather than a place.

The appraisal process incorporates elements of confession. In the appraisal process, both appraiser and appraisee prepare by filling in a competence profile, or questionnaire related to the competences. They then meet to discuss the issue, match profiles and agree a development plan for the individual. In some cases the examination may not just be from above, but may take the form of 360 degree appraisal, where the appraisees' peers, subordinates, and sometimes customers are asked to make judgements about the appraisee. As the Head of Human Resources noted at organisation C:

> A senior manager would get their questionnaires done, then that information is fed back to them in an anonymous way, except that if you have only one boss it is fairly obvious who filled in the form. What we would do with the person is then sit down and look at that and identify strengths and weaknesses.

In all companies, individuals were expected to draw up individual development plans following the appraisal process, thus providing the foundation for the 'examination' through appraisal that takes place on an annual basis. In this way, the examination will make individuals responsible for their own development:

> In a sense, just by opening up we are encouraging senior managers to really think deeply about their development. Hopefully we are going to make them better at doing that for other people ... we are hoping that the process we are going to drive through is also going to embed seeds and make the performance development link.

The Enterprising Self

At the heart then, of the competence approach is the individual's assessment of their own competences, supported by human resource technologies. In the majority of the appraisal processes I have witnessed (with the notable exception of one which shall be discussed in Ch. 8) individuals become involved with their own self-development by filling in their own appraisal before the actual interview takes place. At the interview stage, the manager and subordinate discuss the appraisal, find the gaps and 'contract' with each other (and the individual with herself) to 'develop' these gaps in 'competence'. Such contracts usually manifest as 'personal development plans' which individuals keep, but which are usually deposited centrally with the human resources department, enabling the organisation to keep track of 'organisational learning'.

In this way aspects of individual subjectivity are incorporated into selection procedures, and filed away in the drawers of the human resource department. As the Head of Personnel at the Trust noted:

> The appraisal process will identify development needs, potential and that will be turned into a personal development plan, which will set targets and objectives for development for that particular individual ... it is not going to be left for a year for reappraisal, that plan will have targets, objectives and timetables, and so the actual delivery, if you like, of the personal development plan will be an on-going process.

During the appraisal process:

> They are able to discuss well 'Why did you put yourself here', 'Show me why you think you should be higher or lower and I will tell you what I have seen in you that you are actually better than you are, or that you haven't displayed x or y to me.' So there is feedback everywhere, it is not aimed at one individual, there is discussion around, in terms of team, and it might be between the person above the manager and also the manager and the person with the direct report, so it cross-checks in a lot of places.

The individual becomes, then, in a sense, the central focus of surveillance and discipline. Where 'upward appraisal' is in place, this 'self-policing' becomes a contract between subordinate and manager, so that the whole process is a tightly knit nexus of individual and departmental control. Since in the appraisal the competences are generally 'profiled' against the job role, the individual, although encouraged to believe that they are developing themselves, may not be aware that they are only focusing on those competences which are appropriate to meeting the exigencies of the business plan.

In the organisations, this is reflected in the differences both in terms of the competences, in the way in which they were implemented, the degree of control as characterised by the rigour with which they intertwined with other human resource technologies. Indeed, in some organisations, such as organisation D, and to a lesser extent in others, the competence approach is not far removed from a contemporary form of managerial Taylorism. Competences, although founded in the language of liberation, empowerment, devolution and anti-bureaucracy, can result in an increase in control and an increase in surveillance of managers' behaviour. With increased specification of roles and individuals, in minute behavioural terms, the quality of manager's performance can be far more readily gauged. Monitoring and assessment were built in as routine by-products of the competence architecture. The statements of the relevant competences at the various levels were clear; they were available. Staff were trained in using them by applying them during training to specific roles or to carefully described hypothetical managers. Monitoring and evaluation became a normal part of the manager's role, and both are not only facilitated by the competence approach, they are usually elements of the management competences themselves. As the Chief Executive of the Trust noted:

> Start to talk about people's behaviours, and up goes the barriers, and the skin gets thicker and the resentment, and there is a lack of ease. This [Behavioural Anchored Rating Scales] provides a tool, where people could look at the BARS, and where they felt they fitted into the skills, where their job fitted into the skills, and then when we sat down to talk about it, they had already *subjected themselves* to the process. [My italics]

Here is an interesting use of the term 'subjected'. The Chief Executive uses Foucauldian notions of 'subjectified individuals' to describe how the process works.

6.4   LANGUAGE

All respondents noted the importance of the language of competence in shaping their understanding of the concept. However, very few moved beyond this recognition. Structuralist, post-modern and feminist critics have long recognised the crucial role that language plays in shaping reality. Far from merely reflecting an already given social reality, language, by framing cognition, constitutes reality for us. By constituting this reality, it plays a critical role in creating and maintaining the social structures within which we operate. Language is one of the constitutive, if not the most important, constitutive processes by which social structures are maintained, and through which power relations filter. By its very nature, language has the effect of 'shutting out' other meanings. Thus, by building a hierarchy of values, it has the effect of positively positioning one 'truth' over another. The following discussion, using the analytical tools set out in Appendix 1, shows how, far from stating 'objective truths', as many of the respondents believed, the language of competence was actually constructing their view of reality.

The 'Text' of Competence

The following analysis is based upon a set of texts relating to competence. They were identified through the Open University Bath Information System (BIDS) using the word 'competence' as a search. Texts were selected over three years (July 1992 to July 1995), plus other articles which had stimulated the search in the first place. The sample comprised 61 articles.

The purpose of the analysis is to demonstrate how the language of competence, which respondents felt shaped their understandings, subtly transforms meaning, and consequently their subsequent actions to reinforce structured sets of understandings.

For ease of reading, extracts from the articles used as data are set in a different typeface.

Characteristic of the texts of competence is the projection of the organisation as a 'caring institution' with the best 'needs' of the employees at heart. Thus assessment centres, rather than measuring the performance of individuals in line with the business plan:

offer a more accurate and comprehensive appraisal of the individual's potential and development needs. (Dulewicz 1991, p.50)

Asking a different question of this statement reveals a subtle transformation of meaning: whose needs? Here, the individual is attributed with 'potential' and 'needs' that can be satisfied by the employer. In fact, the 'needs' are not those of the individual – it is the 'needs' of the organisation which are being addressed. This technique I will call '*introjection*'. It serves to hand over responsibility for 'self-development' to the employee, though it is not clear why the individual should take such responsibility. In some cases, the responsibility may not be so subtly handed over:

The successful application of competency-based action learning to the development of effective learning managers, relies upon a judicious marriage of the inner strengths of participants, with reflections upon learning from experiences of action in the real world of work and life. (Smith 1993, p.47)

The metaphorical reference to 'judicious marriage' carries with it the notion of a moral obligation to the organisation. Interestingly, in this article, which is claiming the benefits of competency-based action learning for individuals, the organisationally-based projects that form the basis of the programme:

> provide the organisation with the side benefit of using this project as an assessment centre to prepare and test a manager's ability to operate in a new situation or on a new task at a higher level. (p.47)

While the individual is developing from the action learning programme, the organisation will still be in a position to examine the progress being made. Trust is betrayed by judgement. The 'objective' counselling techniques are combined with judgemental methods with profit as the objective.

This notion of the 'caring' organisation is achieved through the constant juxtaposition of notions of assessment and appraisal (control) against ideas of empowerment of individuals, thus demonstrating the power of *paradox*. The notion of empowerment emerged strongly from all articles as a major theme, and was also implicit in the overarching reference to management education and training. Consider the following extract:

> The second competency deals with the workforce to be led and managed. Employees must not only be free to maximise their contributions to the corporation, they must be encouraged and motivated to do so. They must be freed from the shackles of bureaucracy. Every individual has within him or her the reservoirs of creativity and imagination – all waiting to be released. The executive of the future must tap these reservoirs in each and every employee.
>
> Freeing the individual is not enough. This competency must go beyond – it must motivate the individual to reach further, to fly higher, and in order to do this, individuals must be empowered to maximise their contributions to the organisation. The ability to empower individuals with the reward of self-fulfilment is a must for the *Complete Executive*. (Zimmerman 1993, p.389, original author's italics)

This extract appeared in an article published in *Human Resource Management*, a reviewed journal. The modal tone of exhortation to action – repeated use of 'must' – is characteristic of the prescriptive management school of 'excellence' – but there is here an inherent paradox. In a significant construction of absence, there is no indication of how individuals will be motivated. No guidance is given as to how the 'complete executive' rewards the individual by self-fulfilment. Further the modal tone of exhortation 'must' reflects and reconstructs the 'directive' behaviours, even while 'individuals' are to be empowered. Such a paradox strongly reinforces 'masculine' ways of being that could serve to divide the workforce along gendered lines.

Characteristic too, of the language of competence is the reference to bureaucratic forms of government as prisons. Significantly absent here, is any reference to the academic debate which is currently challenging the association of bureaucracy with inefficient or uncaring management practices (Du Gay 1996). It is this association of competence with the 'enterprising organisations' which must lead many of the organisations in our sample to make the 'culture change' claims that we saw earlier.

One of the areas of resistance to competence came from professionals. The competence approach involves a contest for control between professionals and managers, threatening the power which professionals have accumulated over the past century. The voices of professionals are significantly absent from the discourse. Within the lists of competences identified at a generic level, there is generally a consensus of agreement over which are fundamental to a manager's job. These are rarely those traditionally associated with those of the professional. The discourse, and the competences themselves are characterised by repeated and condensed use of words such as 'concept formation', 'interpersonal search', 'managing interaction' which are all examples of the creation of new 'word meanings'.

The following passage uses a combination of creating word meaning, and shifting of attribution to subtly take away power from those specialisms traditionally considered as having 'professional' expertise to a new breed of generalist managerial professionals:

> As entire work processes are *reengineered*, work roles become *cross-functional* and bear little resemblance to the traditional job-based roles ... *Training and development professionals* typically define a learning organisation as one whose members are continuously and deliberately learning new things. Members demonstrate what they have learned in terms of improvements in the product or service quality, the processes involved in making the product or providing the service, the quality of the work environment, and the performance of members and teams. (Burdett 1993, my emphasis, p.25)

The new word 'reengineered' with its 'taken-for-granted' meaning that it is scientific, and therefore 'efficient' sets up the argument that 'training and development professionals' will be 'defining the organisation'. Here, the attribution of the word 'professional' to the training and development function demonstrates how, in the discourse, the general management function is seizing the autonomy and prestige traditionally associated with specialist professional groupings.

Such a debate may well, through paradox, undermine the power of the professional groupings. Take the following example:

> Thus there is the need for the development of skill sets that are appropriate and unique to the organisation and that will provide core competencies and competitive advantage. This raises numerous issues around how to best manage individuals so they develop and maintain the correct skill sets and how to rapidly change the organisation as the old projects disappear and new ones appear.
> ... professionals may find skill-based systems especially attractive [they] tend to be keenly interested in increasing their expertise, thus a skill-based pay system pays these employees for what they want to do in the first place. Greater expertise also

> affords the employee some measure of professional security in an era when fewer
> and fewer employees can expect to spend their entire career in one company.
> (Lawler 1994, p.7)

Here, the skills of the professional are being subtly subsumed into those of the
organisation rather than those of the occupational profession, which is set up
as a sectional group. The skills to be used are those required to meet the needs
of the organisation, not those required to help further the professional's career.
The individual is encouraged to develop 'form specific' as opposed to
'transferable skills' thus rendering the economic contract between individual
and organisation more beneficial for the organisation. However, the
professional will welcome such a change since they are being paid for 'what
they want to do in the first place'. And further, even though the skills to be
developed are unique to that particular organisation, acquiring these skill sets
will afford them 'some measure of professional security in an era when fewer
and fewer employees can expect to spend time in one company'. The
professional who has already acquired a set of skills is thus being urged and
will, apparently, welcome (note here the technique of ventriloquism) having to
acquire a set of skills that may only be appropriate to one organisation. Note
that throughout this particular text the words 'competence' and 'skill' are used
interchangeably in a rather subtle version of 'neither/norism' so that the
appropriation of status from professional to general is not noticed.

The language of exhortation and metaphor are also used to develop this
picture. For example:

> The stepladder is gone, and there's not even the implied structure of an industry's
> rope ladder. Its more like vines, and you bring your own machete. You don't know
> what you'll be doing next. (Drucker, quoted by Harris 1993, p.117)

> ... No amount of knowledge of marketing, finance, operations, Human Resources
> (HR) and Strategic Management techniques will suffice in the tough, changing
> world of Contemporary Management, unless it is built on a firmly based self-
> concept. (Smith 1993, p.46)

The tough and challenging world of the explorer is fully evoked here to engage
the readers in an exciting quest for new and better managerial skills. Note too
how the modality is direct, and uses the 'will' form to bring the message home.
Further, how will the mother, used to developing skills outside the home, with
her own particular brand of 'nurturing skills' respond to the language of the
'machete'?

Inherent in the discourse is the assumption that 'skill' is unproblematic; that
it can be measured and paid for on entirely objective grounds. This is
particularly clear on articles relating to pay. There is an assumption that
'market rate' is an objective measurement. Ultimately, many organisations are

working towards rewarding employees on a competence basis. Yet the discourse of competence completely ignores the problems that many organisations have faced in creating 'equal value for equal jobs'.

The most striking absence from the body of articles however, is that of women's voices. Equal opportunities is only mentioned once as a theme in any of the literature. Only one of the articles mentions the possibility that men and women may not be treated fairly in appraisal and assessment (Townley 1990) while only two (Robertson and Kinder 1993; Arnold and Davey 1992) address the possibility that there may be problems in the 'scientific' and 'objective' assessment of individuals' personality and behaviour.

This discussion has highlighted the variety of ways in which language can frame cognitions and expectations. This happens both through extensive nominalisations, and, in particular, the creation of new 'word-meanings'. While organisations may not *necessarily* use the nominalised form of communication in their own organisational communications, it has become fairly standard practice for these nominalisations to become taken up as the common form of exchange in organisational life.[1]

Materials from Case Studies

The same 'technologisation of language' can be seen in the textual material of the organisations in the sample. Here, for example, is the opening text of the glossy brochure produced at the semi-privatised utility for their competence framework. On the front of the brochure is a picture of a male lion and it is entitled:

Development and Career *Planning* in XX
Part of XX *Performance Management*
(my italics)

Here are four nominalisations. But we can ask the questions, whose development? Whose planning? Whose performance, and who is managing? Nominalisation here creates the 'taken-for-granted' organisational view that employees will 'be' 'developed', and that this is not subject to debate. The anonymous tone of the brochure is set clearly from the start. Power is removed from the agenda.

On the inside front cover is a letter from the Chief Executive. This is written as follows:

Dear staff member
    I would like to stress to you the importance the Board and I attach to ensuring adequate attention is being paid to individual development and career planning within XX.

> To further our goal of being a significant player in the global energy marketplace, we are totally dependent on the drive, energies and capabilities of our people. With a rapidly changing business environment I believe this means personal development must be an ongoing process for all of us.
>
> I am also aware of the responsibility I share with the Board, to ensure our investment in people is enhanced by careful management of our valuable people resource. The Corporate Management Review is a vital process which enables us to achieve this on a regular and structured basis. It is playing a key role in ensuring we have effective teams and that we can respond quickly to emerging business needs. I commend it to you

It is notable here that employees have now become 'staff members' to emphasise their important role in the team. 'Member' is generally a term one would use for sports or leisure activities. This is obviously intended to engage the employee in the agenda of the business. Unlike most of the other texts, this is written in the first person. Despite this, however, he immediately goes on to distance himself by saying 'the Board and I' – not only is he distanced but the message is imbued with greater institutional power. This is reiterated in the third paragraph, again notable by the nominalisation. Even though it is in the first person, a sense of agency is removed. A different way of writing this might be:

> The Board and I need to make sure that we get the most out of every penny we spend on staffing. To do this we shall be regularly reviewing your performance in a structured fashion. This way we can be sure that we can build [and disband] teams quickly to respond to business needs [e.g. downsizing]. Please comply.

It is also worth noting that the choice of a lion as a theme that runs through this brochure, and reference to the word 'survival' is one that plays on individuals' fears, delineating not a calm and relaxed working environment, but one where death hangs round each corner.

Thus, it seems that language works to create and 'transform' meaning, and can subtly position one group over another. All of the respondents said how important it was to gain an understanding of the language and engage in its 'shared meaning'. 'Shared meaning' is, however, not as objective, or indeed as benign as it appears to be. 'Constitutive processes' of language shape meaning and reality such that inequities may persist or be constructed.

6.5   CONCLUSIONS

It seems that, when examining the discursive practice of competence in more detail, far from creating a new culture change, the competence project was more likely to reflect the organisation's past as much as its chosen future, that its implementation could be critiqued in terms of objectivity, and rather than empowering employees through constructing the enterprising manager, competence frameworks could be used for partitioning, ranking and enclosing individuals. These were underpinned by the disciplinary practices of examination and confession through assessment and appraisal. Further, the language of competence was not the neutral textual tool that managers imagined. Indeed, a different 'reading' of its language showed how the textual transformations invite the reader or employee into the surveillance of the competence frameworks.

Far from being objective, the competence approach, for all its apparent simplicity, could be interpreted as a disciplinary practice. However, perhaps because of the effective nature of the discipline, most respondents were enthusiastic about the project. Where the implementation process was seen to be failing, however, attention was focused not so much on the process itself, but on the 'technical' problems of interpretation or problems of consistency of application. In other words, the competence process itself was rarely questioned. Thus the reasons of why competence was introduced was not seen to be an issue – even though, when asked, many people had not even thought through what 'competence' actually meant. The technical nature of the competence process was deemed to the '*raison d'être*' of its introduction. The competence frameworks were drawn up so that organisations became more efficient, not for the benefit of the employee. Instrumental rationality was the order of the day, and discussions about values were rarely raised. Indeed, the technicality of the competence processes closed down any discussion about values.

ENDNOTE

1. I myself have spent several years as a 'publishing consultant' in organisations, both as editor of an HR magazine, and drafting and producing in-house communications and training materials. Acting as a gamekeeper turned poacher in this book, I have to say that I have always been very aware of using 'jargon' in order to get messages across. The dressing is more important than the message within it. Often, when clients have wanted to get the message across, the question 'What do you mean?' tends to floor people. Unreflective use of a particular 'technical' language tends to be part and parcel of organisational life.

7. Writing out gender

Modern managers, technical experts and consultants have become the 'organic intellectuals' of our own time. Their performance management 'systems' determine what is 'normal' in organisational life. Competence frameworks were introduced by consultants, communicated through the organisational system to managers, and not surprisingly, the reasons for introducing these frameworks were rarely questioned. Where there was debate, this was around the technical nature of the frameworks. This chapter digs deeper into the competence processes to examine what their likely impact is to be on women managers. Two aspects of the competence frameworks are questioned here. First, do the practices of competence build in disadvantage at a structural level for women who carry the burden of domestic duties, and if so, how? And second, to what extent do the competence frameworks favour directive over nurturing behaviours? In the first part the practices associated with competence (drawing up the competence frameworks and subsequent practices of assessment and appraisal) are examined to see what the implications are here for those people (mostly women) who may use a predominance of nurturing behaviours, and who may also have structural constraints of caring for children, the old or the sick. In the second part, I analyse the competence frameworks themselves to see whether the actual behaviours outlined reflect directive or nurturing behaviours.

7.1   THE PRACTICES

In order to see how women may be disadvantaged through the 'objective' practices of competence, we need to see where 'discursive closure' may be taking place – one way of this is to examine the assumptions that are underlying the frameworks.

There are (at least) three assumptions made when introducing these practices that could lead to the disadvantage of women: firstly the assumption of objectivity in deriving the competences; secondly the assumption of objectivity in the assessment and appraisal process; and thirdly the very nature of the appraisal process itself

Assumption of Objectivity in Deriving Competences

Whether an organisation uses generically-derived or organisationally-derived competences, claims are made, as we have seen, that the methods used for identifying such competences are 'objective'. Organisations use critical incident interviewing techniques so that the competences use the 'voices' of the employees. These are then carefully analysed, and incorporated into lists of behaviours that are 'observable' and hence 'measurable' and quantifiable. However, as we have seen earlier, there are numerous points in this 'objective' strategy where subjectivity and relations of subordination come into play. In the case of generic managerial competences it is important to examine the profile of the managers from whom desired behaviours are elicited. Given the occupational and managerial breakdown of the workforce, it is likely that such competences were derived primarily from unrepresentative incumbents of managerial posts. This applies equally to organisationally-derived competences. Despite the claims to objectivity, there was considerable variability and tolerance in the way in which the competences were clustered, even though responses had come from critical incident interviews with employees. For example, the way in which the consultant clustered the competences in the Trust after 18 months of rigorous interviewing was somewhat suspect – especially as the 'understanding, knowledge and learning' which apparently underpinned the process had largely been learned from her partner, a competence consultant. The competences then, may well reflect and reinforce the organisational norms that existed prior to the implementation of competence frameworks, and will reinforce the existing gendered substructure.

Assumption of Objectivity in Appraisal and Assessment

The cornerstone of the competence initiative is the assessment and appraisal techniques, yet the potentially gendered aspects of these processes were never raised. Many organisational researchers argue that widespread assumptions, about, for example, gender difference, are embedded in beliefs about personal skills and traits, rendering the ideal of objective selection impossible (Alimo-Metcalfe 1994, 1995; Collinson *et al.*, 1990; Rubin 1999). Even where women are behaving in ways which match the organisational norm for success, such behaviour may be negatively perceived in a woman. Such research provides:

> a warning to those who seek to teach women simply to 'fit in' to existing organisational arrangements ... Behaviours important for men's success are not directly transferable to women because identical behaviour is not perceived or treated in the same way. Success is not defined in sex-neutral terms. (Burton 1992, p.195)

Further, one cannot ignore the social nature of the interaction at appraisals and selection; candidates or appraisees may well be 'performing' based on the situation and their expectations. Some women (and men) may well be highlighting those aspects of themselves which they perceive as compatible with the existing, male organisational norm. This may mean excluding aspects of themselves which are more likely to be perceived as typically 'female' (Rubin 1999).

At the same time, in ostensibly gender-neutral assessment, the desire to focus on correct procedure draws attention away from more subtle forms of stereotyping that may be taking place. With the filling out of a large amount of paperwork that accompanies competence-based appraisal, there is a likelihood that both gross and more subtle forms of stereotyping may take place. Further, the increased emphasis on appraisal, and the lack of training or awareness that accompanies this, suggests that women may further suffer from the process. Since the competence methodology centres around the process of appraisal, more and more appraisals will take place. The appraisal process moves further down the line, and lies in the hands of people who are effectively untrained in assessment processes. If research has shown that even trained assessors 'get it wrong', then there is a likelihood that more errors are likely to be made as untrained people attempt to measure and judge performance.

The Nature of the Appraisal Process

A further, and perhaps more insidious way in which women may be disadvantaged through the competence methodology sits within the actual practices associated with competence. Competences are underpinned by yearly appraisal and regular assessment, and require that the individual disclose and discuss where and how she or he is failing. We have already seen that characteristics of women's behaviour include: not blowing their own trumpets, not making an effort to hide errors, and engaging in rituals where one apologises even when not at fault. In a study of 'female modesty' in achievement situations, Heatherington *et al.* (1993) show how women consistently underrated their own performance in public conditions – precisely the conditions which prevail during appraisal – the public confessional. Thus where the appraisal is conducted in a formal, hierarchical way, it would seem that 'nurturing' types of behaviours could be penalised.

Further, women may disadvantage themselves through the 'ritual' itself of confession. Feminist writers are beginning to recognise the dangers of 'therapism' as an over-evaluation of feeling. It is a brand of disclosure that confuses genuine self-revelation with the perpetual manifestation of intimate feelings (Raymond 1986, p.156). Here some women may be more vulnerable to the passion of 'confessing', so that the action of power in the relationship is lost from sight. As Foucault (1976) has pointed out:

L'obligation de l'aveu nous est maintenant renvoyée à partir de tant de points différents, elle nous est désormais si profondément incorporée que nous ne la percevons plus comme l'effet d'un pouvoir qui nous contraint; il nous semble au contraire que la vérité, au plus secret de nous-même, ne 'demande' qu'à se faire jour (p.80).[1]

7.2   THE COMPETENCES

This part of the analysis, the competence frameworks themselves (that is the list of competences drawn up by each of the companies) is examined in the light of two criteria:

- to what extent do the competence frameworks favour directive over nurturing behaviours?
- is there any structural disadvantage built into the competence frameworks that may favour the particular conditions under which most men work, or those of women, who are the primary care-givers in society?

One set of competences (from organisation D) is compared against the set of behaviours drawn up in Chapter 2, which showed the predominant tendencies in women's behaviours, and with a set of competences derived from a study carried out by Lyons *et al.* (1990) at the Emma Willard School (pp.204–5; p.32 in this volume). This work was part of a major study carried out in collaboration with Gilligan and colleagues to assess differences in adolescent girls' ways of thinking. The purpose of the study was to identify how a sample of adolescent girls think about and act as leaders. In the analysis of their responses to questions about leadership, a set of ideas emerged around two different modes of leadership. Each mode points to a different set of values and assumptions about leadership. I am not, of course, suggesting that all girls, and women use the interdependent mode. However, the study showed that this was the predominant mode in the Emma Willard School. I am using these as a point of comparison since they reflect differences which have been noted *before* boys and girls reach the workplace and have been socialised into the gendered norms of the organisation. Further, the list of competences were derived from adolescent girls in leadership positions basing the methodology on that used by Boyatzis (1982). Where appropriate, I shall also use textual tools of analysis listed in Appendix 1.

Organisation D was chosen since it had one of the tightest sets of integrated practices, with competences forming the official basis of selection, appraisal and promotion. It was also concerned, incidentally, about its lack of women employees. This organisation had a set of 18 clusters of competences, broken into separate behaviours, which were themselves defined by indicators and contra-indicators which were used to measure these behaviours. The first part of the analysis looks at one of the clusters of competences relating to 'people/operations' and their definitions, and the second selects two of the competences and looks at indicators and contra-indicators used to measure this behaviour.

I have particularly selected this cluster, since its title 'people/operational' suggests that there could be mixture of nurturing and directive behaviours.

> People/operational cluster
> 10 Technical excellence
> Strives for excellence within the function, works to high quality and technical standards, in the context of business requirements.
> 11 Organisational engineering
> Designs and implements efficient organisation structures, procedures and processes which take into account the interface with other parts of the organisation and give effective achievement of the business plan.
> 12 Management control
> Puts into place systems which provide information for monitoring performance areas such as finance, people, health and safety, environment etc.
> 13 Development of human resources
> The ability to maximise the effective use of human resources. Develops and attracts talent.
> 14 Communications
> Communicates in a way which creates a performance-oriented culture, building consensus when appropriate. Networks and recognises the communication requirements of others. Ensures company strategy is understood and linked to actions.

In this cluster related to people and operations, there is a predominantly 'directive' feel. Here, 'hard' engineering solutions are proposed for 'human' problems. There is an implicit assumption that organisations can be classified, codified and run along entirely rational grounds. The elision of finance, people, health and safety in competence 12 suggests that all these aspects are under control – or can be if they are systematised. It is interesting that 'people' has become a 'performance area' in a new word-meaning. Note also the fairly overt implication that 'management' is an area of 'control'. As far as human resources are concerned ('human resources' itself, of course, a new word-meaning), 'talent' becomes a resource in itself – nowhere is there any sense of 'people'. The workforce has become nominalised. In the competence relating to communication, the prime aim is to create a 'performance-oriented culture'. This nominalisation leading to new 'word meaning' stamps authority on a particular type of communication which is not communication for the sake of meaningful relationships, but communication for an end purpose. Consensus is to be reached only 'when appropriate' – not as part of the culture. One wonders when consensus is considered to be appropriate. Human resources are to be 'controlled' and systematised. People are not considered as human beings with which one has a common shared desire to communicate; rather they are entities with 'communication requirements' (note the nominalisation). This is far from the 'connectedness' of women's way of perceiving the world as noted, amongst others, by Belenky *et al.* (1986). Above all, the communication should lead to meeting the company structure – not to encourage teamworking.

The behavioural indicators of one of these competences in more detail shows the same pattern.

13   Development of Human Resources
     Definition
     The ability to maximise the effective use of human resources. Develops and attracts talent.
     Indicators
     - Analyses future risks, their probabilities and resultant people resource implications
     - Uses human resources flexibly with contingency plans
     - Maintains task objectives uppermost without damaging staff morale
     - Contributes to written people plans and timescales
     - Organises work and people effectively
     - Trusts people and believes in them, people become aware of this
     - Delegates effectively
     - Creates a work climate in which people succeed, empowers people to take action
     - Spends time discussing development issues with staff and acts on the decisions
     - Allows other to take the credit (never signs somebody else's paper), spreads recognition and gives visibility
     - People outside the team seek to join for development opportunities
     - Able to judge personal qualities in people

The emphasis throughout here is on the notion of 'managing people' as a resource. Ideas and plans are devolved directly down from the manager, and people are there as a resource to carry them out. There is no indication here of leading being a 'team activity' with the leader acting as facilitator or coach. The indicators move downwards (probably in importance) from notions of 'human resource' to 'staff' to 'people plans' and it is only more than half way down that there is a sense that people can be 'talked to'. In other words, there is very much a feel that 'people' are the 'objects' that managers 'manage'. The emphasis on 'writing' things down in order that they can be measured resonates with Foucault's dividing practices. Action and not relation is considered to be the way of 'empowerment'.

Comparing these sets of indicators with those derived from Lyons's work with Gilligan, shows that they bear far greater resemblance to the 'autonomous-in-relation-to-others' mode than the 'interdependent' mode which was the predominant mode for the girls at the Emma Willard School. The emphasis on goals, on structuring and getting things done resembles very closely those of the indicators of competence 13 (see above). For example, even the words 'able to judge personal qualities in people' signals that the leader is well in control 'able to *value* personal qualities' would be a more 'interdependent' way of viewing the world. It is interesting to note too, that 'trusts' people is brought out as a 'behaviour'. This denotes, perhaps, an assumption that 'trusting' is not a natural state of being, or suggests an initial position of separateness. Nurturing behaviour has trust has its foundation.

Here is another of this organisation's 18 competences:

Stress tolerance
Definition
Performance does not deteriorate at times of increased work pressures. Able to think laterally when obstacles are encountered, flexible, resilient.
Indicators
- Addresses problems and challenges against a background of clear personal values and stability of relationships
- Thrives on pressure and significance of work
- Performs consistently and quality of written work does not suffer despite high workloads/time pressures
- In a debate maintains logic and persuasiveness of argument despite heavy opposition from others
- Loses temper 'constructively' i.e. to promote action
- Is patient and understanding with others despite being personally under considerable pressure
- Shows willingness to consider other options and approaches and tests them out
- Thinks laterally about problems and identifies potential solutions rather than restating old solutions
- Reviews plans regularly for appropriateness and often suggests minor or major changes
- Reacts positively to major changes of direction
- Employs stress reduction techniques (e.g. Relaxation, Humour, Exercise, Leisure Activities)

One of the contra-indicators for this competence is 'Reports problems in home relationships, eating problems, deteriorating health etc.' Here again, I would suggest, is a predominance of 'directive' behaviours, very much more in keeping with the 'autonomous-in-relation-to-others' mode. The manager is obviously expected to drive things through, perhaps 'losing his/her temper constructively', whatever the opposition. Logic and persuasiveness are to conquer opposition. Relating on a personal level, or for personal relations is positively discouraged. Adopting the 'one-down' position here, as adumbrated in Tannen's list (1994), would result in failure. The work/home divide is clearly reinforced in that employees will be penalised for 'reporting' problems with their home life. There is considerable emphasis on high workloads and pressure which would pose considerable difficulty for women with heavy domestic responsibilities. Other aspects that we might more traditionally associate with home life, such as relaxation, humour etc. are to be employed as a technique to improve performance. The manager is encouraged to take other options on board, but still retain control whilst so doing. The hand never leaves the tiller.

Of course, not all the organisations have lists of competences with quite such a 'directive' feel to them, but on the whole they do reflect certain 'taken-for-granted' assumptions about ways of behaving in organisations. For example, the following competence in the Trust reflects very much the 'command and control' model we saw above:

> Tenacity and resilience
> Resolutely determined. Consistently holds his/her nerve to confront, learn from and capitalise upon corporate challenges and setbacks. Ensures that the Trust stays in there winning and competing.

Here too, there is little in common with the interdependent-in-relation-to-others mode predominant amongst the adolescent girls. The use of terminology such as 'winning' and 'competing' is also redolent of the ways in which boys conduct play at an early age. I am not arguing that the 'directive' approach is necessarily inappropriate. Directive behaviours may be required to get on with the job. What is needed a balance between the two modes.

Structural Assumptions

Little consideration is taken of the structural constraints under which most women operate. For example, in the extensive and glossy documentation which accompanied the competence project in organisation D, the following appeared:

> *Mobility*
> Ticks are used to indicate 'Yes, 'No or 'Don't know responses [referring to the personal report where employees are asked whether they are (a) be prepared to relocate to obtain desired experience (b) prepared to commute to another work location requiring temporary living/multiple overnights]. Use the 'Comments' section to indicate any special conditions. Your answers will not affect any

contractual requirement to relocate, but will be considered when taking account of
your personal circumstances.
Experience profile
Use a tick to indicate areas in which you have worked continuously for a period of
at least six months.
Management training
Courses listed here should be of at least two days' duration.
Major accomplishments
Space is provided for you to record three or four major achievements from the last
ten years of your work.

Clearly, it would be difficult for people with domestic constraints to meet
these requirements and carry out the job required of them. Further, it may be
difficult for women returners, for example, to gain promotion here. The
assumptions upon which these statements are made is that of continuous
service. Even if a woman has managed a one-day course this will go
unrecorded. Any experience that she may have gained outside the workplace
will equally go unrecorded, since achievements have to be work-related, and
to have taken place over the past ten years.

Thus, in the competences themselves questions arise around the inevitable
divide between work and home. Because only commercially quantifiable
value added is considered relevant to competence analysis, the skills and
awareness developed through running a home and bringing up children do not
come into the reckoning, even though they bear a significant resemblance to
'multi-tasking'. The language of the competence framework (for example,
externally aware, delivery of customer care etc.) would not be applied to skills
in the household. Carers outside the workforce fail to value their achievements
in the non-paid environment in which they have to operate. Thus the
competence project can confirm and reinforce the failure to value skills and
abilities gained outside paid employment. Second, the assumptions built into
the framework are premised upon the notion of a 'universal worker' who, it is
assumed can adhere to organisational rules and regulations, and practices.
Being prepared to sacrifice personal life to duty in the organisation is
presented as a virtue, or it is assumed that the appraised has no obligations of
comparable weight in his or her family life.

7.3   COMPETENCE AND MODES OF COGNITION

A further, though more speculative reading is possible. The majority of ways
in which the competence approach was implemented reflected the
characteristics of the paradigmatic mode of cognition. Organisations built up
complex frameworks, focusing on systems of counting, classifying, and
measuring, leading, in individuals, to the construction of the calculating and

compartmentalised self. In the frameworks themselves, once implemented, there was no room for further contextualisation or 'story-telling'. The forms were drawn up, and boxes ready to be ticked. Even in the appraisal process, where 'confession' was encouraged, the 'confession' was to take place in the paradigmatic fashion in which appraisal documentation was framed.

The competence framework, unless it has built-in processes for change and questioning, and exploration in the narrative mode, is part of, and contributes to the paradigmatic mode of cognition. It is likely to entrench further those patterns of behaviour which men are more prone to display. In such conditions women will either have to 'confess' their tendency to behave in different ways, and set themselves on a programme of self-improvement, which may not do justice to the strengths they do have, or alternatively, they may have to leave the enclosure of employment, as many women managers are choosing to do (Rosin 1991). For women, this means either adopting the paradigmatic mode wholesale (as many do) or to a possible loss of self-confidence as their predominant way of thinking and being is denied validation. The closure exercised by paradigmatic modes of cognition restricts the scope of thinking and problem-solving which may not be in the interests of the organisation itself.

7.4 WRITING OUT GENDER

The competence approach, as we have seen firmly accepts the 'dominant liberal model' of equal opportunities which is based on the assumption, found within liberal political theory, that inequalities arise from the interference of individual biases and prejudices in otherwise rational organisational processes.

Thus women's voices are absent from much of the discourse. The liberal model of the level playing field underpins the discourse. Such a model advocates that women be equipped to enter economic competition and perform better on the existing course, in particular through improved training and qualifications. The discourse does not take into account the broader context of women's lives.

Assumptions that underpin preconceptions about work requirements include the notions that responsible work must be undertaken full-time without interruptions, that particular posts on the career ladders must be reached by specific ages, and that employees in 'good' jobs must be capable of mobility at their employer's behest (Nicholson and West 1988). These preconceptions about work requirements are particularly disadvantageous to many women as long as assumptions about the division of labour in the family remain stable or change only slowly.[2] These issues are noticeably not addressed within the competence initiatives.

To disregard personal and domestic responsibilities and to premise the discourse of competence upon parity in the workplace by assuming that each individual is a *tabula rasa* for the time they are in the workplace, is to ignore the evidence on gendered domestic labour and the recognition of the importance this plays in the daily and generational reproduction of labour power. Further, even though much of the literature on the theme of women's work and home lives makes the point that women's experiences of work and family are intricately linked in ways which differ from the experience of men (for example, Knight 1994), setting up human resource systems that ignore these differences may be debilitating for both organisations and for women.

The practices which produce the facade of gender neutrality are, according to Acker (1992) the impersonal, objectifying practices of organising, managing and controlling large organisations. This reproduces the gender substructure of the organisation and larger society. The gendered substructure lies in the spatial and temporal arrangements of work, in the rules prescribing workplace behaviour, and in the relations linking workplaces to living places. This is the most difficult part of the process to comprehend because it is hidden within abstract, objectifying textually mediated relations and is difficult to make visible.

This research has firstly 'deconstructed' the supposedly 'gender neutral' practices of competences, by displaying how, when we apply an understanding of 'difference' (thus dismantling the assumption of the level playing field) both to the competences and to the practices, we can see a different picture emerging. Here we can see that the competences are likely to reinforce the existing structures, which will disadvantage women. Second, it has highlighted the concrete activities which produce such assumptions.

Some critical management theorists have highlighted the way that men in organisations are often preoccupied with the creation and maintenance of various identities and with the expression of gendered power and status in the workplace (for example, Knights 1990; Collinson, Knights and Collinson 1990; Knights and Willmott 1999). Men's gender identities are constructed, compared and evaluated by self and others according to a whole variety of criteria including personal success in the workplace. Competence methodologies, by focusing on behaviours, work explicitly at constructing this particular 'way of being' to the exclusion of other 'ways of being', namely other masculinities and most femininities. This 'way of being', despite beliefs to the contrary, is historically constructed, and reflects the 'way things are done round here' and thus will build in existing inequalities. The practices which help construct these 'ways of being' or 'identities' are, as we have seen, the practices of assessment and appraisal which resemble disciplinary practices of examination and confession, and which are later tied in, to a greater or lesser extent to the human resource structures of selection, promotion and pay, which are themselves dividing practices.

What is particularly striking here, however, is that when the behaviours are internalised through assessment and appraisal, women are usually unaware of the way in which they may be reinforcing and perpetuating gendered identities which already disadvantage them in the workplace. Thus, it seems here that collective identity-securing strategies documented amongst others by Collinson, Knights and Collinson (1990) have been translated onto an individual level. This suggests that competence strategies are likely to be more pernicious in their discrimination through cutting out possibilities of collective resistance. On-going processes of gender construction, it seems then, are part and parcel of the competence approach, despite the beliefs to the contrary.

It seems that the 'objective' practice of competence is working through different sets of relations: at one level it is favouring and indeed constructing one particular 'masculine' way of being and dividing and partitioning along these levels; at a more fundamental level it is dividing and partitioning along gender lines. Perhaps the whole irony of the situation is encapsulated in a comment made by the Human Resource Director in organisation C, who admitting that they have an equal opportunities problem, and while convinced of the equality of the competence programme, noted that, after two years, they had not yet had a woman manager to appraise. As he commented:

We haven't yet had a woman at the Development Centre.

What, however, happens to such 'objective' strategies when the veil of gender neutrality is lifted? The next chapter examines what happens in an organisation where there is an awareness that these strategies are not necessarily neutral.

ENDNOTES

1. The need to confess is so omnipresent that we feel it in the depths of our being, and fail to see the action of power. On the contrary, it seems that the truth, our very deepest secrets, simply have to be surfaced.
2. The effects of increasing male unemployment on the division of labour has yet to be ascertained.

8. Competence: empowerment rather than control

A major critique levelled against critical theory is its rather oblique theorising, and its tendency to 'hypercritique', thus rendering many of its subtle insights of little practical value. To address this issue and to add further insights into competence frameworks, I concentrated on one organisation which had a very different approach to competences, that of a beauty and cosmetics manufacturer and retailer based in the south of England. This organisation differed from the others in that it had very different reasons for introducing competences. It was, moreover, concerned about the so-called objectivity of the frameworks available. Above all, it maintained constant vigilance about whether the competence approach contained in-built bias against women employees. For this reason, I pursued the research deeper into this organisation, in order to explore how the approach was implemented, and what the implications of the approach were likely to be here for women managers. I selected this as a critical case (Smith, Whipp and Willmott 1988) since it provided an exceptional case as a point of comparison.

8.1   WHY AND HOW IMPLEMENTATION TOOK PLACE

This organisation is a publicly quoted manufacturer and retailer of health and beauty goods. It began in 1976 with the opening of the first shop in the south of England and had become an international company rapidly expanding throughout the world. Its rise has been phenomenal. By the financial year ending of 1990 the organisation had 457 shops trading in 38 countries and in 18 languages; 1265 staff were directly employed. By the financial year ending 1995, 1210 shops were operating in 45 countries trading in 23 languages; 3100 staff were directly employed. The rest of the retail outlets are franchised. Its founder and chief executive was a charismatic woman with very firm ideas, particularly about the values of business trading.

Unlike most other organisations in this research, this organisation did not perceive a threat from competitors. They are a known brand retailer, who manufacture their own products, so unlike other retailers, they do not work on short cycles. Traditional problems such as which brand and how the product looks are not issues, since the labels stay the same and the bottles in which the product is sold stay the same. They were the top sellers in their market, and new products were simply extensions of existing ones. Their competitors have a marginal impact on their market, since their customer profile is that of 20–35-year-old females who have an interest in environmental and social issues on behalf of which this organisation campaigns.

Reasons for Introducing Competences

The major reason for introducing competences in this organisation was to build in some structure for the rapidly growing company. Competences were seen as a way of founding an HR strategy and policy since there had never been a unifying logic on which it was built.

The organisation had just undergone a major restructuring, and needed a way of systematising what were rather ad hoc methods of employment. It had also just gone through a pay banding exercise where the existing 550 job titles had been rationalised into five pay bandings. Except in some parts of the company where a 'performance agreement' was used, there were usually no job descriptions except where jobs stay the same (which is rare in a company growing at that rate).

As the Head of Corporate Services and HR Director pointed out:

> I don't think we are a particularly efficient organisation [in terms of productivity of people]. On the whole companies are not usually specific enough in defining what they do and need ... And you know, words like leadership, or 'good with people' or 'good interpersonal skills' are fairly useless in term of criteria for improvement or advancement or performance measuring. So competences ... is to really think through that service ... to be more specific about what you are looking for and targeting, so that it can be assessed.

A further aim was to use the competences as a way of incorporating the rather unusual values into the culture of the company. These values are, fundamentally, very simple, and represent the initial values of the founders. These are that people, in relating to each other act with:

- honesty
- care
- integrity
- respect

However, as the general manager for company culture noted, though these basic values appear superficially quite straightforward, they were notoriously difficult to implement. It was all too easy to campaign passionately for animal rights, for example, and yet not behave with integrity towards one's colleagues. The competence programme was seen as a way of integrating these values into the company, so that it supported behaviours that would allow the company to support social and environmental issues.

Identifying Competences

The first stage was to carry out critical incident interviews with a 5 per cent sample population at senior management, middle management, administrative and operative levels. At the same time, the existing appraisal documentation was reworked to reflect the competences that were identified. This process took about three months to complete.

The interviews were conducted from October 1994 to December 1994, and the competences collated in mid-December. The information from the interviews was then clustered into groups for each level by two people, one who was responsible for introducing performance management, and the other a former employee used as a consultant. I was present on this occasion and witnessed the attempts to make sure that the language used by people was retained as much as possible. There was some surprise at the lack of 'strategic vision' displayed by middle and senior managers and as a result further interviews were later conducted to ascertain whether this had been missed.

At a series of meetings with senior and middle management, the competences were fed back, discussed and adjusted to reflect the day-to-day reality of the workplace. Other meetings were held to discuss the type of appraisal forms and whether or how they might work in the different businesses. At the same time, the person responsible for the 'values programme' in the company spent some time making sure that the values were properly incorporated as an integral part of the competences, rather than as an 'add-on' at the end.

Once the competences had been agreed across the four levels, the implementation group (now comprising the Head of Learning and Development and her team and the person responsible for performance management) presented back to the Board for approval to take the plan forward into appraisal and selection procedures. The plan was generally greeted with approval, but there was great debate over the actual word 'competence' since it suggested that they were seeking the lowest common denominator rather than suggesting a more aspirational approach which would encourage individuals and positively reinforce effective behaviours. The word 'capability' was adopted in its place.

Uses of Competences

By July 1995, a series of workshops were run to introduce the employees to the new appraisal systems, and to give them training in carrying out appraisals. These began with the HR department (corporate) then spread out to the various separate departments within the company. At the same time, the Learning and Development department created the 'Rough Guide to Learning' for distribution among the various departments. This consists of open learning materials, useful addresses, book reviews listed under each capability so that people can plan their own 'personal development plan.'

At the capabilities and appraisals workshops, each participant was given a manual listing the capabilities at each level and a set of appraisal documents which are discussed in the workshop. The appraisal documentation (called performance review), essentially the kernel of the competence approach, consisted of a review of previous performance, list of capabilities/skills and a continuum on which to assess where the employee lies, the mission statement and department objectives, the agreed tasks for the forthcoming year, a page for assessing future needs of the employee, a place to request career advice, a coaching plan to be filled in by appraiser and appraisee, a learning plan, private to the individual which may incorporate broader goals than on the learning plan and a page for comments by reviewer, reviewer's manager and the reviewee.

At the time of the research, the entire organisation was being trained on the appraisal systems, and it was hoped that appraisals would gradually become the norm, though they were not compulsory. Because of the way and the rate in which the company had grown, there was no existing set of formalised job descriptions, and though the human resource department hold 'role profiles' of the jobs created for the pay banding system, there was a feeling that this was too generalised for most jobs. At one of the workshops I attended, one of the participants expressed his frustration at being unable to extract a job description from the HR department.

There was a hope that the capabilities would become a 'way of life' creating a 'web' throughout the organisation. There was on-going debate about whether performance-related pay should be introduced, but the pay banding exercise had led to a certain amount of demotivation since it did not result in increased pay for performance. No proposal or decision had yet been made as to whether competence-based pay should be introduced. There was fear that the vitality of the appraisal system would be lost if pay became tied into it. Though not formally incorporated into recruitment and appraisal, it was hoped that eventually the competences would be used as guidelines for recruitment. The appraisal forms allowed the employee to ask for career advice, so they could be used for succession planning, and also be used with 360 degree feedback, though this again was optional.

Although not formally introduced into recruitment as yet, the competences were being used as a basis for 'fair selection workshops' that were run from

November 1995 into 1996 throughout the company to ensure managers were selecting in an unprejudiced, unbiased and objective manner. They had also been used as the basis for discussions with the sales development managers, responsible for liaising with franchisees. This development arose spontaneously from discussions between sales development managers and franchisees. It was hoped that the capabilities would be used as the basis for developing their own technical capabilities, so that they could use them:

> as mechanisms for clarifying and consolidating their role ... [the process] highlights and focuses on key behaviours, but it also helps to shape expectations and behaviours with their customers ... you almost find you are negotiating your own customer service agreement.

8.2   THE PERCEPTIONS OF COMPETENCE FRAMEWORKS, DISCIPLINE AND RESISTANCE

Culture Change

The reason for introducing competences in this organisation, was not to change the culture, but to create more formalised systems and reporting mechanisms. There was a great concern to retain a balance between the fluidity of their current 'ways of being', and the need for some structure to give them a sense of direction. Because of its spectacular growth and its very particular values, this organisation had evolved in a very ad hoc manner. A major reason for introducing competences was to create a system that could cope with the growing numbers of employees and expanding markets.

One of the issues that was seen to cause this lack of structure was the lack of a business plan. This was much bemoaned at the workshops, and frequently became a topic of discussion. As one employee noted on the lack of a mission statement:

> We will be very fortunate not to sell motor cars in Y, because there is no mission statement which says, 'Thou shall not sell motor cars'. (Executive Manager, Colourings)

Other managers expressed anxiety about the lack of system:

> We need to know what framework we are working on.

> It is like being in quicksand.

> Flexibility can be a problem, [if people don't have the same manager] I had four or five different Board members in the last year and I wouldn't feel confident enough to turn around and be appraised because they wouldn't know me enough and I would not feel right.

Therefore, while other companies saw competence as a means of changing culture, in this organisation, the approach was seen as a way of systematising some of the fluidity, and was welcomed as such. Clear commitment to the values and enjoyment of the culture of the company was also frequently referred to in the workshops, even when people were expressing their dissatisfaction with the lack of structure.

Chapter 7 showed how, at its most thorough, the competence approach implies the implementation of systems and structures which incarcerate or 'fix' ways of being that are aligned with the organisation's goals. The tensions and sense of paradox, and the struggles that this organisation experienced in attempting to implement the project while retaining a 'fluid' sense of being perhaps exemplifies the difficulties that many organisations face when attempting to retain a balance between structure and creativity. We could speculate that the discussions that I witnessed here, both in workshops and meetings, represented a 'surfacing' of the many unspoken fears and anxieties that the over-systematic frameworks in other organisations were suppressing.

Objectivity

Every effort was made to ensure that the competence framework did not 'crystallise' into a set of 'fixed views' as to how employees were expected to behave. In keeping with the rather 'fluid' culture of the company, there were many points at which change could be effected, and where discussion took place. Few claims were made about the objectivity of the approach in this organisation. Unlike the other organisations, the 'scientific' status of the competence framework was considered to be more an encumbrance than of value. The organisation neither adhered to the 'scientific' model nor did they balk at changing the competences themselves when necessary.

For example, the organisation diverged quite radically from the 'scientific model' in that the competences were altered quite explicitly after the critical incident interviews. When the human resource department discovered a lack of 'strategic planning' at senior levels, further interviews were held to probe for this capability. The process was continued when the new Head of Learning and Development arrived and noticed that the competences were reflecting historic rather than 'wished for' performance measures. However, there was an awareness that, despite the apparent objectivity of the exercise, they were bringing their own concepts and experience to bear in drawing up the clusters – which in itself was more open than happened in other organisations (for example, in the Northern Ireland Trust, the consultants exclusively drew up the competences which were a 'reflection of years of learning and experience', and although they were fed back to the Board and adjusted in a minor way, there was little other discussion about the final competences themselves among the staff). While this may be interpreted as an attempt by the HR department to appropriate power, this was not what I saw at this organisation. Indeed, I was myself invited by two of the senior managers to help cluster the competences at the beginning of the process.

The competence framework was handed wholesale over to the company culture and social audit projects for comments. I was present when senior managers examined, discussed the framework, and changes were made. This process took far longer than anticipated and was conducted with a great deal of care. During the first year of the research, the competences changed at least four times.

The notion of appraisal itself was up for discussion. When the competences and revamped appraisal documentation were discussed at a meeting of senior managers, much time centred on what the actual purpose of appraisal was. This discussion continued at the workshops where the competences and appraisal documentation were presented to the middle rank of managers. At these meetings the team were still prepared to listen and change the appraisal documentation and the processes involved in it. Although the implementation of the appraisal process was to be left to different departments, the HR department stands by as a resource, not a monitorer. As one of the team pointed out:

> None of this is set in stone ... It does very much depend on what people want and need as well doesn't it? I mean we can't impose something that people aren't happy about, because they will fight it ... what we want to do is to let those areas of the business which are happy with their current documentation carry on using that.

Compare this with the Trust in Northern Ireland, where, after introducing their competence framework, one of the participants at an appraisal training meeting asked what would happen if the appraisee disagreed with the appraisal. Where, she asked, was a place of appeal. The Personnel Director then replied that there was no recourse to the Human Resource Department and the last resort would be dismissal.

Empowerment and the Enterprising Manager

Unlike other organisations, competences were being introduced not to 'empower' people, but to help set up a system wherein the enterprising manager could manage effectively. What was interesting was that over the previous three years 40 per cent of the people then in the management structure had joined the company, which was probably bringing, on the one hand, the need for more structure, and possibly ideas about the competence approach that were more relevant in a more traditional organisation. For example, here was the comment of the newly recruited Head of Learning and Development:

> It is about people having flexibility to move across different parts of the business so that you can utilise a number of skills … So many organisations are taking out levels of management now, that there aren't the hierarchies that you used to have … what we are doing here is just actually saying this is what professional good behaviour would be, in this context … then asking individuals to rate themselves on a scale from one to six … and you know it is not a scientific model, but what it does do is to enable an individual to actually work through themselves.

This resembled the expectations of competence projects displayed in organisations in the previous chapters more than comments from people who had worked with this organisation for a longer time. For this respondent, competence was considered as 'professional good behaviour', individuals are 'enabled' by the model so they can work on themselves to produce this 'professional good behaviour'. Also the language in which this comment is framed is far more resonant with the 'language of competence'.

This organisation has grown from its very own, idiosyncratic, homespun philosophies. The model of the 'enterprising manager' does exist in this organisation, but only inasmuch as this model is congruent with the fluid nature of the working environment. At the time of interview, the organisation had a sufficient 'critical' mass of people to take managerial concepts and mould them to their own conceptions of 'being'. How far the organisation could sustain this idiosyncratic way of being, while taking on board people from outside with more accepted views on management was open to question.

Potentially, the approach in this organisation could be used to manage people en masse. However, the constant debate meant that where there was a possibility that 'division' or 'enclosure' might take place, this became explicit and therefore was addressed at a conscious level. There were significant differences in whether the approach could potentially partition and rank individuals. First, there was not the degree of emphasis on individuals being defined and hence spatially and temporally located as there was in other approaches. As I saw in one workshop, rather than job descriptions being drawn up by the HR department, the HR department declined to take up this role, claiming that the incumbent was the best person to know what the job was. It was felt that the page of 'key tasks' and 'objectives' as it appeared on the appraisal form should be the place where the job was described. While in fact, except in well-defined roles, job descriptions are not always available in many organisations, one of the claims of the competence approach is that promotion and selection along competence dimensions are 'profiled' alongside job roles. For example, in the Northern Ireland Trust, the entire organisation was undergoing role profiling, from the Chief Executive downwards.

In this organisation, on the other hand, the facilitators from Learning and Development and HR departments consistently gave this message:

> This doesn't mean you can't move the goalposts ... you may sometimes have to make provisions as you go along
>
> People can 'add in' some extra [capabilities] if that is appropriate ... we [Learning and Development] can come and work with you further on developing some of the technical and specialist areas of capabilities.

On the appraisal form itself capabilities could either be ranked on a line or by number – it is up to the appraiser to decide. Such a loose method of measurement means that scientific comparison and coding and classifying in the Foucauldian manner could not take place. Neither were the forms themselves compulsory:

> It doesn't really reflect what you do, pick them out, and mix them up. Make it work for you, that's the difference ... not to put them in boxes and say that is not my criteria.
>
> But equally it might be that we are happy working with different forms, as long as we are constantly reviewing around the same group criteria, ... then really to some extent the discussion is the most important thing, not the documentation and that is there to make sure that the appraisal process happens, and if only we had these discussions, we wouldn't have to go through this tedious exercise writing. (Workshop Facilitator)

There were, however, differing views as to how ultimately the competences would actually be incorporated in the system. The new Head of Learning and Development saw it as being computerised, with jobs 'banded' so that people could 'mix and match' their skills in order to move either horizontally or upwards in the organisation. A long-serving member of the Executive Committee viewed the competences as eventually becoming so much a 'way of life' that people would 'live and breathe' the behaviours. These long-term views of the competences reflect the tension that exists in this organisation. The outsider view, with the computerised 'mix and match' is more similar to approaches in other organisations: the insider view represents the more fluid approach. How this tension will be resolved was still to be seen – but as the organisation was at a critical stage in its growth, and employing senior managers from the outside with different experiences of working environment, then other managerial discourses from outside could come to predominate.

Although not expressed in the Foucauldian sense of examination and confession there was clear disquiet about the possibility that appraisal could be used as a disciplinary technique. In the many discussions this was expressed as a real concern:

> It is also very demoralising … I think if you are not careful they are very negative forms of discussion, formatted discussion, and they have to be treated very sensitively. (Manager, Colourings)

> I think we really need to understand the purpose of an appraisal. (Finance Manager)

In this organisation, 360 degree feedback rather than becoming another potential form of examination and confession, was encouraged but in the following sense:

> It is the manager's responsibility, to go and find out a bit more, if they have got a team, from the team and their customers, from their colleagues in a positive way, not to use as ammunition to make their point, but seeking open-mindedly opinions that can be expressed in appraisal.

The appraisal is not viewed as a time to 'examine' employees, but rather as a responsibility for the manager:

> If you are a manager and are responsible for a team, you have a commitment to provide and develop time to work with that team and not to leave them. (Workshop Facilitator)

Although the appraisal in this organisation is unlikely to be implicitly reinforced by techniques of examination and confession, the commitment required of employees is probably significantly greater than that required in other organisations:

> Because, I think, I very strongly support the idea that the business environment should be no more no less than an extension of the rest of your life, so it is not as if you leave part of your personality at home, and only have to bring your personality into the working place, and the environment here definitely encourages people to bring all of themselves into the working environment …We always try to explain that if you leave your suit at home, you do not come in jeans … you leave your suit at home and walk into the building naked … that is how it feels at this place. (Head of Product Promotion)

It is clear from this statement that there could be a possibility of a different, more subtle, type of 'subjectification' taking place in this organisation – in that the total commitment required of employees is closer to the 'enterprising self' through self-policing policies built around the subject's identification with social and political issues. However, this is beyond the remit of this research and would require a different methodology in order to explore the question.

Language

There was also a very acute consciousness of the importance that language played in implementing and understanding competences. Here there was generally a greater overall awareness of how people's expectations and behaviour would be shaped by the choice of language used, and more significantly, a desire to move away from the constraining nature of such language. The prime example is the fact that, though the word 'capability' has equal limitations, there was at least an attempt to get away from the 'taken-for-granted' meaning of competence from the outset. The Chief Executive was heard to say to her husband, one of the Directors, at the Board Meeting on the introduction of competences, that she would not want to be called a 'competent wife' (at which point he said he would not call her one either).

Not only was there debate about the actual word itself, but there was a great deal of discussion about how to frame the competences, about how to get away from technical jargon, but also how to make sure that the competences themselves were framed in the language used by the actual people who were interviewed.

> I am very conscious of not really knowing what I think I mean about competences, even though I talk to people about it, and I had it kind of lucidly explained ... the word is stupid. It is such a crappy word, it is such a demeaning word ... It is uninspired ... Oh no I don't, I really know I don't understand it. (Consultant responsible for Board Development)

> ... when you try to formulate something accurately, ... if you read it back a day later it always sounds really formal and rigid, because you have literally tried to corner off what you are trying to say ... And I find it a real challenge to communicate something effectively without losing your audience, because you know you end up with political sounding language ... the language of politicians ... (Head of Product Promotion)

> I think it is almost because people stay at almost a sort of headline level of knowledge sometimes, and talk in terms of communication, motivation, buzz words if you like, and not to think more deeply than that, as to what does communication means ... and so it was taking them into that deeper level of understanding of what communication involves. (Person who conducted critical incident interviews)

> She [Chief Executive] needs to be talked round about the language ... is interesting ... there is an extremely strong reaction to the word 'competence' ... probably driven by [Chief Executive], but also language is very important. (Head of Technical Production and Executive Committee Member)

> People are now really trying to focus on what defines success and the ability to stay ahead, leadership skills or whatever, and you have to define what you mean by that, and ... think through what the true implications of what you are actually talking about, rather than just talking through on the surface. (Head of Corporate Services)

What is striking here, is the awareness about how language can shape perceptions, and the strong desire not to encapsulate anything in a concrete, 'measurable' form. There seemed to be a genuine desire to understand the real 'meaning' of competence. Further, the language used to frame the competences themselves was gone through with a fine toothcomb by many of the directors, senior managers and equal opportunities manager to ensure as far as possible that they did not reflect 'male' values.

Despite the tight planning, the implementation ran about 3 months behind schedule, due to the many changes and discussions that took place. In this organisation, only one respondent actually expressed any doubts about the notion of competence itself. This was the person responsible for the management development of the Board:

> I don't think there is a huge drive to do competences in a different and wonderful way, that is in a way why I keep prodding at it, because I would like it to be done differently, ... I don't think we do ourselves much honour as a human race, if what we do is to make people into mechanical things ... But this notion that you can decide what you are doing at the top of an organisation, and then break it down progressively into little parts, always struck me again, as something I just didn't want to be part of. ... But certainly I would be interested in pushing as far as I can the idea of a more different human developmental approach to competences.

This did not mean that there was not fierce discussion around the nature of the competence framework and the implementation process. It was perhaps the openness of debate that made such a striking difference between this company and other organisations. It was this constant discussion that actually made the process slower than anticipated. In this case, opposition could be expressed openly and was not muttered in the back corridors of the building.

8.3 IMPLICATIONS OF THE APPROACH FOR WOMEN MANAGERS

Was this organisation subject to the same assumptions that we saw in the previous chapter, or did it succeed in moving away from the dominant interpretation of the competence approach, which I suggested may hamper women's progress?

The Practices

In the previous chapter, the practices associated with competence processes disadvantaged women through: assumptions of objectivity in identifying the competences; assumptions of objectivity in appraisal; and the nature of the appraisal process itself. This organisation, it seemed was already aware of some of these dangers.

For example, there was no assumption about objectivity. Indeed, even though derived through critical incident interviewing, considerable changes were made in the competences throughout the implementation process. One of the most significant ways in which changes were made was to ensure that the competences reflected the very particular values of this company. At first these were clustered separately, but later they were woven into the other sections so that the values became an integral part of the way of working and rewarding people.

A separate section entitled 'active citizenship' for activities related to matters of social concern was later added to this clustering. The ability of the competence model to absorb the values was a source of great excitement for many people. In the interviews I held, the values were frequently, unbidden, mentioned:

> That is what this company is all about, because there is lots of debate here about whether people are too much on the value side. If you haven't got these values, then you might as well work at Unilever. (Executive Committee Member)

> Because the real values of Y should automatically be reflected in the competences. If we really have the values they are in everybody's mind and soul, if they are not reflected, then I question then whether we have got them anywhere else than on a piece of paper. (Executive Committee Member)

This flexibility and openness around the assumptions of objectivity had two important implications for women managers. First, there were no discernible 'hidden' assumptions embedded within the process itself; and second the fact that the values that are added are constantly up for debate. The values themselves could not be maintained unless each individual is responsible for questioning and contextualising them in every situation. However, this is not at all easy as the person responsible for promoting and encouraging these values noted.

The notion of appraisal itself was hotly contested. There was an awareness of how such a process could be used as a means of 'discipline' rather than empowerment. This arose at all the workshops and meetings that I witnessed. This was particularly acute at a meeting of senior managers when appraisal documentation and procedure were debated. For example the business manager of one product line who had spent a great deal of time establishing his own appraisal system noted that:

> I don't really think that it can be given out to everybody, because the appraisal is a very, very sensitive document, and it has to be treated so ... appraisals if you are not very careful are a very negative form of discussion, ... and they have to

incorporate a time span which enables managers to get it done ... I know how valuable they can become, but to make a huge operating document, I think is just wrong.

This company certainly differed greatly in the way in which the appraisal process was introduced to managers, and the thoroughness with which they were shown the pitfalls of appraisal. Videos and books were available at the Resource Centre should managers wish to further their experience and knowledge of appraisals. The equal opportunities manager had also run further fair selection workshops for all managers based on the competence framework.

The Competences

Set out below are extracts from the framework of competences. They are discussed in the light of nurturing/directive behaviours (see later for further discussion of these differences). I have made little comment since I think largely they speak for themselves.

Managing People
i) Setting goals
+VE Holds regular meeting with their team, communicating day-to-day and future objectives. Ensures information provided is accurate and detailed. Ensures the team are all working to the same goals. Links goals to mission statements – both corporate and departmental.
Prepares their communication using their knowledge of individual team members' likely responses. Plans how they will make a request in order to get a positive response from others. Arrives at mutual agreements with individual and team over future objectives.
Asks for feedback and questions to clarify and understand fully. Gives their own opinion which will be supported by information from their own experience.
Feeds back the requests and concerns of the team to senior management, acting as a two-way communicator. Always follows up with an answer to employees' queries.
–VE Lacks urgency in providing employees with up-to-date information and dealing with their feedback/concerns. Rarely, if ever, holds communication meetings.
Takes an aggressive approach to communication, bulldozing across others' opinions. Imposes conditions and decisions with no explanation.
Insists and expects others' support without persuasion or explanation. Makes threats to others if support not forthcoming.

The emphasis here is on openness and listening. A caring approach, compatible with nurturing behaviour is encouraged in the attention that should be paid to ensuring that the team constantly receives feedback. Further, the time taken to ensure that the style of communication will be perceived positively by the team reflects the prime importance given to relationships rather than meeting goals. The major goal here is 'understanding, thinking and feeling' together as reflected in the emphasis on joint decision-making. The goals and plans are arrived at through jointly talking through issues and problems – which clearly reflects the interdependent-in-relation-to-others mode (mode 1).

ii) Delegation

+VE Uses the skills of others to effectively manage the business, sharing workload among the team.

Examines existing workload, present skills and motivation to do the task, before delegating to a particular team member. Uses delegation as an opportunity for individual's development and explains this to employees.

Where skills are lacking, ensures that the individual is properly trained before taking on a new responsibility.

Takes time to regularly review progress on tasks. Reviews at a distance, allowing the individual to have ultimate responsibility. Gives feedback on progress.

–VE Has no trust in the skills of others, and tries to do everything themselves. Interferes and will not let go of the task.

Abdicates work – dumps tasks on others without proper training and guidance. Blames others for any resulting mistakes.

Here, the motivation for delegation is to help develop employees, not to offload unwanted work. The act of delegating is done from a distance, so the person who delegates is not in a 'control' position. The 'blaming' and 'controlling' behaviour on the negative side tends to be more 'directive' – more in keeping with the 'not taking the one-down position' of men that we saw in Chapter 2, than the maintaining of harmonious relationships more typical of women.

iii) Team motivation

+VE Promotes team spirit and identity, through promoting common team goals and creating a family atmosphere.

Creates an environment within which creativity can flourish.

Encourages and enthuses the team, projecting excitement into tasks. Openly celebrates team successes, speaking in terms of 'we' not 'I'.

Gets actively involved in work and social events with the team. Uses fun, games and exercises to make the job more enjoyable, without distracting from work objectives.

Motivates individuals through giving rewards and responsibilities which match their personal wants and needs.

Empowers others – gains their commitment and co-operation by allowing them to set objectives, organise their work routine and take responsibility in decision-making.

Creates a common purpose/encourages teamworking and co-operation across functions and other related areas of the business.

–VE Wants to achieve by riding on the backs of others' efforts. Takes personal praise and credit only, neglecting to share it with the team.

Neglects the interests, wishes and needs of the employees in their desire to get the job done. Sees task achievement as all important, as opposed to team and individual contentment.
'Spoon-feeds' the team withholding real responsibility, Makes key decisions alone, without employee involvement.

These behaviours encouraged the 'nurturing' way of behaving such as thanking (here, celebrating), praising (here, giving rewards and responsibilities) and supporting others' actions and remarks. Individuals and team members are also placed higher than getting the task done (an inherently caring attitude). Emphasis is placed here on the relationship with employees, rather than in meeting the task. Indeed the third of the negative behaviours listed above 'Sees task achievement as all important, as opposed to team and individual contentment' was considered a positive one in the semi-privatised utility: 'maintains task objectives uppermost without damaging staff morale'.

iv) Employee support
+VE 'Open door' policy – will take time to make themselves approachable to others to deal with their requests and queries and anxieties.
Takes an interest in employees's lives outside [the organisation] e.g. has some knowledge of family life/circumstances.
Genuinely compassionate, considerate and understanding of employees as human beings. Looks after the interests of both the team and individuals – will act as a spokesperson on the team's behalf, when appropriate.
Gives knowledgeable advice and support to management on counselling and disciplinary issues. Takes responsibility for these areas within their own team – uses a mixture of sympathy and practicality to help people work out issues for themselves.
Cares for individuals – not afraid to act from the heart.
Acts as an intermediary to help resolve disagreements within the team and with others. Will confront a conflict as and when it occurs and deal with it neutrally.
Has concern for well-being of individuals, is aware of factors which will affect well-being – stress/ill-health/occupational health issues.
Actively supports Department Environmental Advisor (DEA) Safety Representatives, Communicators, etc., providing opportunities at communications meetings and regular encouragement.
–VE *Physically distant from team – stays at their desk or in their offices. Unavailable, has no time for people problems.*
Reluctant to follow through with necessary counselling and discipline – afraid of making themselves unpopular with the team. Allows problems to fester and affect team motivation and morale.
Fails to support departmental representatives.

With its emphasis on the emotional (acting from the heart) and caring (has concern for the well-being of individuals) and using a mixture of sympathy and practicality, with the ability to 'confront', this competence reflects a broad mix of nurturing and directive behaviours. Interestingly, the negative aspects (fear of being unpopular) is also a nurturing characteristic – demonstrating that this organisation, while encouraging both masculine and feminine behaviours, is equally aware of the negative sides of both behaviours. The specific point about 'physical distance' is also interesting, since, as I indicated in Chapter 2, this is a behaviour into which most boys are socialised at an early age. Further, the emphasis on knowing the individual outside the organisation, with his or her problems represents an attempt at breaking down the private/public divide which tends to privilege men over women. Compare this with one competence in the semi-privatised national utility where, in the personal effectiveness cluster 'reports problems in home relationships, difficulties sleeping, eating problems, deteriorating health' is included as a negative behaviour.

v) Developing people

+VE Interested in what their people want to achieve and will talk with them about their plans.

Celebrates individual success.

Looks for individual employees' potential, providing incentives and opportunities for individuals to develop. Tries to ensure team members receive opportunities for promotion.

Manages change positively.

Operates a regular, formal, two-way appraisal system, providing praise and constructive feedback.

Has a training plan for their own department. Monitors and reviews progress of this plan.

Encourages risk-taking and innovation.

Takes the role of informal mentor and teacher, encouraging employees to accept achievable challenges, giving practical help, training and advice.

Shares learning with others to develop skills and knowledge.

Acts as a role model in encouraging self-managed learning.

–VE *Doesn't devote time and energy to develop employees. Has a low skilled workforce and does not create opportunities for team members' progression.*

Unwilling to give honest feedback – prone to raising false expectations to keep employees temporarily happy.

Does not recognise that taking time to PLAN, DO and REVIEW learning is a valid work-based activity.

Expects training and development to be a passive exercise and a completely separate activity with no link to the workplace.

The emphasis here is on sharing, caring and learning together. This may be something of a truism in a competence called 'developing people', but the emphasis leans most heavily towards the person, as opposed to the business plan. There is again emphasis on praise, typical of nurturing behaviours. The contra-indicator, 'Unwilling to give honest feedback' is a negative side of nurturing behaviour, as is 'prone to raising false expectations' reflects the importance of nurturing behaviours overall in this organisation: Equally, the 'nurturing' is balanced by the emphasis on the more directive 'planning' types of behaviours.

vi) Leading by example
+VE Leads by example, setting high standards of professional conduct as a role model for employees and especially by demonstrating including all value issues in decision-making processes.
Hands-on approach. More than happy to get stuck in to solve a problem, without interfering with or stifling others' efforts. Willing to answer phones, take messages or photocopy if the appropriate person is busy.
Actively encourages active citizenship (has community projects).
Would not ask team members to do something unwilling to do themselves.
–VE Doesn't practise what they preach. *Likes to direct, rather than do.*

It is particularly interesting to note that here 'values discussion' is positively encouraged in the leadership role. It is precisely the lack of values discussion that Habermas and other critical theorists decry. There is a real attempt to remove 'hierarchical' and 'divisive' behaviours and to encourage a working together.

The other competence clusters reflect the same balance between directive and nurturing behaviours, with the positive and negative sides of both included. What is also important here is that the competences acknowledge and reflect the positive and negative aspects of both types of behaviours. Thus 'not speaking one's mind' is perceived negatively, but equally is a behaviour which many women manifest if their 'interdependence' is based on fear rather than strength. Again, positive characteristics of directive behaviour are encouraged in the 'calls for action' in the risk-taking and innovation and in the positive sides of seeking equality and fairness in relationships. Further, the potential domestic constraints of individuals are positively taken into account. For example, under 'Commitment' one of the positive behaviours is: 'makes sure junior employees can exercise commitment without doing long hours. Makes full allowance for family caring duties'. Overall the competences reflect a balance of narrative and paradigmatic modes of cognition; the emphasis throughout lies on seeking information around the situation in order to contextualise problems, rather than imposing predetermined rules and regulations.

8.4 INCLUDING WOMEN'S VOICES

There was an ongoing concern that gender equality was not built into the competence strategy. Women's voices were noticeably present, in the implementation and in the discussions surrounding the implementation of the project. The process was monitored by the Equal Opportunities Manager. I was welcomed here as being able to help 'pick up' anything that I felt was undermining for women. The Equal Opportunities Manager did not believe that they had gone far enough yet to ease out gendered expectations. Despite the capabilities and the emphasis on equal opportunities policies, she believed there was still an attitude that long hours was a sign of commitment, and that part-time working was not considered as fully committed. For example, though not included for obvious reasons in the final list of capabilities, some of the managers in the critical incident interviews did cite long hours as a sign of commitment. Such a tension was expressed in the then debate about the fact that the nursery only took full-time children for 42 and a half hours. As she points outs:

> Now, if there is an expectation for you to progress career wise ... the management are really saying you have to work more than 42 and a half hours a week, and this is really what it is all about. I mean, is the company going to be honest, and just come out and say you have to work extra hours if you want to progress, or are we going to stop that, and say no, we are going to be family friendly, and be more flexible, and say you can work from home, and it is the quality of the work you produce, and not the quantity of time you spend doing it. This is certainly something that is going on at the moment within the organisation, it was interesting that it came up in the process.

Of course, these competences reflected the employee profile. Women were significantly better represented in this company when compared with the national averages. For example, as of June 1995, three of the nine Board members were women, and one of the two non-executive members was a woman. Of the Executive Committee, five were women, and ten were men. This compares with the national average which showed that in 1994, only 2.7 per cent of board members were women. At senior management level (heads of department and general managers), 77 per cent are men, and 23 per cent are women. At middle management level 44 per cent are men and 56 per cent are women. At junior level 37 per cent are men and 63 per cent are women. Overall, then, excluding Board and Executive Committee members, 44 per cent of managers are women. These figures related to the total company which includes manufacturing and retailing. A total of 65 per cent of the entire company were women and 35 per cent men. In the corporate section, where this research is based, senior management comprised 28 per cent women, middle management comprised 64 per cent women and junior management comprised 68 per cent women. Overall, in the corporate section then, 53 per cent of the managers were women. This compares with the national average (1994) which showed that, among managers, 11.3 per cent were women. Although the percentage of women employed in this organisation is higher than the average, the figures represent a significantly higher representation overall.

However, the dispersal of women managers still reflected national patterns (increasing underrepresentation at the top of organisations), and gave cause for concern. In the middle band there were still more women than men, however, the situation had reversed at top management. Equally, there was a predominance of male managers in manufacturing as opposed to the entire company, despite the fact that the numbers were practically equal at the lower end of the scale. It is interesting that the slide downwards is reversed at Board and Executive Committee level – this may be a reflection of the fact that the founder is a woman. Overall salary scales were £18000–£23000 for junior managers, £23000–£40000 for middle managers, and £40000–£80000 for senior managers. Again, these did not reflect national norms, where female-dominated occupations such as teaching and nursing were less well-rewarded than other occupations.

In October 1994 a manager was appointed with responsibility for standardising the employment conditions and setting up an equal opportunities policy. This resulted in the production of *The Manager's Handbook* which set out procedures and systems for terms of employment. This covered recruitment, employee benefits, employee welfare, equal opportunities, employee rights and pay. This was preceded by the human resources mission which was:

> To create and sustain a successful community of individuals actively committed to meeting each other's needs.

The equal opportunities section covered harassment, maternity and paternity leave, child care support, special leave, health and disability policies, job sharing and flexitime. These were more than the statutory requirements and included 10 days paternity leave. There was a crèche available on site at HQ, and the organisation was considering in what way they may contribute to childcare costs. Job sharing and flexitime (between core hours of 10.00 to 4.00) was available. There were plans to run equal opportunity awareness days for all members of HR, and further days on understanding company policy on maternity and a series of recruitment and equality interviewing days for managers to ensure they followed a fair selection process.

8.5 CONCLUSIONS

The first stage of the case study showed that the process of implementation itself, viewed at a superficial level, was not dissimilar from that in other organisations. However, the environment in which the approach was implemented meant that the implications of its use were very different for women managers. Although the competence approach did serve to partition and rank, there was a degree of flexibility so that this partitioning was not 'fixed'. The extensive discussions and debate about the purpose of appraisal, and the flexibility with which the appraisal documentation was treated, meant that there was less scope for examination and confession of the disciplinary type to take place. Although still struggling with ingrained attitudes, managers were attempting to offset the structural disadvantage which renders women in the double bind of bringing behaviours to the workplace which are undervalued, and equally facing systemic disadvantage from their domestic constraints.

Feminist discourses here contested and challenged the more 'paradigmatic' approaches to competence to break down 'conditioned' ways of behaving and thinking – in particular expectations about how women and men behave and the underlying 'taken-for-granted' capitalist assumption that making a profit is the major objective or organisational life. This organisation has shown that an environment can be created where the work/home duality is broken down and preconditioned expectations eliminated, and yet still for the organisation to survive in a competitive capitalist system. It was in maintaining a balance between structure and process, between the paradigmatic and the narrative, that this organisation differed from others – and it was here that space opened up for other voices to be heard.

9. Finding a way forward: competence as organisational learning

Rather than falling into the trap of one-dimensionalism or negativity that bedevils much critical management theory, this chapter is an attempt at drawing some lessons from the research that may be useful for the pragmatic agenda of management. It draws together the findings from the spread of organisations and sets out a 'learning' model for organisations wishing to introduce competences, but also seeking to avoid the traps of 'disciplinary' practices. Organisations need systems and processes. They consist of the system and the lifeworld. Competence models, in themselves, may be useful tools for organisations – but there needs to be space for reflexive practices in the competence processes. Drawing on the experiences set out in the empirical material, I further adapt the original competence process such that there is opportunity for 'learning' to take place. This chapter brings together the findings to open up possibilities of pragmatic ways in which organisations may enhance the use of competence frameworks.

9.1 DIFFERENCES AND SIMILARITIES IN FRAMEWORKS

This initial comparison showed how competence frameworks varied in their depth and rigour, depending on the environment in which the company was operating, the culture of the company and the reasons for introducing competences in the first place. These are reproduced in Table 9.1. Depth and rigour is equated with the extent to which the competence strategies were closely locked into human resource structures of recruitment, selection and appraisal, how far down the organisation the competence approach penetrated, and the extent and rigidity of the company documentation and appraisal systems accompanying the implementation.

The depth and rigour of the competence frameworks, to a great extent, seemed to be closely associated with an organisation's espoused desire for culture change. Thus the semi-privatised utility was seeking to render its workforce less formal, with a need to start 'behaving differently'. However, this was equally associated with an enormous downsizing exercise where

Paradigmatic ←

Table 9.1 Competence frameworks on a paradigmatic/narrative continuum

Organisation	Reason for implementation	Use in recruitment, selection, appraisal and pay	Use as training and development, organisational restructuring, performance management	Characteristics of current organisational culture and desired change	Time scales	Depth of dividing practices and disciplinary techniques	History of trades union disputes
Semi-privatised national utility	Privatisation, downsizing. Flatter organisation, change in culture	Recruitment, selection, appraisal	Training and development, organisational restructuring, performance management	Formal, bureaucratic, status conscious, move to first name terms! Need to start 'behaving differently'	4 years	Extensive and rigorous documentation. 18 carefully broken down competences, combined with psychometric testing	Extensive
National Health Trust and Social Services Trust	Break down 'traditional demarcations' between social services and health services, create culture change and market-driven culture	Recruitment, selection, appraisal	Training and development, organisational restructuring, performance management	Bureaucratic. Desired 'fast, fluid and enterprising culture'	3 years, still on-going	Extensive and rigorous. 34 competences at 6 levels	With various professional groupings

Multinational oil company	Need for culture change, downsizing	Not formally, but recruitment models aligned with it. Selection at lower levels. 360° appraisal	Training and development, performance management	Fairly fluid, wants to be peopled by 'enterprising selves'	4 years, evolving process	More as guidelines	
Multinational construction company	Recession created need for new management skills	As guidelines	Training and development	Currently formal. No plans for change through competences	2 years	Guidelines, use of development and assessment centres	
University	Change in higher education, need for academics to be 'managers'	Hope to use it for recruitment and selection. 360° appraisal	Training and development	Fragmented: academic, administration, technical. Need to create senior management ethos'	18 months (still on-going)	Not yet incorporated into HR strategies. Greater appraisal	None
Beauty goods manufacturer and retailer	Need to become more systematised with growth	Recruitment, selection, appraisal, possibly pay	Training and development, organisational restructuring, performance management	Fluid, political and open. No desire to change	2 years (still on-going)	Yes, in terms of documentation. Much greater room for discussion and debate. Less gender bias	None

149

managers were being called upon to take more and more responsibilities. Thus the reason for the espoused culture change lay behind a drive for more and greater efficiency, not a more 'empowered' environment for the individuals within it. The Trust required a similar orientation towards the 'customer' underpinned by 'market-driven' values. However, though the espoused culture change was to become 'flexible and fast', this was belied by the rigidity of the competence framework. In the middle of the scale, on the other hand, the University, although hoping to create a greater 'senior management ethos', did not express any particular wishes for a collective change of organisational culture. At the far end of the scale, the cosmetics manufacturer was hoping to reinforce the values of the company, and impose a more 'systematised' way of working. There was no desire to change the culture – quite the opposite.

The two organisations at the top end of the spectrum had extensive documentation, rigid appraisal systems, hierarchical reporting lines, and an assumption that the competence approach would not be challenged. In the cosmetics manufacturer, the company had extensive documentation and plans for the system to be used in selection, promotion and recruitment. However, the constant questioning, especially around the notion of appraisal itself, and the flexibility allowed in the use of the final framework, meant that there was a willingness to change the new system should that be necessary.

Overall, despite the apparent cohesiveness of the competence approach, different organisations had very different experiences of its implementation. Thus in companies A and D competences were still in their infancy, and there was no sense of urgency about the implementation process, however, in organisations B, D and E the relationship with selection, recruitment was much tighter. All three of these organisations were undergoing considerable change (downsizing, need to respond rapidly to market forces) and hence were open to more resistance and industrial relations problems.

Despite the different espoused aims of the organisations, then perhaps the most interesting observation is that the tighter the controlling practices required (understood in terms of previous industrial relations problems, downsizing, or realigning professional groupings) the tighter the approach is locked into HR structures. This was apparent in the semi-privatised utility and in the Trust. Paradoxically, they did not appear to be moving towards the 'empowering culture' which underpinned the approach, and was highly emphasised in both organisations. It would seem that in both these organisations the language of 'enterprise' was necessary to ensure the 'complicity' of the employees in the espoused aims of the competence initiative.

Competence as Discipline

The four issues that emerged from the different organisations were an association of the competence project with culture change, a conviction that the competence project was 'neutral' and 'scientific' and would indeed help create 'enterprising individuals', with an emphasis on the importance of learning, understanding and using the language of competence. The one exception to this was the beauty and cosmetics retailer who was happy with the existing culture, but wished to impose more 'system' on the company.

However, despite the claims that competences would bring about culture change, this did not take place. The methods of deriving the competences, and the lack of objectivity meant that in most organisations the competences and their implementation reflected the organisation's past as much as its future. The claims of neutrality were equally debatable. In several parts of the 'technical' process, 'subjectivity' crept in through the back door. One of the most important areas where this occurred was the point at which competences were clustered after interviews with the staff had taken place. There was variation as to how many, and whom were interviewed, and at the point of clustering changes were made to the competences as they were drawn up. Despite attempts at rendering the process objective, the competences reflect constructs that are already defined within the minds of senior managers or consultants.

When analysed in the light of 'dividing' practices, the individual could be seen as a calculable self, constructed by techniques of recording, classifying, combining and comparing data. Those organisations with the tighter knit systems of selection, recruitment and promotion had in place even tighter systems of appraisal, with extensive documentation. In these organisations, the rewards were good for those who took themselves in hand and actively developed themselves through filling in the gaps that appeared between their performance and what was required of them in the role. Even the language of competence was not the neutral textual tool that managers imagined. Embedded in the language was a set of relations which placed various groups of workers over others: autonomous business managers over professionals, HR function over line manager, and, by significant construction of absence, men over women.

A deeper level of analysis examined whose interests the competences were likely to favour. This was to examine where 'relations of dependence' had become solidified – and how these interests (in these cases those of men) were constantly met. One of the ways in which this happens is when some form of discursive closure has taken place, and is continually taking place, but because it is hidden, it cannot be transformed.

Buried in the competences themselves were specifications and expectations that would favour most men over most women. The practices associated with competence frameworks were equally likely to disadvantage women. Competence strategies are invariably accompanied by an increase in on-going assessment and appraisal. The objectivity of such processes was not questioned. However, research has clearly indicated that appraisal and assessment is not the objective and scientific exercise that is assumed. The competences themselves, although seemingly objectively derived, did privilege directive over nurturing types of behaviours. Women, bringing as they do, a differently constructed sense of self to the workplace, have no option other than to attempt to emulate these required behaviours, or confess in the appraisal process when they fail. At a structural level, embedded in the competences themselves, are assumptions that workers can devote themselves over and above the required working time to pursue the organisation's aims. Such an expectation can only be met by those men and women who do not have domestic constraints. Since it is women who primarily bear the burden of childrearing and other domestic considerations, they are likely to be disadvantaged by these assumptions. The cycle reinforces itself.

The illusions of neutrality were created by practices which claimed to construct 'the enterprising self' and by a language which contained in itself, embedded relations of power. Both the practices and language of the competence methodologies drew agents into the agenda of competence, such that they internalised the behaviours required, took action based on this internalisation, and thus recreated the practices which constrained them. Where there was evidence of resistance, this was expressed more in the form of a disheartened cynicism, rather than an active attempt at making the model work.

9.2 BREAKING DOWN THE DISCIPLINE – MAKING WOMEN MANAGERS VISIBLE

One organisation had, however broken the mould. The major distinguishing factor of this organisation from the others was the constant reflection and questioning of the 'way we do things round here', and a desire to underpin the organisation with core values of:

- honesty
- care
- integrity
- respect

These values encouraged the contextualisation of a problem before applying a solution. In other words, a solution was not imposed in a paradigmatic fashion, using abstract principles, but was first 'narrativised'. Here there was a balancing between the 'fluid' way of being and a need for 'structure', but it was in the maintenance of this tension that energy was generated. In a sense, this tension could be said to emulate the tension between paradigmatic and narrative, which resulted in a framework that combined nurturing and directive behaviours. The fluidity was apparent in the lack of structures and hierarchies, and in the constant ebb and flow of the process of implementation.

It was this fluidity of approach that created the possibility for balancing structure and process, nurturing and directive behaviours. Whilst the approach was introduced to 'systematise' more elements of the existing culture, the fluid way in which this was being done meant that there was an on-going dialogue between system and individual action/cognition.

This was maintained by the passion people expressed in working for the company. This passion was transferred to the competence process itself, so that it neither became the sole 'baby' of any of the organisational functions, nor did it fall on the wayside as yet another management initiative, which was a possibility in two of the other five organisations (the University and the construction company).

However at the same time, they do not duck the issues of discipline:

> I have a completely ambivalent relationship with the company, it is the most extreme example of a love/hate relationship that I can remember, ... I think it is very cutting edge compared to other companies to see how this company is wrestling with finding the right balance between what tends to be called the masculine approach, versus the more feminine approach to tackling and solving problems. (Head of Product Promotion)

Such passions were evident from the top down, and many statements were prefaced with 'I've been working here for xx years, and I wouldn't leave'. There was a sense in this organisation that everyone was part of one team, from the person in the reception to the people serving in the 'diner' to the drivers of the small buses on the company tour. This was further reinforced by the consistently changing, dramatic decor both outside and inside the building. For example, at the time of the research, there was a plea for signatories to the 'domestic violence' debate, and at other times there was a telephone in reception for anyone to ring up the Nigerian embassy about the plight of Ken Sara-Wiwa. The company newspaper reflected and reinforced this passion and called for action on issues of social importance. Thus, in this organisation, other discourses came to predominate.

Despite, or perhaps because of, this passion and people's obvious attachment to the company, many people were open about the fact that politics was a 'way of being':

> It is not true that this is not a political company, there are politics here. It is far more, I mean with [the chief executive], when she gets her knife in, it is not devious, it is all very open, and the politics I found at [xx] were all driven by career aspiration.

> ... My feeling is that the politics here tends to be driven by the desire to be seen as a valued person ... but it makes it nicer, it is a nicer kind of politics, less harmful. (Head of Technical Production)

> It is an incredibly political environment ... I think that subconsciously there are number of people who have come into the company from highly structured big organisations, and they see the lack of organisation structure and apparent chaos within this company, and they think, of ' Wow I can build my own little empire here'. They start to gather up other little groups of people and try to control them, in most cases only to discover that one day that the whole groups of people they should be controlling has shot off in different directions, and are not very impressed any more with their input. ... a number of people have gone through major personality changes in this place. (Head of Product Promotion)

What is interesting here was the number of people who equated politics with change, and discussed the change in personality that some people needed to go through in order to survive in this company. It was clear that there was very little divide between home and work. Total commitment was a prerequisite in order to enjoy and thrive in the job. It would seem that here there is no need for techniques of discipline: employees identify strongly with the company from the outset. In some senses, then, the employee and managerial profile was self-selecting. If you wanted a clear work/home divide, then the culture would not permit it. How and whether this manifested on the shopfloor and in the retail outlets however, could be the basis of further research.

A further theme in this organisation was the need to balance business needs against values. This is seen as a constant tension between having systems in place, or maintaining the fluidity:

> ... you know it is big, it is international, and there are just simple rules of logistics that you can't get round ... You have to rely on meetings, systems, coding, disciplines [otherwise] the business just collapses into chaos ... maybe it is good that people in [this organisation] should feel uncomfortable and question, it is quite right, but they shouldn't be Luddites and think that we don't want any systems and procedures because that isn't us, then *us* had better stop growing because we are not going to cope. (Head of Technical Production)

There was also a great desire for equal opportunities, though, of course, there was an acknowledgement that some people would earn more than others, and that opportunities were not boundless

As the Head of Corporate Services points out:

> There is always a drive that ties us all in, everybody is in the same boat, no differentiation, which applies from everything through to the salary bandings, through for example, travel, and there is an attempt to be completely egalitarian, everybody is going to do it, and we are all held up to the same standard ...The culture of [this organisation] is always very individual, and we have to look for

people who are going to fit in, and we are very egalitarian ... so somebody who is
wanting to be sitting behind the desk with a big fat cigar, and order everybody
around is simply not what we are about here ... most of the individuals are fairly
spontaneous and have got their own opinions, and all that adds up to something
radically different.

Such a comment does suggest that there is a certain 'type' of individual who
would want to be employed, and would indeed be selected for this
organisation. So that, though there is a feeling of egalitarianism, it might be
argued that employees are self-selected in the first place. Indeed, in one of the
workshops, two people wanted to sit in the middle of a semi-circle in order
that they were not 'first to go' with a type of 'reporting-in' activity that
precedes these workshops. They admitted that they felt uncomfortable with
such a procedure.

In addition to observations of workshops and the interviews that I carried
out in this organisation, my reflections about this organisation have been
framed by the openness with which I as researcher was welcomed into the
organisation. This radically changed my initial cynicism. From the outset, I
was allowed access to all files, to all meetings (including those of the Board)
and any further statistical information that I required. My views were also
often sought on matters of language and on how other companies were
managing competence implementation. This was in marked contrast to some
of the other companies, where I felt that I had to tread very carefully in order
to elicit information. For example, in the semi-privatised utility, I had to
undergo 15 minutes of hard grilling by the Head of Human Resources and
Head of Training on the 'value' of my research before I was allowed to
conduct the interview. At the Trust, it was only after a year that I was allowed
sight of the actual competences, and this had to be returned. I was never given
a copy of the accompanying Training and Development Manual.

Whether, how and why this 'way of being' arose and continued to exist
would be the subject of further research – it is no doubt due to a combination
of factors: the fact that the organisation was created and run by a woman; the
predominance of women in the company; the very particular values that are
the critical base on which the company is run; the lack of competitors; the lack
of strong functional groups and so on. What is important here was the absence
of taken-for-granted assumptions of a level playing field, and the attempts to
balance nurturing and directive behaviours (though not explicitly stated as
such). This meant that the implications for women managers were far more
promising. Here, processes of gender construction were on the surface and
open to question. Gender issues were already being questioned when I arrived.
But this was not a naive approach. There was a genuine desire to balance
corporate goals and individual achievements – but unlike orthodox thinking
about and in organisations, there was an understanding that the first would not

be met unless the second was being satisfied. Whilst there was an awareness of the need to balance values and profit, it was felt that the values would lead to profit.

However, the approach is not without its dangers. In its constant attempt to differentiate itself from others, it could breed an assumption of types of behaviours that could exclude others who may be just as effective. As the consultant to the Board noted about the organisation:

> There is a myth about Y, and I mean myth not in the sense of a false notion, but in terms of a collective story ... there is an ideal that Y is held up as certain kinds of things, radical, friendly, against animal testing ... there is a picture which is conjured up about it and some of it is true ... but in some ways Y is an organisation like any other, that has to get work done and so forth ... so there is a fantasy that Y will do things differently, but it is a struggle ... it is something you shouldn't take for granted.

Its attempts to be different at organisational level meant standing out from the crowd. Such an assumption may be taken up at an individual level, where employees, in order to demonstrate their commitment, need also to 'stand out.' This has three dangers: first, those with quieter, but perhaps more balancing qualities may be missed; second, the organisation may not use its reflexivity in order to take in learning from the external environment, thus 'throwing the baby out with the bath water'; and finally the organisation risks becoming simply a group of individuals rather than an integrated group of people working with a common aim.

However, this organisation has shown that there was an open discussion about values, the gendered substructure of the organisation was much open to contestation. By rendering the practices implicit in the gender substructure open to challenge and debate, the management here were offering some way in to opening up areas where 'relations of dependence' may have become solidified.

9.3   COMPETENCE AND REFLEXIVE AWARENESS

From this 'retelling' of the competence story a new picture emerges. In the spread of organisations, the competence strategy tended to act as a central relay mechanism between structure and individual. This created asymmetric relations where board govern managers, and, among the 'managed', masculine 'ways of being' were privileged over feminine 'ways of being'. Where the competence initiative was implemented in a manner where care was taken to offset the disciplinarian aspects, the competence strategy was used as a tool for reflexivity and not a tool for control.

What might we learn from these findings? And how might we help organisations avoid the dangers of 'closing' out alternative voices? If we map out these processes onto an organisational learning model we can see possibilities for ensuring that 'reflexivity' takes place. The learning model is useful since it introduces a notion of inquiry into organisational life, and thus offers up the possibility for mutual change. According to Schon:

> ... managers live in an organizational system which may promote or inhibit reflection-in-action. Organizational structures are more or less adaptable to new findings, more or less resistant to new tasks. The behavioural world of the organization, the characteristic pattern of interpersonal relations, is more or less open to reciprocal reflection-in-action – to the surfacing of negative information, the working out of conflicting views, and the public airing of organizational dilemmas. Insofar as organizational structure and behavioural world condition organizational inquiry, they make up what I will call the 'learning system' of the organization (1983, p.242)

Reflection-in-action is one way in which members of an organisation may achieve greater degrees of consciousness of self and other. We already saw from Chapter 1 that 'consciousness' was considered to be a useful strategy for women. Indeed, it may well be a useful strategy for both men and women, and enable them to bring more of themselves into organisational life.

By drawing up a model which sets up the conditions for this 'reflection' to take place, then there may be room for more voices to be heard – or indeed for more of each individual to be heard and given space. The flow diagram highlights the possibilities of using the competence strategy as a tool of incorporating more 'voices' into the competence strategy.

Organisational learning (that is, possibilities for change and for hearing alternative voices) can take place when there is sufficient flexibility in the practices themselves for reflexivity and action to take place – in other words when the concepts and practices of other discourses can challenge the dominant discourse.

In all of the organisations, the process of drawing up competences (critical incident interviewing) articulates the tacit knowledge (that is, ways of being) in the organisation. In the Trust, although critical incident interviewing took place, the influence of the consultant at the clustering stage was very strong, so the competences probably did not reflect the tacit knowledge to the degree to which it could have done. These were equally altered with the beauty retailer, but through additional processes of challenge and debate with the people in the organisation.

The way in which the competences were then implemented may, to a greater or lesser extent, be reinforced by disciplinary practices (control). Thus in the semi-privatised utility and in the Trust, accountability was heavily reinforced by controlling management. In the construction company and the

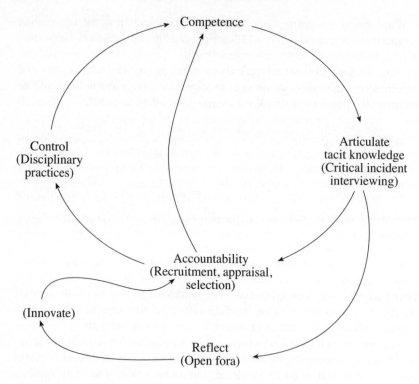

Figure 9.1   Competence as a tool of organisational learning

multinational oil company, though there were controlling practices, these did not run as deeply. In the University there was clear evidence of reflexivity, and little to suggest, for the academics at least, that the competences would become disciplinary. Here, there was already a great deal of awareness about the possibilities of control. In the beauty and cosmetics manufacturer, there was a great deal of scope for reflexivity.

Thus, where, in management terms, control is of more importance than flexibility (for example in the semi-privatised utility where the product itself does not change) such a system may well be effective – in management terms, management development is deemed to be successful if managers are working efficiently and productively, particularly in periods of extensive downsizing. In the Trust, while used ostensibly for management development, the competences themselves did not necessarily reflect the views of the employees, rather they represented the views of the consultant who felt, with the chief executive that a market-driven culture was required. Despite the extensive number of interviews that were carried out, it seemed here that the competence framework did not even surface 'tacit' knowledge, and there was certainly not the opportunity to reflect and innovate. Here the competence approach is not used as a tool of learning, but as a tool to change behaviours to meet the goals of the organisation.

Thus where there were opportunities for reflexivity and change, the approach seemed valid as a tool of organisational growth. One of the differentiating features of both the University and the cosmetics and beauty goods manufacturer was the amount and depth of the questioning around the competence implementation. In both organisations, there were pathways for the competences to be changed, should the need arise. However, there was a danger in the University that the competences were viewed cynically, so the debate here was not necessarily fruitful.

Competences can be a powerful tool for organisational change and control. This is because the approach systematically locks together structures and behaviours, and can therefore be used both to objectify in terms of spatial enclosure, partitioning and ranking of employees, and subjectify through the appraisal process and the linked-in processes for self-development. Equally, as we have seen, it does have the potential to be used creatively as in organisation F. Here the objectifying practices are tempered by challenge and debate. They themselves are open to change.

The road to achieving organisational- and self-reflexivity is hard and unremitting. Hard for employees and managers. Nevertheless, those organisations who are genuinely seeking harmonious working conditions in the sense of true equality would do well to question where and how there is room for reflexivity and change in their managerial models, and be prepared in practice to have the courage of their convictions. It is heartening at least to see that genuine attempts to foster this ethos can be successful.

9.4   REFLECTIONS ON THE RESEARCH PROCESS: POLITICS, ETHICS AND ACCESS

The fact that the research formed part of a larger project gave me a significant advantage in gaining access into organisations. Even where organisations perceive that they may have a problem of gender imbalance, there is often a great deal of fear about tackling it. Those male managers who attempt to do so often find that they come up against the same fears that many women have of articulating dissatisfaction with equality of employment. Women who articulate this dissatisfaction may be labelled as 'harpies', 'feminists', 'whiners' and so on, while men who attempt to tackle the situation may be labelled 'new men', 'wimps' etc. There is no choice but to run the gamut of such 'gender constructionism' or simply continue to collude.[1] More importantly, with one exception, gender issues were not considered to be a 'problem' within the competence strategies since the approach, as the literature shows, is claimed to be gender neutral. I do not believe that I would have had much success in asking organisations for their opinions purely on gender in relation to competences since none of the respondents, apart from in organisation F, considered that this was a problem. As my theoretical outline hypothesised, it is the very fact that gendered processes are concealed that renders them so pernicious. How these processes came to be believed to be objective, and what the implications were for women managers needed to be inferred.

Access was gained through various contacts of mine built up from six years as editor of a human resource magazine. This process began in June 1994, and in August, I had set up interviews with the six organisations featured here. In all cases, save two, contact was first made with a senior human resource manager, if not the head, of, human resources. In the multinational oil company, contact was made with the Head of Leadership Programmes, and in the case of the Northern Ireland Trust, contact was made through the consultant, and then directly with the Chief Executive.

The majority of the organisations were accessed either through my contacts with consultants, or in one case, as a result of a contact made on a seminar held at the Institute from which the major competence project was funded. Only the multinational oil company and the beauty and cosmetics retailer were approached cold, though one of my male colleagues had earlier carried out some work with the latter. Two organisations actually went cold during the project. The first was a major supermarket chain who had offered us an initial interview. It transpired that they were well ahead with competence initiatives, but issues of confidentiality and competition were paramount. The fruits that we were offering (publications, company seminar) were obviously not enough to risk unsettling what was obviously already a well-devised and secure implementation. The second company was the semi-privatised utility which gave a full two-hour interview, and an opportunity to follow-up, but did not want an in-depth case study as they were undergoing yet another period of change, and felt that research would interfere with their objectives.

Access could have been a problem if I had not already had some contacts. I also feel that I could not have reached so high up in the organisations without these initial contacts, and also without the experience of having worked for several different organisations as a freelance publishing consultant. This gave me a certain credibility, and encouraged managers to want to 'divulge' what they had been doing, with a certain amount of pride, mixed with trepidation at the results. Further, organisations were extremely interested in what other organisations were doing so they could 'benchmark' their efforts against others. The shared knowledge that I was in a position to offer was perceived to be of great value.

Given the nature of the research, questions of politics and ethics loomed high on the agenda. There were two issues here. The first was the fact that in essence, the broader competence project, in focusing on the 'construction of the competent manager', came up against issues of control. However, organisations gave permission to undertake research in the hope that we may be able to offer some insights into the relative merits of different competence models. My ethical position on this was clear, though not always that easy to uphold. When asked what I was attempting to do, I was open and prepared to discuss the more 'sociological' side of the research, but tended to focus more on the value of the research as evaluating competence models. This indeed was true, at the end of the project we were in the position of giving organisations valuable information on competence models, and indeed, at several points, my advice was asked throughout the research. On the whole, organisations were not interested in my views on 'constructing the competent manager'. If I started talking about this sociological aspect of the research, people did not seem to 'hear' what I was saying. Perhaps I was also subconsciously not wishing to enter into this dialogue, and therefore presented it in an oblique way. Whilst at first I felt slightly uncomfortable with this dual role, since one had to be very aware of this position throughout the interviewing, I felt that as long as neither organisations' nor individuals' positions were threatened by what I was doing, then I had done everything possible to ensure that data gathering was focused, and integrity maintained. Sensitivity too, had to be maintained around issues of what information about organisations could be divulged to others. There were varying degrees of openness about giving information of this sort. The multinational oil company did not wish to reveal its competences at the interview, though they subsequently released these to me a year later. In the Trust, I waited nine months before the competence model was actually given to me, and when it did arrive, the following words were written in capitals across the front:

STRICTLY FOR USE ONLY WITHIN XX TRUST

THIS DOCUMENT IS ONLY APPLICABLE TO STAFF WITHIN XX. IT MUST NOT, **UNDER ANY CIRCUMSTANCES**, BE PHOTOCOPIED. IT MUST REMAIN IN YOUR POSSESSION AT ALL TIMES.

The fear around releasing this information came from two camps. The first was the consultant who hoped to implement the project elsewhere in the NHS, and the second was from the Chief Executive, who believed that the framework of competences had value, and could be 'sold' to other Trusts. Although this example is perhaps extreme, it does reflect some of the issues and fears that one constantly meets when conducting research at this level of organisation.

A further issue that arose in one of the case studies was that of trust. Gaining the trust of respondents is critical in effectively teasing out resistance, or underlying attitudes that may resist projects. In a few cases, people were simply 'waiting to see' how the competence strategy would work before 'buying-in' to the project. Invariably, as my own experience has shown by working with organisations over a period of time but as an outsider, people tend to confide in you, and as researcher or consultant, one becomes, in a sense, the repository of much confidential information.

The second issue was that of tackling gender issues along with the main competence project. As I noted earlier, I do not believe it would have been possible to gain access on this issue alone. The only way this may have been achieved would have been by offering organisations research into their own organisation, and then action research in the form of a plan for changing what I found. However, I first needed to find out the overall problems, contextualised in a wider environment before I would have been in a position to do this. One cannot offer solutions before knowing what the problems are. As it was, it was relatively easy to ask questions about gender in the context of the wider project, giving people the option to offer what they wanted. Since the focus of the analysis was on ways in which the strategy was perceived and implemented, any more probing questions would probably have been too 'interventionist' and changed the nature of the research. As it was, those who had reflected on the issue, discussed it; others simply noted that the competence strategy was 'objective' and therefore gender relations not a problem. As we shall see later, it is this 'taken-for-granted' assumption that is likely to be most damaging for women managers. Further, as this research is focused at digging out 'taken-for-granted' assumptions, I had, of necessity, to be fairly oblique in my approach.

Gender Dynamics in Research

This piece of research was carried out as part of a larger research project. I was responsible for the bulk of the field research, and set up the organisations listed here. I was working with two male colleagues, who occasionally carried out some interviews with me. The status and gender of the researcher undoubtedly affected the research process and the data elicited. When I was working with my male colleagues, the focus of the interview rested very much on the more 'abstract' modelling of competences along the more 'paradigmatic' way of thinking that I discussed earlier. In this case, how this related to feature of enterprise. Managers proudly discussed how the competence models worked, and in some cases, made overt comments as to how they could be used to control. For example I will not forget walking into the Head of the Human Resources office with one male colleague. The air was clouded with tension. (The fact that this particular respondent had already been nicknamed 'Rottweiler' may have prejudged how the interview was to take place.) This was also the only interview in the entire period where we were not allowed to use a tape recorder. Whether or not this would have happened had I interviewed on my own was another question. The same phenomenon occurred when I interviewed the Head of Human Resources and Head of Training at the multinational oil company. After an initial grilling of over 15 minutes on why this research would be any better than any other, the two began to open up about the process, there was a sense of 'vying' for the kudos of how competences worked, and indeed how many employees had been lost in the downsizing exercise. Further, I could have been a flower on the wallpaper when my male colleague and I interviewed the Vice Chancellor. This may have been due to the longevity of my male colleague's employment, at this establishment, along with his reputation.

When I interviewed on my own, however, after the initial probing on how competences had been implemented, the interview focused more on how people 'felt' about the competences, and whether they thought they might work. Whilst this is an entirely subjective account, and attempts not to make any value judgements about the value of either approach, I do think it merits attention as a factor in any type of organisational research. Gender, both in the sense of interviewees and interviewers is often taken as given. But my experience shows, along with Hammersley and Atkinson (1983), that 'The researcher cannot escape the implications of gender: no position of genderless neutrality can be achieved' (p.84). The only solution is to attempt to retain constant awareness and openness both during interview and in the subsequent presentation of these issues.

ENDNOTE

1. The strength of gender identification and fear of raising gender issues in organisations was brought home to me when I visited, with a female colleague the Chairman and Vice Chairman of a prestigious consultant engineers. They had noticed that they were losing women engineers in mid-career, and couldn't understand why. We had been invited to discuss how they might set about enquiring into this problem, and to propose some solutions. They had two major concerns: 'What would we tell the workforce that "the ladies" from Cambridge were doing?' and where should we send our proposal so that no-one caught sight of what was going on at this early stage. Thus, even a genuine desire to promote equality becomes hampered by fear of being seen to be doing so. If the Chairman and Vice Chairman need to go to such lengths for secrecy, what chance is there for a middle, or even senior manager to get anything off the ground of any significance?

10. Embodying the subject: integrating separation and connection

This book is particularly concerned with women managers. In keeping with the spirit of critical theory, it has attempted to render the connections between how knowledge is generated (that is, how we perceive competent managers) and whose interests this serves, more visible. In this concluding chapter, I offer up some reflections on some of the issues that emerged from the empirical work and relate these back to the theoretical framework that I set out earlier. In particular, I hope that the connections made between critical theory and feminism may mark a way forward to open up organisational life to more 'voices', and that this may be useful to those struggling in the midst of the organisational complexities, particularly in this ever-changing, globalising world where we need to communicate across and through diversity.

10.1   THEORY EMERGING FROM PRACTICE

The research set out to expose concrete practices by which organisational strategies 'hid' and possibly reinforced a gendered substructure. Three issues emerged from this research. The first, which I had anticipated, was the strong influence of language on creating 'taken-for-granted' assumptions. The second was somewhat unexpected – this was the use of the myth of culture change as a means of hiding processes of gender construction. Finally, a third, perhaps more unexpected issue, was the break between paradigmatic and narrative cognition and the implications of this for women managers.

The 'Technologisation' of Language

Language played a critical role in shaping perceptions, cognitions and action such that practices of gender construction remained hidden. While post-structuralists have for a long time understood the importance of language in shaping reality for us, with few exceptions (for example, Martin 1990; Fairclough 1991, 1992) the importance of language has not undergone empirical investigation in organisations. This study showed how individuals were constrained within the language they used, and how the language, in a sense, closed down other possibilities of understanding. It backs up the findings of Garnsey and Rees (1996) who showed how the language of 'equal opportunity' actually constrained thinking about progress for women managers. It seemed that, unless there is a great deal of self- and organisational awareness, agents are constrained within the discourses in which they operate.

Above all, however, the creation of a particular type of language seemed to have become a practice in itself of constituting reality, more than just the medium through which other practices operate. Interviewees themselves talked about how necessary it was to 'learn' the language before they could understand the processes. There was evidence here of the 'technologisation of discourse' as identified by Fairclough (1992, pp.215–18). Growing use of world-wide information systems must render this an important area further research. The use of e-mail as a major mode of cross-cultural communication, and the domination of this medium by the predominant use of English renders this more urgent.

The Culture Myth

The second issue, that of the use of the term 'culture', both as a means of description, and its close association with organisational change, was somewhat unexpected in its wholesale adoption, but universal in all but one company. Respondents used the term, loosely to describe 'ways of being' in the organisation, and this included both the structures (for example, hierarchical structures, flat structures, teams and so on) and behaviours (ways of relating on a daily basis with one another, ways in which meetings are handled and so on). The term did however, seem to have more than a descriptive element. Most significantly, the term 'culture' was almost synonymous with that of organisational change, and in some cases downsizing. While there has been a huge literature in this area, both at practitioner and academic level (which would account for the use of the word) there is 'a remarkable dearth of serious critical analysis of this phenomenon' (Willmott 1993, p.517). The research has highlighted the way in which 'corporate culturism' has invaded organisational life both as a metaphor for description, but more importantly as a means and a justification for incorporating managerial practices, which, as we have seen, far from empowering employees, may lead, to greater systems of control.

Such a finding accords with the theoretical critique of 'corporate culture' provided by Willmott (1993) who suggested that:

> ... corporate culturism aspires to extend the terrain of instrumentally rational action by developing monocultures in which conditions for the development of value-rational action, where individuals struggle to assess the meaning and worth of a range of competing value-standpoints, is systematically eroded. (p.518)

Competence strategies seemed to draw on the corporate culture metaphor to legitimate and justify their existence. In the semi-privatised industry, claims were made that the culture was to be changed; though lip service was played to this idea (introduction of use of Christian names, for example) in fact, the competence documentation, and the practices inscribed within the approach perpetuated the 'command and control' system that was in place. In the Trust, there was a move from a service to a market-orientated culture, but the market culture was not the 'empowered' one usually associated with the claims of Thatcherite enterprise. Far from it, here the competence approach most closely resembled Taylorist-type practices.

The research did show however, that where other discourses predominated, such as that of feminism, or professionalism, then the authority of the corporate culture was not necessarily so dominant. This was very apparent in the beauty and cosmetics manufacturer, where the environment was characterised not so much by strong adherence to another set of values, but by allowing the individual to question, constantly, the values by which he or she worked. Thus it was not so much the values themselves that were important – rather it was creating the environment in which values could be challenged.

In essence, this differentiation reflects the contrast in social action as delineated by Weber. Weber delineated four types of social action, of which *Zweckrationalitat* and *Wertrationalitat* (value rational action) are considered to be the most important for analysing modern society (Willmott 1993). In brief, a person whose actions are determined by *Zweckrationalitat* derives subjective wants from a set of values which are already given. A person whose action is guided by *Wertrationalitat* makes a 'self-conscious' formulation of the values that orient his or her conduct. It is precisely this 'critical self-reflection' that is called for by Habermas (1968/1971) in the third constitutive area of knowledge, and it is just this distinction which existed in the beauty and cosmetics manufacturer.

Willmott argues that:

> ... *if* we are persuaded by the idea that the indeterminacy of human existence *demands* that actions are shaped by meanings and not just by drives, the central *moral* issue then becomes: what kind of *social institutions* respect and foster the capacity of human beings to recognise and contemplate a variety of competing standpoints, and to appreciate the existential significance of the opportunity to make informed choices between these value standpoints?

Without attempting to provide anything like an adequate response to this question, it can be suggested that the ability to develop a 'self-conscious formulation' of the values that orient our conduct is conditional upon (i) access to knowledge of alternative standpoints and (ii) a social milieu in which their competing claims can be explored.

My experience at the beauty and cosmetics manufacturer and retailer suggested that people were encouraged to develop a 'self-conscious formulation' of their values, and equally given the space and time in which to explore them. This allowed alternative standpoints of feminism and environmentalism to exist, and thus meant that the potentially controlling aspects of the competence strategy were diluted.

Paradigmatic and Narrative Modes of Cognition: a Way of Reinforcing the Gendered Substructure?

In Chapter 2, I discussed the growing recognition of the importance of narrative modes of cognition in constructing accountability, and how the current principal technologies of organising consistently undervalue and often suppress narrative modes (Boland and Schultze 1996). Bruner (1986, 1990) suggested that the paradigmatic form dominated cognitive psychology, just as it has been accepted as the mode of cognition in all forms of human reasoning As such it has become the primary mode of functioning in organisations (Boland and Schultze 1996).

Such a mode of cognition would seem to have underpinned research and formal organisation structures of the last decade. Use of the paradigmatic mode of cognition is exemplified in the Taylorist approach to people-management, with its fragmentation of jobs into minute and measurable tasks. The majority of ways in which the competence strategy was implemented reflected the paradigmatic mode of cognition. The research showed how organisations built up complex systems, focusing on systems of counting, classifying and measuring leading in individuals, to the construction of the calculating and compartmentalised self. People internalise norms and notions of perfection, based on paradigmatic cognitions, and accountability becomes a system of one-way visibility: the gaze of the panopticon.

Hierarchical forms of accountability that we have seen in the competence approach have equally been related to Foucauldian concepts of disciplinary power (Boland and Schultze 1996). It is possible that where more disciplinary practices are in evidence, the more likely this organisation is likely to favour, or give allegiance to people working in the paradigmatic mode of cognition. The narrative self, situating experiences in time, taking into account relationships with others, building beginnings, middle and ends, bears a greater resemblance to women's psychological and moral development as explored by Chodorow (1978) and Gilligan (1982). It may be, therefore, that indirectly, the dominance of paradigmatic thinking in organisations is likely to be a reason for women's inabilities to progress further up the managerial ladder. Bringing as they do, a set of behaviours whose value is largely unacknowledged, and the rationale for which stems from undervalued narrative modes of cognition, they, and men who reason as they do, are deprived of space in which to express their own experience of the world. For women, this means either adopting the paradigmatic mode wholesale (as many do) or a possible loss of self-confidence as their predominant way of cognition is not validated. For the organisation too, it may entail a loss of opportunity. While paradigmatic thinking is an essential part of civilisation, its use to excess and to the exclusion of narrative forms of reasoning, as Bruner and Boland show, can be stultifying. The creativity and flexibility of modern organisations are paradoxically endangered by methods that attempt to capture these qualities in paradigmatic form.

This research has highlighted the possibility that paradigmatic modes of cognition may predominate in modern organisations (especially those that are market-oriented) and may be a rich area for further theory building and empirical research.

Acker (1992) points out that gendered processes are both overt and covert. Gendered processes are often resources in organisational control and transformation. However:

> Underlying these processes, and intimately connected to them, is a gendered substructure of organizations that links the more surface gender arrangements with the gender relations in other parts of the society. Ostensibly gender neutral, everyday activities of organizing and managing large organizations reproduce the gendered substructure within the organization itself and within wider society. I think that this is the most important part of the process to comprehend, because it is hidden within abstract, objectifying, textually mediated relations and is difficult to make visible. The fiction of the universal worker obscures the gendered effects of these ostensibly neutral processes and helps to banish gender from theorizing about the fundamental character of complex organizations. Gender, sexuality, reproduction and emotionality of women are outside organizational boundaries, continually and actively consigned to that social space by ongoing organizational practices. (p.259)

If objective managerial practices are dominated by the paradigmatic modes of cognition as the research here suggests, it could be here that women's 'voices' or perhaps better women's 'presence' is lost. The very particular case set out here, that of competence, reveals how the gender substructure is reproduced through a language which creates and confirms the myth of culture change, but which by its very nature (that is, working through paradigmatic modes of cognition) consigns the more narrative style of women's thinking to the tick boxes on the appraisal forms. Unless there is room for the 'narrative' approach in drawing up the competences (as was the case in the cosmetics retailer) competences will reflect the organisation's gendered history rather than open up spaces for a creative future.

10.2   EMBODYING THE SUBJECT: TRANSCENDING AUTONOMY AND RELATEDNESS

While the study draws its inspiration and goal of emancipation from critical theory, it is also informed by feminist and post-modern thinking, thereby broadening out the possibilities of critical theory to introduce a notion of the 'embodied subject' into communicative practices. The main drive of critical theory is to surface whether and how competing ideas, methods and findings are developed and sanctioned as authoritative, and to surface the social relations that construct them as so. In particular, it is concerned with whose voices are heard in the processes by which structures are developed, and whose interests are likely to be most enhanced by those processes. I was interested here in pushing out the boundaries of critical theory to encompass a more 'embodied' subject, and draw upon the findings in the research to take this possibility further.

The major drawback in Habermas's conceptualisation of the subject is the sole emphasis on the social rather than the individual, such that particular aspects of individuality are consigned to questions of individual psychology or nature. This leads to 'anonymity' of critical theory and Habermas's inability to overcome the opposition of universal and particular in his theory of communicative action. Leonard (1990) suggested that critical theory must 'break from "universalistic assumptions"' and give way to a 'plurality of critical theories'. However, it is not enough to reassert the importance of the plural. Feminism, he suggests, is such a critical theory in action since it 'embodies a commitment to both solidarity and plurality' (p.212). It is less concerned with the theoretical elaboration of emancipatory practice than it is with the 'practical demands that theory must meet' (p.213).

Following these possibilities, I posited a different and more provisional understanding of the 'subject'. Gender was understood not only as the psychic ordering of biological difference, but also the social ordering of that difference. For the purposes of this research I have assumed that the subject had some degree of agency, while at the same time she was placed within particular discursive configurations.

I proposed a set of differences that enabled a more biological and psychological subject to enter the frame, and set these on a nurturing/directive continuum. By ignoring such differences, we saw how the competence practices, overall consigned the more 'nurturing' aspects of human experience to the edge of organisational life, and with it, all those individuals for whom this way of relating is paramount. This has the effect of reinforcing a hidden gender substructure, which, though hidden, provides us with the modes of interpretation through which we relate to ourselves and to the world. If, as Benhabib suggests, a gendered substructure can be considered as: 'the grid through which the self develops an embodied identity, a certain mode of being in one's body and of living the body' and 'the grid through which societies and cultures reproduce embodied individuals' (Benhabib 1986), then what might be the implications of our findings at a more generalised level? This would suggest that, if individuals are to feel truly 'empowered' at work, and not hampered by restricted and power-soaked ways of relating, then we need to question the pervasiveness of particular types of competence strategies, and other types of performance management systems.

How might this be tackled? Alcoff (1988) suggests that 'consciousness' would be a useful strategy. But this raises the question, conscious of what? Raising consciousness is not new politically or ethically. Marxist analysis tries to bring to light the systems that subvert and lock subjects into false consciousness. Feminism began by 'consciousness-raising'. On the whole, this has meant raising consciousness about the external conditioning that constrains us into habitual patterns. At a different level, subjectivity, consciousness, identity (classed, gendered or raced) means coming to terms with, or learning to inhabit one's body. This is not a psychoanalytical project, nor the basis for some unifying essence, but rather it is 'an ongoing process, a continual renegotiation of the relationship between self and others. It is both a "sensual" and a cultural project which cannot be evaded through evocation of the "autonomous" ego who somehow manages to transcend the bodily aspects of existence (Marshall 1994, p.113).

A gendered identity is thus an interpreted identity, mediated through social systems and indeed textual relations, and also by the possibilities of growing awareness of the subject in relation to his/her body. Challenging the mind/body dualism inherent in Habermasian thinking, means challenging the accepted autonomous relationship between culture and biology. This study showed how a tension and opposition between autonomy and relatedness favoured men's ways of being over women and thus was more likely to perpetuate male managers' interests over female managers' interests. If we can break down the opposition between autonomy and relatedness, we can see that this becomes integral to the development of subjectivity – becomes a route to greater self- and thereby organisational consciousness.

Further, if we can see this tension as a tension between self and other then we can also see how this is a fundamental organising principle of human society, and which perhaps helps explain the pervasiveness of gender relations. Bologh (1987) writes: 'The tension between a commitment to individual rights and a commitment to relationship must be maintained as a tension internal to moral reasoning itself' (p.151). Thus the relationship between individual and society must be seen partly as an internal tension, and not fully externalized as classical sociological theory would suggest. The tension between public and private, political and personal, mind and body, masculine and feminine, must be seen as an internal struggle in the construction of identities, as well as one that is externally manifest in debate. The struggle over masculinity and femininity is a moral and ethical struggle, and one in which we all need to engage. Further, this engagement needs to take place both externally and internally, and therefore implies a self-reflexive practice.

The critical theory approach here gives a context for emancipation, a way of looking at the relationship between system and lifeworld, but in place of the disembodied and universalist subject of Habermasian thinking, or the fragmented subject of post-modern thinking, I have introduced an embodied subject, shaped and conditioned by the mutually interacting forces of culture and biology. With this more 'embodied subject' the study has shown us how competences are used to construct behaviours, and encouraged employees to 'identify' with particular constructs of the manager. Disciplinary practices ensure that these 'objectify' and 'subjectify'. Introducing feminist and post-modern approaches has helped 'flesh out' the subject, and thus opened up critical theory to be able to work with intersecting systems of patriarchy, as well as political and class systems. It could be suggested that the 'universalistic' subject of Habermasian theory has itself contributed to on-going processes of gender construction by veiling this additional quality of subjectivity.

However, the more we can understand that the tension between separation and connection is a question of values, the more we can question and open up channels of communication, through an understanding of this difference, rather than its denial; the more our capacity grows to overcome a conditioned response. The more we understand that this tension is a tension that is inherent to both males and females, and one that needs to be resolved internally as well as externally – it is one that is to be resolved by inquiry into the self, and inquiry into how one relates to the 'other'.

Hopefully, the recognition of these complex and intersecting processes may lead us to further question our own conditioning, and more importantly our own actions, so that we may act compassionately in organisational and social life. We have seen how the goal of subjectivity – or self-consciousness – can be moved towards by integrating autonomy and relatedness, and that we need to do this through learning how we relate to ourselves as men or women, and thus at one level, how we relate to our bodies. If we wish to free ourselves of the hidden gendered substructure, then as men and women we need to adopt the strategy of developing self-consciousness for ourselves. Organisations could provide the conditions in which such self-questioning can take place. They may become, not the place of emprisonment and control, with the chief executive and the customer as jailor and warder respectively, but places where men and women can together attempt to shape a future where a shared humanity endeavours to create a world that is both self-sustaining and spacious enough to accommodate the richness of diversity.

10.3   SELF-TRANSFORMATION

This research has taken place over a period of some ten years. Throughout that time, my views and positions have changed considerably. I have been changed both by the reading of the literature, by my experiences in organisations, and by my own life path. There has been a constant iteration between theory and practice. My insistence on managing the interdisciplinary nature of this project, of keeping theoretical plurality, has meant that my 'career' as such has suffered in the sense of the time taken to get this work into the public domain. Theoretical plurality is difficult to retain, when a 'tight' empirical project is required. It is no surprise to me that there are few empirical demonstrations of critical theory. Due to the time taken in bringing together these theoretical perspectives, I have been in the unfortunate position of losing a fellowship at a prestigious UK university, due in part to the delay. Undoubtedly, one is always making trade-offs between breadth and depth. Unfortunately, the current approach to research is one where one has to make trade-offs between breadth, depth and a career. Currently, I have chosen to work in an institute for less money, where I have more time to pursue the complexities of interdisciplinary research. At a personal level, this gives me more insights into the 'relative' truths, more perspectives, and thereby I find more meaning in the work that I do pursue. My work is informed by a daily meditation practice where I myself am under the microscope. This helps me break down the 'mind/body' duality and begin to learn to relate from the totality of my being rather than from this dichotomised and conditioned split. There are no claims to objectivity here, but merely an intention to become more 'aware' of myself in relation to my environment, and how I myself have become constructed. I have no other tool than this.

The Research and Narrative Position

I have also been, as far as possible, aware that I have my own preconceptions and judgements. I am myself constrained within my own predominant discourses. I have stressed throughout this book, my understanding that research implies a political position, and this will be reflected in the initial boundaries I set around the analysis. I make no claim to neutrality. Some of my preconceptions have not been affirmed. I approached organisation F with a great deal of cynicism due to the excessive free publicity they generally receive as a result of their unique approach. I felt that they were trading on the rhetoric of their values. This I found not to be the case, and though there are tendencies to excessive 'talk' and focus on external moral issues rather than their own there is a real awareness amongst some individuals of what they are trying to achieve, and the pitfalls which they are likely to meet. Equally, I approached organisation E with a certain degree of optimism generated by the enthusiasm I initially met from the consultant responsible for implementation, that some of the chaos that had befallen the National Health Service due to governmental reform may have been improved through the competence approach and result in the delivery of a better service. However, the rigid imposition of competences, and the market-driven language of consultants and top managers suggested to me that issues of care would be a long way down the agenda.

10.4 CONCLUSIONS

> Once we abandon the concept of women and historical victims, acted upon by violent men, inexplicable 'forces' and societal institutions, we must explain the central puzzle – women's participation in the construction of the system that subordinates her. (Lerner 1986, p.150)

The problem addressed here was the continuing inequality of women in the workforce – in particular women in management. The path which I have taken in order to address this has emerged from the persistence of one recurring observation: that women through their actions, appear to be colluding in their own subordination. I have never lost sight of this observation, and consequently, the path I have taken has been long, complex and exploratory. It has taken me through the literatures of women in management, labour market process, organisation theory, gender and cultural studies, psychological and linguistic studies, and feminist and post-modern thinking, and critical theory. It has taken me on my own path of self-discovery. As I began to see the ingrained structures that perpetuate this illusion, so I had to break down how these were ingrained in my own cognition and repeated patterns of behaviour, and how I myself contributed and contribute to my own and others' subordination.

Men and women are active agents in historical construction, but the analysis here has shown how interests can become objectified into structures. Given certain historical conditions, women may make what appear to be very reasonable choices (or perhaps the only choice available). The consequences of this is to produce and reproduce the conditions for subordination. Thus a woman may 'choose' to work part-time in a nursery, even though this is demanding and badly-paid work, and the consequences of her choice is that the job contines to be badly paid, since she has then contributed to building up 'supply'. Competence frameworks, once implemented, specify in advance the characteristics required of 'good' management. The 'choices' for women are to behave in ways in which they may feel uncomfortable, and for which they may be perceived to be 'incompetent', possibly eliminating other richer ways of behaving, or to adopt these other ways of behaving, for which they will be little rewarded institutionally. Undoubtedly, there are other 'groups' which will suffer too. However, when we shed the light of awareness onto these practices, then we can open up more creative solutions. We need structure and we need process, but above all, we need an intent constantly and compassionately to illuminate and challenge the provisional relationship between these two.

This book has essentially been written from a critical modern position that welcomes post-modern and feminist insights. I cannot remove myself from the research. I have written it within an unashamedly emancipatory agenda. This makes it open to criticism from many quarters. However, the perniciousness of gender inequality demands that a more 'holistic' approach is taken, otherwise, as I have shown elsewhere (Garnsey and Rees 1996), equal opportunity initiatives are simply washed away from the sand on which they are constructed.

Afterword

The perniciousness of gender inequality is a problem with which many organisations and individuals constantly struggle. This research has begun to show how deeply rooted are the processes by which inequality is perpetuated. It explains why policy at a structural level rarely works. It also shows quite clearly that the problem is not one of 'women in management': it is one of gender relations. These gender relations intersect with capitalist, patriarchal and intra-organisational relations. The problem cannot be addressed by making minor adjustments here and there. Only if we can employ a broader understanding of the systemic processes by which inequality is perpetuated, and undertake to raise our own awareness of where we may 'collude' with these processes, can we empower ourselves as men and women to tackle the inequalities that persist in our places of work.

I am a different person from the one who set out on this journey ten years ago. And yet ... as I write these final pages I see that as I have sought to emancipate myself from my own constraints, my understanding of how deeply these constraints go is only just unfolding. I realise that true emancipation can only emerge from a deep and compassionate listening – in the first instance to my own body – to what it truly means to be a human being and a woman, and to see where I have constrained and still do constrain my own feelings and actions – and to be prepared to act upon these observations.

The key issue here, it seems to me, is that of awareness. As men and women, we are largely unaware of the processes by which our subjectivity is constructed. We are unaware of the conditioned way in which we enter and leave situations, workplaces, relationships. We are unaware of how we construct, confirm and are the system which oppresses us, men and women alike. We are unaware of how we enter into and confirm relations of domination. Most importantly, we are unaware of our mind's relationship to our body. It is only by examining our own repeated patterns of behaviour and incessant cycles of cognition and reinforcing action that we can discern the ropes that constrain us. Only then can we begin to see and understand our suffering. Only then are we free to take compassionate action.

ON THOUGHTS

Just as the butterfly
flits
from bud to bud

the swan
cuts
through the shimmering water

As the dew
balances
on the verdant leaf

So our thoughts
run
swiftly through our minds

And, just as the butterfly momentarily
rests,
We can but attend,
a moment.

Not ours to hold, our thoughts,
Know them, and
gently let them go

Enriched
As the snail leaves its silvery stream
to grace
another

And as the stream runs deeper, clearer
So we grow together.

Ever deeper. Ever simpler.
Ever freer.

Appendix 1

List of interviews, observations and questions

(M or F indicates whether the respondent was male or female, and the number in brackets the number of interviews that took place with each individual)

Organisation A: University
Head of Human Resources (M) (x2) (one with male colleague)
Vice Chancellor (M) (with male colleague)
Operations Director (M) (with male colleague)
Consultant (F) (telephone interview)
Dean of Social Science (M)

Organisation E: Trust
Consultant (F) (x4)
Chief Executive (M) (x2) (with male colleagues)
Head of Human Resources (M) (with male colleague)
Head of Personnel (M) (x3) (one with male colleague)
Members of Project Implementation Group (2F, 1M) (3 separate interviews)
Observer/participant at focus groups introducing competences and appraisal to managers (one day)

Organisation F: Beauty and Cosmetics manufacturer and retailer
Head of Corporate Services, HR Director and Executive Committee member (M)
Performance improvement developer (F) (x2) (one with male colleague)
Equal Opportunities Manager (F) (x2)
Head of Learning and Development (F)
Second at Learning and Development (F) (x3)
Person responsible for drawing up 'The Rough Learning Guide'(F)
Head of Product Promotion and Marketing (F)
Head of Technical Production and Executive Committee member (M)

Consultant to the board (M)
General Manager for company values (F)

In addition observation and/or participation at various stages of the process.

1. Observer, then participant at initial clustering of competences
2. Observer at meeting when various senior managers were presented with clustered competences
3. Observer/participant at one-day meeting when human resource specialists throughout the company were introduced to the scheme
4. Observer/participant at one-day meeting when different departments were introduced to the scheme and to the different appraisal techniques

Checklist of Issues for Interviews

- respondent's role and responsibilities in organisation
- respondent's first encounter with competences
- why competences were introduced (environmental pressures, competition etc.)
- how they tied in to business plan
- what the overall schedule of the competence framework was
- how competence frameworks were tied to recruitment, selection, promotion
- what the projected future of the competences was, and whether this was realistic
- how the organisation had responded so far
- whether there were any drawbacks/difficulties of implementation
- what respondents understand by 'competence'
- how they responded personally to the introduction of competences
- whether they felt that their and other people's behaviours had/would change?
- whether the introduction of competences have any effect on the employment of women in the organisation

Questions used for Interviews

Questions for initial meetings

1. General context (environment, response to competition, current and perceived threats)
   (providing a broader societal context and historical positioning
2. How far the competence process and framework reflected the general competence model as drawn up in Chapter 1 (how did the model match up to the prescribed framework, were there any changes?)

3. How the competence model had evolved over time (i.e., historical aspect)
4. What respondents understood by the term 'competence' and how they personally felt about the framework
5. Whether respondents perceived any difficulties with the framework and its implementation both in their own terms and other groups such as subordinates who were affected by it (were subjects actively welcoming/resisting change?)

Subquestions/issues to 'unearth' gender substructure

*   whether and how competence strategies work at the level of individual identity as a means of control (to what degree competence strategies are tied in with human resource structures of recruitment, promotion and selection, and how do processes of appraisal and assessment work which underpin the competence strategies)
*   whether and how competence strategies were constructed as gender neutral
*   whether they work at a further level of identity construction by favouring a 'directive' type of behaviour over a nurturing type both in the practices and structures, thereby 'writing out' many women's particular experience of the world
*   how competence strategies are implemented in organisations, and how these are tied in with human resource technologies of recruitment, promotion and selection and whether and how these are underpinned by appraisal and assessment
*   what sense people make of the competence strategies and whether they felt they were neutral and gender-free
*   what the practices are which create these beliefs, if this is the case
*   how these beliefs become accepted as part of the organisational 'norm'
*   whether and how the competence strategies are likely to favour those employees (mostly men) who tend to use a predominantly 'directive' style of behaviour

Appendix 2

Analytical tools for textual analysis

I have drawn selectively on linguistic techniques that have been identified by linguists/cultural analysts/discourse analysts such as Barthes (1956), Astroff and Nyberg (1992), Sorenson (1991), Fowler (1991) and Fairclough (1992). These tools were first published in Garnsey and Rees (1996).

TEXTUAL TRANSFORMATIONS: RHETORICAL TECHNIQUES

The following section outlines various techniques used for discourse analysis. These are techniques that exist both at the level of the 'content' of the discourse and can be used both across and within texts, and also linguistic techniques that encode various relationships within a text in such a way as to appear natural and unremarkable.

They are by no means exhaustive, since the analyst must always be prepared to identify and name new techniques that may arise.

Across-text Analysis

1. **La vaccine** (or inoculation) is a technique identified by Barthes (1956) as acknowledgement that a phenomenon has undesirable aspects, but through admission of an incidental aspect and in such a form as to obscure major, intrinsic ill effects (Barthes 1956, p.238). Garnsey and Rees (1996) show how, in the discourse of Opportunity 2000, a problem is admitted in the underrepresentation of women in management, but reassurance is immediately offered in terms of an achievable solution and the underlying factors are not examined. Imbalance in numbers of women is admitted, but as though it were an incidental feature, without an examination of causes, in a way which conceals structural inequalities. Sorenson (1991) shows how such a technique 'depoliticizes and dehistorizes' discourse (p.228).

2. A second mechanism is that of **paradox**, whereby contradictory

information from other discourses is appropriated and disarmed. Astroff and Nyberg (1992) for example, show how in the (anti-socialist) US media coverage of the French elections, the media insist that the French, while voting for Mitterand in the first round of the presidential election, did not really mean to elect him. They equally go on to show how selected aspects of French history are used to set up a paradoxical situation: thus the history that is not selected or that is carefully pruned is the history of the French left. For example, throughout there is only one reference to Jean Jaurès, father of the French left. The Socialist party is thus consistently presented as a contradiction rather than rooted in French history (p.16).

3. **Repetition and condensation** of 'unpacked' concepts is another device that can be variously employed to establish 'taken-for-granted' meanings. It has long been recognised that culture industries depend on 'the constant reproduction of the same thing' and the same is true of academic and business discourse. Garnsey and Rees (1996) show how the repeated use of short-hand terms such as 'recruitment and selection' or 'family-friendly' policies, without defining or unpacking the terms, fails to take into account the domestic constraints that many women face.

4. A further rhetorical technique identified by Barthes is that of **'Neither-Norism'**. Through this technique, two equally unacceptable choices are juxtaposed in order that both may be rejected. Sorenson (p.238) show how this technique is used in mass media discourse on the Horn of Africa. For example, Jonathan Dimbeldy reporting on Eritrea for the Spectator, attempts to undermine any perception of the EPLF's legitimacy through repeated, gratuitous references to Pol Pot characterizing the situation as 'a suicidal stalemate where the self-righteous rhetoric of both sides about our "just cause" floats ludicrously back and forth over the corpses'.

5. **Techniques of appropriation** can be used to deny various groups of people any voice. For example the voices of the subjects about whom the discourse is written can be absorbed into the neutral and authoritative voice of management and government. Nominalisation (verbs and adjectives turned into nouns, see below) and repeated use of passive constructions can deprive subjects of any influence. Further, such techniques can be used to negate any sense of causality, and attribution of responsibility.

6. A further technique identified by Sorenson is that of **ventriloquism** where people are either quoted or invented in order to speak the appropriate phrases required by the hegemonic script of the author (p.237). Sorenson shows how a reporter notes, in discussing popular images of Africa constructed at the height of imperialist expansion, that

the European press claimed that masses were in favour of imperialism but were prevented from co-operating by their selfish leaders.

7. The use of **metaphor** in language may well be ideologically loaded, but often will have become so profoundly naturalised within a particular discourse that people are often quite unaware of them most of the time and find it extremely difficult, even when their attention is drawn to them, to escape from them in their discourse thinking or action. Note, for example, the use of the metaphor of war in 'he attacked me at every weak point' (Fairclough 1992, p.195).

8. Repeated use of '**key words**' which have a general and local significance is another device that may be employed. Here there is constant and repeated use of words that have significant potential of different meaning. As producers we are always faced with choices about how to use a word, and how to word a meaning and as interpreters we are always faced with decisions about how to interpret the choices interpreters have made. These choices and decisions are not of a purely individual nature but are socially variable and contested (Fairclough 1992, p.185). Thus texts may be characterised by ambiguities and ambivalences of meaning. Fairclough shows how, for example, the word 'enterprise' has been exploited in this way in the speeches of Lord Young, Secretary of State for Trade and Industry in the Thatcher government (1985–8). Different speeches highlight different senses of the meaning of the word, not by promoting one sense to the exclusion of others, but by establishing particular configurations of meaning particular hierarchies of relationships among the different meanings of enterprise, such that private enterprise is associated with culturally valued qualities of 'enterprisingness'. I will, like Fairclough, call this **word meaning.**

9. The second aspect of the many-to-one nature of the word-meaning relationship is the multiplicity of ways of '**wording**' a meaning. Thus there are always alternative ways of 'signifying'. As Fairclough indicates, the wording of immigration as an 'influx' or 'flood' as opposed to a 'quest' for a new life, can in a real sense change the meaning. New wordings can generate new 'lexical items' (Fairclough 1992, p.191) because this captures the idea of expressions that have achieved a degree of fixity and stability. This often happens when a process becomes nominalised. For example:

    • They held meetings to encourage people to become more conscious of their lives
    • They held consciousness-raising sessions

Thus, as Fairclough shows, creating lexical items brings particular perspectives on domains of experience into wider theoretical, scientific, cultural or ideological purview.

10. Newly identified in this book is the technique of **'introjection'** where anonymous individuals are attributed, repeatedly with 'needs' and 'potential' that can be satisfied by the employer. Here language is used such that the reader will internalise the language and the agenda of the compentence agenda and take responsibility for developing themselves in line with the business plan.

11. Cutting across many of these techniques is that of the **'construction of significant absence'** (Sorenson 1991, p.230). In identifying the construction of absence we draw attention to what is not being said. Thus, what is significant is how all texts identified in a particular discourse fail to say the same thing. Thus they may fail to acknowledge particular structural inequalities that may disempower one group over another.

Within-text Analysis

Most of the above techniques can be identified 'across' a corpus of texts. We can, however, also analyse a text at a closer level using techniques of critical linguistics developed by Fowler (1991) to see how the language used is 'working' discursively to perpetuate common sense assumptions. These tools were used by Garnsey and Rees (1996) to 'deconstruct' the promotional text of Opportunity 2000 to show how excessive use of passive tenses and nominalisations resulted in there being little need for organisations to actually take any action on behalf of Opportunity 2000. This section provides a brief exposition of some of the main constructions used in analysing discourse. These can be divided into three: transitivity; lexical structure; modality.

1. **Transitivity** is the foundation of representation, the way the clause is used to analyse events and situations. There are two important ways in which transitivity is used to inform and transform a text, (a) the use of active and passive voice and (b) nominalisation.

   (a) When we write texts we often unconsciously (or consciously) choose a particular style to help us transmit our message. In academic writing, for example, we are taught to use the passive as a stylistic technique. In fact, this is more than a stylistic technique. Using the passive can have the effect either of positioning the agent syntactically (i.e. in word order) at the right hand side of a clause, and thereby reducing our perception of the agent as causing an effect, or it can remove the agent altogether.[1]

   (b) The second aspect of transitivity is nominalisation, '… a radical syntactic transformation of a clause which has extensive structural consequences and offers substantial ideological opportunities' (Fowler 1991). English is a nominalising language: that is it is structurally possible and common practice for predicates (verbs and adjectives) to be transformed into their derived nominals. Thus from 'to allege' we find 'allegations', 'development' from 'develop'. Also, in basic English, there are many nouns which are strictly speaking actions or processes, rather than objects. Such a strategy is endemic in English, and, ideologically speaking, can have the effect of mystification (who is doing what to whom, when, where etc.) or reification (conceiving of actions, processes as things). The term 'organisation' is a well-known example of the construction of entities through linguistic usage.

2.   Critical linguistics can analyse **lexical structure** to identify hierarchies of vocabulary, each of which bring with them an associated conceptual schema. Continued use of vocabulary in particular contexts reinforces preoccupation with particular concepts and shapes agency so that people will act (and think) in predictable ways. To explain this, Fowler uses the analogy of a 'map'. A map is a symbolic representation of a territory – the signs used figure the area in terms of features which interest the consumer, and thus maps can vary considerably. In the same way, vocabulary can be seen as mapping out segments of the undifferentiated flux of the material world. Continued use of each term crystallises and normalises the areas that are mapped out in particular ways.

3.   Another construction is **modality,** revealing the 'comment' or 'attitude' of the writer. Fowler distinguishes four types of modality, conveying: truth; obligation; permission; desirability. Modality is encoded through the use of what are called in traditional grammar 'modal auxiliary verbs' – such as 'will' (truth), 'must' (obligation) 'can' (permission) or use of a range of evaluative adjectives and adverbs – such as mad, effective, efficient – (desirability).

ENDNOTE

1.   Compare for example:
    (a) Senior managers also told the more experienced part-time staff that unless they too could work a two-shift day, management would have to replace them with full-time staff
    with:
    (b) The more experienced part-time staff were also told that unless a two-day shift could be worked more full-time staff would be taken on.
    In the first example, the message of who is doing what is clearly put across, whereas in the second agents are removed from the picture and causality shifted to unknown factors.

Appendix 3

List of articles used for analysis of competence discourse

Alderson, S. (1993), 'Reframing management competence: focusing on the top management team', *Personnel Review*, **22** (6), 53–62.

Allen, K. (1991), 'Personnel management on the line. How middle managers view the function', *Personnel Management*, June, 40–43.

Arkin, A. (1991), 'Turning managers into assessors', *Personnel Management*, November, 49–51.

Arnold, J. and Davey, K.M. (1992), 'Self-ratings and supervisor rating of graduate employees' competences during early career', *Journal of Occupational and Organizational Psychology*, **65** (3), 235–50.

Brown, R.B. (1993), 'Meta-competence: a recipe for reframing the competence debate', *Personnel Review*, **22** (6), 25–36.

Burdett, J. (1993), 'Crafting tomorrow's leadership today. A practitioner's view of succession and replacement planning', *International Journal of Manpower*, **14** (8), 23–33.

Cockerill, T. (1989), 'The kind of competence for rapid change', *Personnel Management*, September, 52–6.

Cofsky, K. (1993), 'Critical keys to competency-based pay', *Compensation and Benefits Review*, **25** (6), 46–50.

Dulewicz, V. (1989), 'Assessment centres as the route to competence', *Personnel Management*, November, 56–9.

Dulewicz, V. (1991), 'Improving assessment centres', *Personnel Management*, June, 50–55.

Evans, J. (1994), 'Sorting out HR matters on site', *Personnel Management plus*, March, 28–9.

Evans, P. (1990), 'International management development and the balance between generalism and professionalism', *Personnel Management*, December, 46–50.

Fletcher, C. (1993), 'Appraisal: an idea whose time has gone?', *Personnel Management*, September, 34–7.

Harris, T. George (1993), 'The post-capitalist executive: an interview with Peter F. Drucker', *Harvard Business Review*, May–June, 115–22.

Hofrichter, D. (1993), 'Broadbanding: a second generation approach', *Compensation and Benefits Review*, **25** (5), 53–8.

Horrocks, R. (1993), 'A case for developing generic management standards in Australia', *Practising Manager*, **14** (1), 18–23.

Hurley, B. and Cunningham, I. (1993), 'Imbibing a new way of learning', *Personnel Management*, March, 42–5.

Iles, P. (1993), 'Achieving strategic coherence in HRD through competence-based management and organization development', *Personnel Review*, **22** (6), 63–80.

IPM Consultative Document (1994), summarised in *Personnel Management plus*, December.

Kakabadse, A., Alderson, S. and Gorman, L. (1992), 'Cream of Irish management', *Journal of Managerial Psychology*, **7** (2), 18–47.

Kanungo, R.N. and Misra, S. (1992), 'Managerial resourcefulness: a reconceptualization of management skills', *Human Relations*, **45** (12), 1311–31.

Keller, D. and Campbell, J. (1992), 'Building human resource capability', *Human Resource Management*, **31** (1 & 2), 109–26.

Kilcourse, T. (1994), 'Developing Competent Managers', *Journal of Industrial Training*, **18** (2), 12–16.

Kinder, T. and Robertson, R. (1994), 'Do you have the personality to be a leader?', *Leadership and Organization Development*, **15** (1), 3–12.

Knightley, R. (1992), 'Ringing the changes: BT's use of development centres in redeployment', *Journal of European Industrial Training*, **16** (1), 17–19.

Lawler, E. (1994), 'From job-based to competency-based organizations', *Journal of Organizational Behaviour*, **15**, 3–15.

Lewis, R. (1993), 'A Jungian guide to competence', *Journal of Managerial Psychology*, **8** (1), 29–32.

Mansfield, B. (1993), 'Competence-based qualifications: a response', *Journal of European Industrial Training*, **17** (3), 19–22.

Miller, L. (1991), 'Managerial competences', *Industrial and Commercial Training*, **23** (6), 11–15.

Miller, P. (1991), 'A strategic look at management development', *Personnel Management*, August, 45–7.

Mole, G. *et al.* 'Developing executive competences: learning to confront, confronting to learn', *Journal of European Industrial Training*, **17** (2), 3–7.

Moravec, M., Gyr, H. and Friedman, L. (1993), 'Upward feedback. A 21st century communication tool', *HR Magazine*, July, 77–81.

Nemerov, D. (1994), 'How to design and competency-based pay program', *Journal of Compensation and Benefits*, **9** (5), 46–53.

Nowack, K. (1993), '360-degree feedback: the whole story', *Training and Development*, January, 69–72.

O'Driscoll, M.P. and Eubanks, J.L. (1993), 'Behavioral competences, goal setting and OD practitioner effectiveness', *Group and Organization Management*, **18** (3), 308–27.

Parry, S. (1993), 'The missing M in TQM', *Training*, **30** (9), 29–31.

Pickard, J. (1993), 'The real meaning of empowerment', *Personnel Management*, November, 28–33.

Reagan, P. (1994), 'Transform organisations using competency development', *Journal of Compensation and Benefits*, **9** (5), 25–31.

Rhinesmith, S. (1992), 'Global mindsets for global managers', *Training and Development*, **46** (10), 63–8.

Riley, K. and Sloman, M. (1991), 'Milestones for the personnel department', August, 34–7.

Robertson, I.T. and Kinder, A. (1993), 'Personality and job competences: the criterion-related validity of some personality variables', *Journal of Occupational and Organizational Psychology*, **66** (3), 225–44.

Russeveldt, J.V. (1993), 'The concept of "competences" in human resouce and industrial relations theory', European Centre for the Development of Vocational Training.

Seegers, J. (1987), 'Assessment centres for identifying long-term potential and self-development', in Herriot, P. (ed.), *Assessment and Selection in Organizations*, Chichester: Wiley, pp.745–71.

Shuttleworth, T. and Prescott, R. (1991), 'The hard graft way to develop managers', *Personnel Management*, November.

Sloman, M. (1993), 'Training to play a lead role', *Personnel Management*, July, 40–45.

Sloman, M. (1994), 'Coming in from the cold: a new role for trainers', *Personnel Management*, January, 24–7.

Smith, B. (1993), 'Building managers from the inside out', *Journal of Management Development*, **12** (1), 43–8.

Solomon, C. (1994), 'Staff selection impacts global success', *Personnel Journal*, **73** (1), 88–101.

Stewart, J. and Hamlin, B. (1994), 'Competence-based qualifications – a reply to Bob Mansfield', *Journal of European Industrial Training*, **18** (1), 27–30.

Stewart, J. and Hamlin, B. (1992a), 'Competence-based qualifications: the case for established methodologies', *Journal of Industrial Training*, **16** (10), 9–16.

Stewart, J. and Hamlin, B. (1992b), 'Competence-based qualifications: the case against change', *Journal of Industrial Training*, **16** (7), 21–32.

Stewart, J. and Hamlin, B. (1993), 'Competence-based qualification: a way forward', *Journal of Industrial Training*, **17** (6), 3–9.

Stewart, J. and Page, C. (1992), 'Competences – are they useful to trainers?', *Industrial and Commercial Training*, **24** (7), 32–5.

Storey, J. (1994), 'How new-style management is taking hold', *Personnel Management*, January, 32–5.

Townley, B. (1993), 'Performance appraisal and the emergence of management', *Journal of Management Studies*, **30** (2), 221–38.

Townley, B. (1990), 'A discriminating approach to appraisal', *Personnel Management*, December, 34–7.

Wills, S. (1993), 'MCI and the competency movement. The case so far', *Journal of European Industrial Training*, **17** (1), 9–11.

Wills, S. and Barham, K. (1994), 'Being an international manager', *European Management Journal*, **12** (1), 47–58.

Woodruffe, C. (1991), 'Competent by any other name', *Personnel Management*, September.

Woodruffe, C. (1993), 'What is meant by a competency?', *Leadership and Organization Development Journal*, **14** (1), 29–36.

Zimmerman, J. (1993), 'The demand of the future: "The complete executive"', *Human Resource Management*, **32** (2 & 3), 385–97.

References

Acker, J. (1992), 'Gendering organizational theory', in Mills, A.J. and Tancred, P. (eds), *Gendering Organizational Analysis*, London: Sage, pp.235–48.

Acker, J. (1998), 'The future of "gender and organizations": connections and boundaries', *Gender, Work and Organization*, **5** (4), 195–206.

Alcoff, L. (1988), 'Cultural feminism versus post-structuralism: the identity crisis in feminist theory', *Signs*, **13** (3), 405–36.

Alderson, S. (1993), 'Reframing management competence: focusing on the top management team', *Personnel Review*, **22** (6), 53–62.

Alimo-Metcalfe, B. (1994), 'Waiting for fish to grow feet! Removing organizational barriers to women's entry into leadership positions', in Tanton, M. (ed.), *Women in Management: A Developing Presence*, London: Routledge, pp.27–46.

Alimo-Metcalfe, B. (1995), 'Women in management: organisational socialisation', *International Journal of Selection and Assessment*, **1** (2), 68–83.

Alvesson, M. and Deetz, S. (1996), 'Critical theory and postmodernism approaches to organizational studies', in Clegg, S.R., Hardy, C. and Nord, W.R. (eds), *Handbook of Organization Studies*, London: Sage, pp.191–297.

Alvesson, M. and Deetz, S. (2000), *Doing Critical Management Research*, London: Sage.

Alvesson, M. and Willmott, H. (1992), *Critical Management Studies*, London: Sage.

Alvesson, M. and Willmott, H. (1996), *Making Sense of Management*, London: Sage.

Arnold, J. and Davey, K.M. (1992), 'Self-ratings and supervisor rating of graduate employees' competences during early career', *Journal of Occupational and Organizational Psychology*, **65** (3), 235–50.

Astroff, R. and Nyberg, A. (1992), 'Discursive hierarchies and the construction of crisis in the news: a case study', *Discourse and Society*, **3** (1), 5–23.

Bacchi, C. (1990), *Same Difference*, London: Allen and Unwin.

Barham, K. and Conway, C. (1988), *Management for the Future*, Berkhamstead and London: Ashridge Management College and Foundation for Management Education.

Barker, J. and Downing, H. (1980), 'Word processing and the transformation of patriarchal relations of control in the office', *Capital and Class*, **10**, 64–99.

Barthes, R. (1956), *Mythologies*, Paris: Seuil.

Beechey, V. and Perkins, T. (1987), *A Matter of Hours*, Cambridge: Polity.

Belenky, M.F., Cinchy, B.M., Goldberger, N.R. and Tarule, J.M. (1986), *Women's Ways of Knowing: The Development of Self, Voice and Mind*, New York: Basic Books.

Benhabib, S. (1986), *Critique, Norm and Utopia*, New York: Columbia University Press.

Best, S. and Kellner, D. (1991), *Postmodern Theory. Critical Interrogations*, Basingstoke: Macmillan.

Beynon, H. and Blackburn, R.M. (1991), *The Study of Work in Industrial Sociology*, Working Paper No. 5, Cambridge: Social and Political Sciences.

Bicknell, S. and Frances, J. (1998), 'Auditing brand and service behaviour', *Topics*, **1**, 15–18.

Boland, R.J. and Schultze (1996), 'Narrating accountability', in Munroe, R. and Mouritsen, J. (eds), *Accountability: Power, Ethos, and the Technologies of Managing*, Boston, MA: International Thomson Business Press.

Bologh, R.W. (1987), 'Marx, Weber and masculine theorizing', in Wiley, N. (ed.), *The Marx-Weber Debates*, London and Newbury Park, CA: Sage, pp.145–68.

Bowlby, J. (1988), *A Secure Base: Clinical Applications of Attachment Theory*, London: Routledge.

Boyatzis, R.E. (1982), *The Competent Manager: A Model for Effective Performance*, New York: Wiley.

Braverman, H. (1974), *Labour and Monopoly Capital*, New York: Monthly Review Press.

Brewster, C. and Hegewisch, A. (eds) (1994), *Policy and Practice in European Human Resource Management*, London: Routledge.

Brown, R.B. (1993), 'Meta-competence: a recipe for reframing the competence debate', *Personnel Review*, **22** (6), 25–36.

Bruner, J. (1986), *Actual Minds, Possible Worlds*, Cambridge, MA: Harvard University Press.

Bruner, J. (1990), *Acts of Meaning*, Cambridge, MA: Harvard University Press.

Burdett, J. (1993), 'Crafting tomorrow's leadership today. A practitioner's view of succession and replacement planning', *International Journal of Manpower*, **14** (8), 23–33.

Bureau of National Affairs (1983), *Performance Appraisal Programs*, Washington, DC: ENA.

Burgoyne, J. (1989), 'Creating the managerial portfolio – building on competency approaches to management development', *Management Education and Development*, **20** (1), 56–61.

Burton, C. (1992), 'Merit and gender: organizations and the mobilization of masculine bias', in Mills, A. and Tancred, P. (eds), *Gendering Organizational Analysis*, London: Sage, pp.165–85.

Calas, M.B. and Smircich, L. (1992), 'Using the "F" word: feminist theories and the social consequences of organizational research', in Mills, A.J. and Tancred, P. (eds), *Gendering Organizational Analysis*, London: Sage, pp.222–35.

Calas, M.B. and Smircich, L. (1996), 'From the Woman's Point of View: Feminist Approaches to Organization Studies', in Clegg, S., Hardy, C. and Nord, W. (eds), *Handbook of Organization Studies*, London: Sage, pp.218–57.

Checkland P. and Scholes, J. (1990), *Soft Systems Methodology in Action*, Chichester: Wiley.

Child, J. (1964), *British Management Thought*, London: Allen & Unwin.

Chodorow, N. (1978), *The Reproduction of Mothering*, London: University of California Press.

Cockburn, C. (1983), *Brothers: Male Dominance and Technological Change*, London: Pluto.

Cockburn, C. (1991), *In the Way of Women*, London: Macmillan.

Cofsky, K. (1993), 'Critical keys to competency-based pay', *Compensation and Benefits Review*, **25** (6), 46–50.

Cohen, J.L. and Arato, A. (1992), *Civil Society and Political Theory*, Cambridge, MA: MIT Press.

Collins, W.A. and Russell, G. (1991), 'Mother–child and father–child relationships in middle childhood and adolescence: a developmental analysis', *Developmental Review*, **11**, 99–136.

Collinson, D. and Knights, D. (1986), '"Men only": theories and practices of job segregation in insurance', in Knights, D. and Willmot, H. (eds), *Gender and the Labour Process*, Aldershot: Gower.

Collinson, D. and Hearn, J. (1994), 'Naming men as men: implications for work, organization and management', *Gender, Work and Organization*, **1** (1), 2–22.

Collinson, D., Knights, D. and Collinson, M. (1990), *Managing to Discriminate*, London: Routledge.

Connell, R.W. (1985), 'Theorising gender', *Sociology*, **19** (2), 260–72.

Connell, R. (1987), *Gender and Power*, Cambridge: Polity.

Constable, J. and McCormick, C. (1987), *The Making of British Managers*, London: BIM/CBI.

Coyle, A. (1982), 'Sex and skill in the organisation of the clothing industry', in West, J. (ed.), *Work, Women and the Labour Market*, London: Routledge, pp.10–46.

Craib, I. (1992), *Anthony Giddens*, London: Routledge.

Craig, C., Rubery, J., Tarling, R. and Wilkinson, F. (1982), *Labour Market Structure, Industrial Organisation and Low Pay*, Cambridge: Cambridge University Press.

Cressey, P. and Jones, B. (1992), 'Business strategy and the human resource; last links in the chain?', in *B884 Human Resource Strategies*, Milton Keynes: Open University Press.

Crompton, R., Jones, G. and Reid, S. (1982), 'Contemporary clerical work: a case study of local government', in West, J. (ed.), *Work, Women and the Labour Market*, London: Routledge, pp.44–60.

Dant, T. (1991), *Knowledge, Ideology and Discourse: A Sociological Perspective*, London: Routledge.

Deal, T.E. and Kennedy, A.A. (1982), *Corporate Cultures: the Rites and Rituals of Corporate Life*, Harmondsworth: Penguin.

Deetz, S. (1992), 'Disciplinary power in the modern corporation', in Alvesson, M. and Willmott, H. (eds), *Critical Management Studies*, London: Sage.

Derrida, J. (1973), *Speech and Phenomena and Other Essays on Husserl's Theory of Signs*, Evanston, IL: Northwestern University Press.

Dex, S. (1988), 'Gender and the labour market', in Gallie, D. (ed.), *Employment in Britain*, Oxford: Blackwell, pp.281–381.

Donnell, S.M. and Hall, J. (1980), 'Men and women as managers: a significant case of no significant difference', *Organizational Dynamic*, Spring, 60–77.

Du Gay, P. (1996), *Consumption and Identity at Work*, London: Sage.

Du Gay, P. and Salaman G. (1992), 'The Cult(ure), of the customer', *Journal of Management Studies*, **29** (4), 616–33.

Du Gay, P., Salaman, G. and Rees, B. (1996), 'The conduct of management and the management of conduct: contemporary managerial discourse and the constitution of the competent manager', *Journal of Management Studies*, **33** (3), May, 263–82.

Dulewicz, V. (1989), 'Assessment centres as the route to competence', *Personnel Management*, November, 56–9.

Dulewicz, V. (1991), 'Improving assessment centres', *Personnel Management*, June, 50–55.

Eagleton, T. (1983), *Literary Theory*, Oxford: Blackwell.

Ely, R. (1995), 'The power in demography: women's social constructions of gender identity at work', *Academy of Management Journal*, **38** (3), 589–634.

EOC (2002), *Women and Men in Britain: Management,* January.

Fairclough, N. (1991), 'What might we mean by "enterprise discourse"?', in Keat, R. and Abercrombie, N. (eds), *Enterprise Culture*, London: Routledge, pp.38–57.

Fairclough, N. (1992), *Discourse and social change*, Oxford: Polity.

Fay, B. (1987), *Critical Social Science*, Cambridge: Polity.

Fletcher, C. (1993), 'Appraisal: an idea whose time has gone?', *Personnel Management*, September, 34–7.

Fletcher, S. (1992), *Competence-Based Assessment Techniques*, London: Kogan Page.

Flood, R.L. (1993), *Beyond TQM*, Chichester: Wiley.

Foucault, M. (1976), *La volonté de savoir*, Paris: Editions Gallimard.

Foucault , M. (1977), *Discipline and Punish: the Birth of the Prison*, London: Penguin.

Foucault, M. (1980), 'The History of Sexuality' (trans. R. Hurley), New York: Vintage.

Fowler, R. (1991), *Language in the News*, London: Routledge.

Fromm, E. (1932/1978), 'The method and function of an analytic social psychology', in Arato, A. and Gebhardte, E. (eds), *The Essential Frankfurt School Reader*, New York: Urizen Books, pp.477–96.

Game, A. and Pringle, R. (1983), *Gender at Work*, Australia: George Allen & Unwin.

Gammie, A. (1997), 'Developing competence: a framework of performance and its links with culture', *Topics*, **4**, 15–18.

Garnsey, E. and Rees, B. (1996), 'Discourse and enactment; gender inequality in text and context', *Human Relations*, **49** (8), 1041–64.

Giddens, A. (1991), *The Consequences of Modernity*, Cambridge: Polity.

Gilligan, C. (1982), *In a Different Voice*, Cambridge, MA: Harvard University Press.

Gilligan, C., Lyons, N.P. and Hanmer, T.J. (1990), *Making Connections: The Relational Worlds of Adolescent Girls at Emma Willard School*, Cambridge, MA: Harvard University Press.

Golombok, S. and Fivush, R. (1994), *Gender Development*, Cambridge: Cambridge University Press.

Habermas, J. (1968/1971), *Knowledge and Human Interests* (trans. J. Shapiro), Boston: Beacon Press [origin. pubd. as *Erkenntnis and Interesse*, Frankfurt am Mai: Suhrkamp].

Habermas, J. (1979), *Communication and the Evolution of Society*, Boston: Beacon Press.

Habermas, J. (1984), *The Theory of Communicative Action*, Vol. 1: Reasons and the Rationalization of Society (trans. T. McCarthy), Boston: Beacon Press.

Hammer, M. (1990), 'Reengineering work: don't automate, obliterate', *Harvard Business Review*, **90** (4), July–August.

Hammersley, M. and Atkinson, P. (1983), *Ethnography: Principles and Practice*, London: Routledge.

Handy, C., Gordon, C., Gow, I. and Randlesome, C. (1987), *Making Managers*, London: Pitman.

Harris, T. George (1993), 'The post-capitalist executive: an interview with Peter F. Drucker', *Harvard Business Review*, May–June, 115–22.

Hearn, J. and Parkin, J. (1992), 'Gender and organizations: a selective review and critique of a neglected area', in Mills, A.J. and Tancred, P. (eds), *Gendering Organizational Analysis*, London: Sage, pp.46–67.

Heatherington, L., Daubman, K., Bates, C., Ahn, A., Brown, H. and Preston, C. (1993),

'Two investigations of "female modesty" in achievement situations', *Sex Roles*, **29** (11/12), 739–54.

Hill, S. (1991), 'Why quality circles failed but total quality might succeed', *British Journal of Industrial Relations*, **29** (4), 541–68.

Hofrichter, D. (1993), 'Broadbanding: a second generation approach', *Compensation and Benefits Review*, **25** (5), 53–8.

Hofstede, G. (1991), *Culture's Consequences*, London: Sage.

Holmes, J. (1991), 'Sex differences and apologies: one aspect of communicative competence', *Applied Linguistics*, **10** (2), 194–213.

Horrell, S., Rubery, J. and Burchell, B. (1990), 'Gender and skills', *Work, Employment and Society*, **4** (4), 189–216.

Iles, P. (1993), 'Achieving strategic coherence in HRD through competence-based management and organization development', *Personnel Review*, **22** (6), 63–80.

IPM Consultative Document (1994), *Personnel Management Plus*, December.

Jacobs, R. (1989), 'Getting the measure of management competence', *Personnel Management*, June, 32–7.

James, D. and Drakich, J. (1993), 'Understanding gender differences in amount of talk: a critical review of research', in Tannen, D. (ed.), *Gender and Conversational Interaction*, Oxford: Oxford University Press, pp.281–306.

Johnson, P. (1976), 'Women and power: toward a theory of effectiveness', *Journal of Social Issues*, **32** (3), 99–110.

Kanungo, R.N. and Misra, S. (1992), 'Managerial resourcefulness: a reconceptualization of management skills', *Human Relations*, **45** (12), 1311–31.

Keat, R. and Abercrombie, N. (1991), *Enterprise Culture*, London: Routledge.

Kerfoot, D. and Knights, D. (1996), 'The best is yet to come: searching for embodiment in managerial work', in Collinson, D. and Hearn, J. (eds), *Men as Managers, Managers as Men: Critical Perspectives on Men, Masculinities and Management*, London: Sage, pp.78–98.

Kilcourse, T. (1994), 'Developing competent managers', *Journal of Industrial Training*, **18** (2), 12–16.

Kinder, T. and Robertson, R. (1994), 'Do you have the personality to be a leader?', *Leadership and Organization Development*, **15** (1), 3–12.

Knight, J. (1994), 'Motherhood and management', in Tanton, M. (ed.), *Women in Management: A Developing Presence*, London: Routledge, pp.141–61.

Knights, D. (1990), 'Subjectivity, power and the labour process', in Knights, D. and Willmott, H. (eds), *Labour Process Theory*, London: Macmillan, pp.297–336.

Knights, D. and Willmott, H. (1985), 'Power and identity in theory and practice', *Sociological Review*, **33** (1), 22–46.

Knights, D. and Willmott, H. (eds) (1990), *Labour Process Theory*, London: Macmillan.

Knights, D. and Willmott, H. (1999), *Management Lives: Power and Identity in Work Organisations*, London: Sage.

Lamb, M. (1977), 'Father–infant and mother–infant interaction in the first year of life', *Child development*, **48**, 167–81.

Lamb, M. (1986), *The Father's Role: Applied Perspectives*, New York: Wiley.

Lamb, M. and Oppenheim, D. (1989), 'Fatherhood and father–child relationships: five years of research', in Cath, S.H., Gurwitt, A. and Gunsberg, L. (eds), *Fathers and Their Families*, Hilldale, NJ: Erlbaum.

Lawler, E. (1994), 'From job-based to competency-based organizations', *Journal of Organizational Behaviour*, **15**, 3–15.

Leaper, C. (1991), 'Influence and involvement: age, gender and partner effects', *Child Development*, **62**, 797–811.

Legge, K. (1989), 'Human resource management: a critical analysis', in Storey, J. (ed.), *New Perspectives on Human Resource Management*, London: Routledge, pp.19–41.

Leonard, S. (1990), *Critical Theory in Political Practice*, Princeton, NJ: Princeton University Press.

Lerner, G. (1986), *The Creation of Patriarchy*, New York: Oxford University Press.

Lever, J. (1976), 'Sex differences in the games children play', *Social Problems*, **23**, 478–87.

Lewis, R. (1993), 'A Jungian guide to competence', *Journal of Managerial Psychology*, **8** (1), 29–32.

Long, P. (1986), *Performance Appraisal Revisited*, London: Institute of Personnel Management.

Lukes, S. (1974), *Power: A Radical View*, London: Macmillan.

Lyons, N. (1990), 'Listening to voices we have not heard', in Gilligan, C. *et al.* (eds), *Making Connections*, Cambridge, MA: Harvard University Press, pp.30–73.

Lyons, N., Saltonstall, J. and Hanmer, T. (1990), 'Competencies and visions. Emma Willard girls talk about being leaders', in Gilligan, C. *et al.* (eds), *Making Connections*, Cambridge, MA: Harvard University Press, pp.183–214.

Lyotard, J.F. (1984), *The Postmodern Condition: A Report on Knowledge*, Minneapolis: University of Minnesota Press.

Maccoby, E. (1990), 'Gender and relationships: a developmental account', *American Psychologist*, **45** (4), 513–20.

Maccoby, E. and Jacklin, C. (1987), 'Gender segregation in children', in Reese, H.W. (ed.), *Advances in Child Develoment and Behaviour*, New York: Academic Press, Vol. 20, pp.239–87.

Machung, A. (1992), 'The politics of subordination: linguistic discourse in organizational hierarchies', in Hall, K., Bucholtz, M. and Moonwomon, B. (eds), *Locating Power: Proceedings of the Second Berkeley Women and Language Conference*, Vol. 2, Berkeley CA: Berkeley Women and Language Group, University of California, Berkeley, pp.362–71.

Madhok, J.J. (1992), 'The effect of gender composition on group interaction', *Locating Power: Proceedings of the Second Berkeley Women and Language Conference*, Vol. 2, Berkeley, CA: Berkeley Women and Language Group, University of California, Berkeley.

Mansfield, B. (1993), 'Competence-based qualifications: a response', *Journal of European Industrial Training*, **17** (3), 19–22.

Marshall, B.L. (1994), *Engendering Modernity: Feminism, Social Theory and Social Change*, Cambridge: Polity.

Marshall, J. (1984), *Women Managers: Travellers in a Male World*, Chichester: Wiley.

Martin, J. (1990), 'Deconstructing organizational taboos: the suppression of gender conflict in organizations', *Organization Science*, **1** (4), 339–59.

Miller, P. and Rose, N. (1990), 'Governing economic life', *Economy and Society*, **19** (1), 1–31.

Miller, P.M., Danahar, D.L. and Forbes, D. (1980), 'Sex-related strategies for coping with interpersonal conflicts in children aged five and seven', *Developmental Psychology*, **22**, 543–8.

Moravec, M., Hall, K., Bucholtz, M. and Moonwomon, B. (1993), 'Upward feedback. A 21st century communication tool', *HR Magazine*, July, 77–81.

Morgan, G. (1986), *Images of Organizations*, London: Sage.

Nadler, M. and Nadler, L. (1987), 'The influence of gender on negotiation success in asymmetrical power situations', in Nadler, L., Nadler, M. and Todd Mancillas, W.R. (eds), *Advances in Gender Communication Research*, MD: University Press of America, pp. 189–218.

Nemerov, D. (1994), 'How to design a competency-based pay program', *Journal of Compensation and Benefits*, **9** (5), 46–53.

Nicholson, N. and West, M.A. (1988), *Managerial Job Change: Men and Women in Transition*, Cambridge: Cambridge University Press.

Novack, K. (1993), '360-degree feedback: the whole story', *Training and Development*, January, 69–72.

Oakley, J.G. (2000), 'Gender-based barriers to senior management positions: understanding the scarcity of female CEOs', *Journal of Business Ethics*, **27** (4), part 2, 321–34.

Pasmore, W. (1999), 'A Hero for the Underdogs: a review of Dave Ulrich's Human Resource Champions', *Organization*, **6** (2), 361–9.

Peters, T. (1987), *Thriving on Chaos*, London: Macmillan.

Peters, T. and Waterman, R.H. (1982), *In Search of Excellence*, Lessons from America's Best Run Companies, New York: Harper and Row.

Pfeffer, J. (1981), *Power in Organizations*, Cambridge, MA: Sallinger.

Phillips, A. and Taylor, B. (1980), 'Sex and skill: notes towards a feminist economics', *Feminist Review*, **6**, 79–83.

Pollert, A. (1981), *Girls, Wives, Factory Lives*, London: Macmillan.

Prahalad, C.K. and Hamel, G. (1990), 'The core competence of the corporation', *Harvard Business Review*, **68** (3), 79–93.

Pugh, D., Hickson, D. and Hinings, C. (1988), *Writers on Organizations*, Harmondsworth: Penguin.

Ragins, B.R. (1989), 'Power and gender congruency effects in evaluations of male and female managers', *Journal of Management*, **15** (1), 65–76.

Raymond, J. (1986), *A Passion for Friends*, London: Women's Press.

Reagan, P. (1994), 'Transform organisations using competency development', *Journal of Compensation and Benefits*, **9** (5), 25–31.

Rees, B. and Brewster, C. (1995), 'Supporting equality: patriarchy at work in Europe', *Personnel Review*, **24** (1), 19–40.

Rees, B. and Garnsey, E. (2003), 'Analysing competence: gender and identity at work', *Gender, Work and Organization*, **10** (5).

Rhinesmith, S. (1992), 'Global mindsets for global managers', *Training and Development*, **46** (10), 63–8.

Robertson, I.T. and Kinder, A. (1993), 'Personality and job competences: the criterion-related validity of some personality variables', *Journal of Occupational and Organizational Psychology*, **66** (3), 225–44.

Roper, M. (1993), *Masculinity and the British Organization Man. 1945 to the Present*, Oxford: Oxford University Press.

Rosin, H.M. (1991), 'Workplace variables, affective responses, and intention to leave among women managers', *Journal of Occupational Psychology*, **64**, 317–30.

Rubin, J. (1997), 'Gender, equality and the culture of organisational assessment: "There's no overt discrimination, but the template for the ideal doesn't wear a skirt"', *Gender, Work and Organization*, **4** (1), 24–34.

Ruderman, M.N., Ohlott, P.J., Panzer, K. and King, S.N. (2002), 'Benefits of multiple roles for managerial women', *Academy of Management Journal*, **45** (2), 369–86.

Sadker, M. and Sadker, D. (1994), *Failing at Fairness: How America's Schools Cheat Girls*, New York: Scribners.

Saussure, F. de (1968), *Cours de Linguistique Générale*, Paris: Payot.

Schein, E.H. (1985), *Organizational Culture and Leadership*, San Francisco: Jossey-Bass.

Schein, V.E. (1973), 'The relationship between sex role stereotypes and requisite management characteristics', *Journal of Applied Psychology*, **57** (2), 95–100.

Schein, V.E. (1975), 'The relationship between sex role stereotypes and requisite management characteristics among female managers', *Journal of Applied Psychology*, **60** (3), 340–44.

Schon, D.A. (1983), *The Reflective Practitioner*, New York: Basic Books.

Schroder, H.M. (1989), *Managerial Competence: The Key to Excellence*, Dubuque, IA: Kendall-Hunt.

Seegers, J. (1987), 'Assessment Centers for identifying long-term potential and self-development', in P. Herriot (ed.), *Assessment and Selection in Organizations*, Chichester: Wiley, pp.745–71.

Sharpe, R. (2000), 'As leaders, women rule', *Business Week*, November, 74–84.

Sheldon, A. (1993), 'Pickle fights: gendered talk in preschool disputes', in Tannen, D. (ed.), *Gender and Conversational Interaction*, Oxford and New York: Oxford University Press, pp.83–106.

Shuttleworth, T. and Prescott, R. (1991), 'The hard graft way to develop managers', *Personnel Management*, November.

Smith, B. (1993), 'Building managers from inside out', *Journal of Management Development*, **12** (1), 43–8.

Smith, C., Whipp, R. and Willmott, H. (1988), 'Case study research in accounting: methodological breakthrough or ideological weapon?', in Neimark, C. (ed.), *Advances in Public Interest Accounting*, Vol. 2, pp.95–121.

Solomon, C. (1994), 'Staff selection impacts global success', *Personnel Journal*, **73** (1), 88–101.

Sorenson, J. (1991), 'Mass media and the discourse of famine in the Horn of Africa', *Discourse and Society*, **2** (2), 223–42.

Spencer, L.M. and Spencer, S.M. (1993), *Competence at Work. Models for Superior Performance*, New York: Wiley.

Spender, D. (1992), 'Information management: women's language strengths', in Hall, K., Bucholtz, M. and Moonwoman, B. (eds), *Locating Power: Proceedings of the Second Berkeley Women and Language Conference*, Vol. 2, Berkeley, CA: Berkeley Women and Language Group, University of California, Berkeley, pp.549–60.

Statham, A. (1988), *The Worth of Women's Work*, New York: State University of New York Press.

Steiger, T.L. (1993), 'Construction of skill and skill construction', *Work, Employment and Society*, **7** (4), 535–60.

Stewart, J. and Hamlin, B. (1992a), 'Competence-based qualification: the case for established methodologies', *Journal of Industrial Training*, **16** (10), 9–16.

Stewart, J. and Hamlin, B. (1992b), 'Competence-based qualifications: the case against change', *Journal of European Industrial Training*, **16** (7), 21–32.

Stewart, J. and Hamlin, B. (1993), 'Competence-based qualification: a way forward', *Journal of Industrial Training*, **17** (6), 3–9.

Stewart, J. and Hamlin, B. (1994), Competence-based qualifications – a reply to Bob Mansfield', *Journal of European Industrial Training*, **18** (1), 27–30.

Storey, J. (1989), *New Perspectives on Human Resource Management*, London: Routledge.

Storey, J. and Sisson, K. (1993), *Managing Human Resources and Industrial Relations*, Milton Keynes: Open University Press.

Tannen, D. (1990), 'Gender differences in topical coherence: creating involvement in best friend's talk', *Discourse Processes*, **13**, 73–90.

Tannen, D. (1994), *Talking from 9 to 5*, London: Virago.

Tannen, D. (ed.) (1994), *Gender and Conversational Interaction*, Oxford: Oxford University Press.

Thornton, G.C. and Byham, W.C. (1982), *Assessment Centres and Managerial Performance*, New York: Academic Press.

Townley, B. (1990), 'A discriminating approach to appraisal', *Personnel Management*, December, 34–7.

Townley, B. (1993a), 'Foucault, power/knowledge and its relevance for Human Resource Management', *Academy of Management Review*, **18** (3), 518–45.

Townley, B. (1993b), 'Performance appraisal and the emergence of management', *Journal of Management Studies*, **30** (2), 221–38.

Townley, B. (1994), *Reframing Human Resource Management: Power, Ethics and the Subject at Work*, London: Sage.

Townley, B. (1999), 'Nietzsche, competencies and ubermensch: reflections on human and inhuman resource management', *Organization*, **6** (2), 285–305.

Tracy, K. and Eisenberg, E. (1990/91), 'Giving criticism: a multiple goals case study', *Research on Language and Social Interaction*, **24**, 37–70.

Trompenaars, F. (1993), *Riding the Waves of Culture*, London: Economist Books.

Van Dijk, T.A. (1993), 'Principles of critical discourse analysis', *Discourse and Society*, **4** (2), 249–83.

Van Maanen, J. (1988), *Tales of the Field: On Writing Ethnography*, Chicago: University of Chicago Press.

Wajcman, J. (1994), 'The gender relations of management', paper presented at the 'Work, Employment and Society' Conference, Canterbury, September.

Webb, J. (1997), 'The politics of equal opportunity', *Gender, Work and Organization*, **4** (3), 159–69.

Weedon, C. (1987), *Feminist Practice and Poststructuralist Theory*, Oxford: Blackwell.

White, S. (1988), *The Recent Work of Jurgen Habermas: Reason, Justice and Modernity*, Cambridge: Cambridge University Press.

Williams, A., Dobson, P. and Walters, M. (1995), *Changing Culture*, London: Institute of Personnel Management.

Willmott, H. (1990), 'Subjectivity and the dialectics of praxis: opening up the core of the labour process analysis', in Knights, D. and Willmott, H. (eds), *Labour Process Theory*, London: Macmillan, pp.336–79.

Willmott, H. (1993), 'Strength is ignorance; slavery is freedom: managing culture in modern organizations', *Journal of Management Studies*, **30** (4), 515–52.

Wills, S. (1993), 'MCI and the competency movement: the case so far', *Journal of European Industrial Training*, **17** (1), 9–11.

Wills, S. and Barham, K. (1994), 'Being an international manager', *European Management Journal*, **12** (1), 49–57.

Woodruffe, C. (1993), 'What is meant by competency?', *Leadership and Organization Development Journal*, **14** (1), 29–36.

Zimmerman, J. (1993), 'The demand of the future: "The complete executive"', *Human Resource Management*, **32** (2 & 3), 385–97.

Index